# Arizona
# Gunfighters

# Arizona
# Gunfighters

LAURENCE J. YADON
AND DAN ANDERSON

EDITED BY ROBERT BARR SMITH

PELICAN PUBLISHING COMPANY
GRETNA 2010

*The word "Pelican" and the depiction of a pelican are trademarks
of Pelican Publishing Company, Inc., and are registered in the
U.S. Patent and Trademark Office.*

**Library of Congress Cataloging-in-Publication Data**

Yadon, Laurence J., 1948-
  Arizona gunfighters / Laurence J. Yadon and Dan Anderson ; edited by
Robert Barr Smith.
      p. cm.
  Includes bibliographical references and index.
  ISBN 978-1-58980-651-1 (pbk. : alk. paper) 1. Outlaws—Arizona—
Biography. 2. Criminals—Arizona—Biography. 3. Arizona—History—
To 1912. 4. Arizona—History—1912-1950. 5. Frontier and pioneer
life—Arizona—Anecdotes. 6. Crime—Arizona—History—Anecdotes.
I. Anderson, Dan, 1950- II. Smith, Robert B. (Robert Barr), 1933- III.
Title.
  F811.Y34 2010
  979.1'052—dc22
                                              2010012937

Printed in the United States of America

Published by Pelican Publishing Company, Inc.
1000 Burmaster Street, Gretna, Louisiana 70053

# Contents

# Preface

Inside a dark, cavernous pavilion still smelling of the circus animals that performed there a few days before, a young boy waited with his father in a line with hundreds of others to meet a legend. It was the late 1950s, and Wyatt Earp had come to Tulsa in the person of Hugh O'Brian, a television actor and leading man straight from central casting. He was up ahead on a brightly lit stage, about half a football field away.

In the commotion, a man slightly larger than the boy's father jumped the line. "You can cut in, if you really want to," his father said, with just a hint of menace, "or you can go to the end of the line like everyone else." The interloper looked at the line of Old West fans growing in the dimness and then quietly led his own son away.

Years later, the young boy realized that his father's insistence on standing up for oneself was tempered in war but fostered earlier in family stories and traditions. These were tales of feuds, wars, and other conflicts in Missouri, Appalachia, and earlier still, northern England, Scotland, and Ireland. Stories which whispered across the centuries: "Don't be pushed around, you are as good as anyone." Stories like those have played out again and again in the American West.

"Wyatt Earp" looked tired that evening, but no matter, the lawman portrayed by O'Brian was a hero to the crowd and millions of others who grew up in the 1950s. Subsequent generations know him even today through movies such as *Wyatt Earp* and *Tombstone*. The legend of Wyatt Earp and the gunfight at the O.K. Corral is just about all some Americans know of Arizona history. Still others know the glitz and glamour of Sedona and Scottsdale resorts but very little about early Arizona.

This is a book about Wyatt Earp, his brothers, and a host of lesser known gunfighters who usually came to Arizona Territory as adventurers, not as shootists. Some sought wealth through cattle, mining, merchandising, gambling, or saloon keeping. Others pursued their dreams through law enforcement, brothels, ranching, rustling, occasional stagecoach and train robbing, or a combination of these pursuits. Many came simply to get a new start. A few came to hide from dark pasts. All too often, these men settled their personal, business, or political differences with guns.

Our trilogy, *100 Oklahoma Outlaws, Gangsters, and Lawmen: 1839-1939, 200 Texas Outlaws and Lawmen: 1835-1935,* and *Ten Deadly Texans,* focused on the emergence of law and order in Oklahoma, Texas, and eastern New Mexico during a one-hundred-year period ending with the Great Depression. Here, we follow the westward migration of the classic American gunfighter from present-day Oklahoma, Texas, and elsewhere in the states to the desert Southwest, California, and beyond. His story begins after the Civil War and ends with the admission of Arizona Territory to the union in 1912. We have focused on the development of southeastern Arizona, particularly Tombstone; the Pleasant Valley War—among the most violent range conflicts in American history—the rise and fall of train robbers; and the role of the Arizona Rangers in ending large-scale cattle rustling in the twilight of territorial days. Although our earlier trilogy was a popular history based largely on secondary sources, in this volume we have relied more upon court transcripts, newspaper accounts, contemporary diary entries, and late life memoirs available to us in January 2009.

Our subjects are the famous and the forgotten. Wyatt Earp and Doc Holliday share the spotlight with lesser known shootists such as William Harrison "Billy the Kid" Claiborne. Bat Masterson gets equal billing with the obscure saloon-keeping shootist Jerry Barton. Cattle rustling, mining-camp quarrels, and range wars were responsible for much of the violence that infected the West. Many of the events described here are controversial to this day; the gunfight at the O.K. Corral, which actually occurred in a vacant lot elsewhere, is only the most prominent example. We have used the generally accepted versions of events while providing credible, alternative versions or interpretations either in the text or in the notes. Names and places are spelled in accordance with common modern usage, with alternatives found in primary sources placed in parenthesis or referenced in notes. Every effort has been made to reference the generally accepted dates of events described here, with alternatives referenced or noted as appropriate. Regrettably, we have not had access to the original transcript of the O.K. Corral Coroner's Inquest, discovered on April 21, 2010, in Bisbee, Arizona, which has not yet been released.

Robert Barr Smith (*Tough Towns, Outlaw Tales of Oklahoma*) has guided our efforts as consulting editor and contributed four chapters. Nevertheless, judgments made concerning the relative credibility of competing sources, dates, and any errors sifting fact from mythology have been our own.

# Acknowledgments

Research for this project was performed in conjunction with our previous works, *100 Oklahoma Outlaws, Gangsters, and Lawmen: 1839-1939, 200 Texas Outlaws and Lawmen: 1835-1935*, and *Ten Deadly Texans*. A number of organizations have assisted the authors in the research for these projects over the past five years. These institutions included but were not limited to the Flying Fingers Typing Service, Sand Springs, Oklahoma; Texas Ranger Museum, Waco, Texas; the Haley Library; Harris County Public Library; Dallas Public Library; El Paso Public Library; Fort Bend County Public Library; Houston City Public Library; Young County Historical Commission; City-County Library, Tulsa, Oklahoma; Oklahoma Historical Society; Western History Collection, University of Oklahoma Library; University of Oklahoma Law School Library; Oklahoma Heritage Association; Oklahoma Centennial Commission; Woolaroc Museum, Bartlesville, Oklahoma; Texas Jack Association; Oklahombres, Inc.; Oklahoma Outlaws, Lawmen History Association; Tulsa Police Department; Public Library, Enid, Oklahoma; Beryl Ford Collection, Tulsa, Oklahoma; Oklahoma Publishing Company; Lenapah Historical Society; the University of Tulsa; Kansas State Historical Society; Will Rogers Museum; National Cowboy Hall of Fame; Gilcrease Museum; Enid Public Library; Boone County Heritage Museum, Harrison, Arkansas; and the Lincoln Heritage Trust, Lincoln, New Mexico.

Individuals who have assisted us in prior projects have

11

included Bill O'Neal, Nancy Samuelson, Bob Ernst, Bob Alexander, Robert K. DeArment, David Johnson, Chuck Parsons, Rick Miller, Phil Sanger, Randy Stainer, Ross Cooper, Ron Trekell, Armand DeGregoris, John R. Lovett, Mike Tower, Michael and Suzanne Wallis, Rod Dent, Gary Youell, Phil Edwards, Terry Zinn, Michael Koch, Diron Ahlquist, Willie Jones, Clyda Franks, Emily Lovick, Lisa Keys, Joseph Calloway Yadon (ardent researcher and author's son), Danielle Williams, Irene and Larry Chance, Glendon Floyd, Curt Johnson, Dee Cordry, Rik Helmerich, and Herman Kirkwood. Thanks are also due Helen J. Gaines, Jim Bradshaw, Adrienne Grimmett, Beth Andreson, Jim Hamilton, Dana Harrison MacMoy, Mary Phillips, Stacy M. Rogers, Rand McKinney, Jana Swartwood, Gini Moore Campbell, and Phillip W. Steele, Dorman Holub, Sgt. Kevin F. Foster, Jane Soutner, Brian Burns, Ashley Schmidt, and Dana Brittain. Special thanks are due to Roy Young and Marshall Trimble, the official state historian of Arizona.

Lastly, without the patient guidance of our consulting editor, Robert Barr Smith, and patient support of Julia Anderson and Martha Yadon, this book would not have been possible.

# Introduction

Arizona was one of the finest lands in the world and all
they lacked was plenty of water and good society.
—attributed to Samuel Woodworth Cozzens.[1]

Mid-nineteenth-century Arizona was not a separate or
distinct place at all. Instead, this remote and often violent
region was part of New Mexico Territory, which had been
created in 1850. The original New Mexico Territory included
most of present-day Arizona, then labeled "Santa Ana County,"
as well as portions of present-day Colorado and Utah.

## Spanish Exploration

From the beginning, the European experience in Arizona
was about souls, silver, and gold, but not necessarily in that
order. During the spring of 1539, a Franciscan missionary
entered the Tombstone region of southeast Arizona looking
for the fabled Seven Cities of Cibola, a myth originating in
about the year 1150 during the Moorish conquest of Spain
holding that seven bishops had fled to a far away land with
all their riches. The Spanish explorer Francisco Vasquez
de Coronado doubted this place even existed, yet taking
no chances on missing a fortune, he led a fruitless two-year
expedition seeking the mythical cities of gold in 1540-1542[2]

and passed within a few miles of rich silver deposits that later would be mined in the Tombstone area.[3] Some forty years later, the former Inquisition officer Antonio de Espejo turned west from the vicinity of Albuquerque into present-day Arizona but failed to find any mineral wealth. Finally in November 1598, conquistador Juan de Onate ordered an expedition to the vicinity of present-day Prescott, where at last rich silver ore was discovered.

The focus of Spanish exploration returned to religious purposes with the arrival of Franciscan missionaries at various Hopi settlements in 1629. Fifty-one years later, in response to the Inquisition and labor exploitation, the natives launched the Great Pueblo Revolt in present-day New Mexico, which prompted the brown-clad monks to seek evangelistic opportunities elsewhere. Eventually, a series of rudimentary Jesuit mission stations known as *visitas* were established to the south in Sonora.

One story relates that in 1736, huge boulders of native silver weighing up to 2,500 pounds were found on a ranch owned by Bernardo de Urrea. The boulders were covered by oak trees and thus referred to as *aritzona*, roughly translated as "the good oak." Silver in significant quantities was also discovered that year at a small village about twenty-five miles southwest of present-day Nogales, called Ali-Shonak, perhaps a Tohono O'odham word for "place of the small springs." The Spanish corruption of this term, "Arizonac," eventually was corrupted again perhaps to become Arizona.[4] A presidio (fort) was built there in about 1751 following a Pima Indian uprising. Later, the presidio was reestablished at present-day Tucson, setting the stage for ranching and mining operations as well as the founding of new missions. At about the same time, a second military presidio was established in 1775 near the later site of Fairbank.[5]

This was all accomplished before a treaty with the

Apaches was arranged in about 1780. When the treaty was repudiated following the establishment of the Republic of Mexico in 1821, the Apaches and other tribes began raiding settlements throughout present-day Arizona, a tradition that continued into the 1880s.[6] Indian raids were particularly devastating for the cattle ranchers. The Hopi Indians, also in what is now Arizona, had grazed cattle centuries before the Jesuit missionaries copied their practices even as they sought to convert the natives to the new religion.[7] The Apaches resented the wide-ranging cattle grazing enjoyed by their new neighbors and contained such efforts in the Santa Cruz Valley. Thus, even though by the late 1840s, parts of southern Arizona were inhabited by feral cattle, there was no large-scale ranching there until after the Civil War.

One of the cattlemen of that era driving herds to California from Texas was stern New Englander Henry C. Hooker, founder of the Sierra Bonita Ranch in the Sulphur Spring Valley, a well-watered place close to two Indian reservations and two military forts. Hooker had established his Arizona Territory cattle ranch with the proceeds from the sale of five hundred turkeys to mining camps in Nevada. Later, he briefly employed Henry McCarty, known to history as "Billy the Kid." Hooker owned about eleven thousand head of cattle by the mid-1870s, according to one report.[8] Smaller ranchers established themselves near present-day Prescott, Wickenburg, and Phoenix. Hooker shared the Arizona grasslands with the Middleton and Ellison families of Pleasant Valley and the Tonto Basin, who began operations in the mid-1870s.

Sheep grazing, which Arizona tribes began in the 1600s, accelerated with the European arrivals. By 1890, approximately seven hundred thousand sheep populated the Arizona Territory.[9]

## The Republic of Mexico Era

Among the first Anglo-Americans to explore the region in the 1820s was Kentuckian James Ohio Pattie, whose account of frontier exploration in the Southwest and California is today considered a mixture of fact and fiction.[10]

The American war against Mexico in 1846 brought Col. Stephen Watts Kearney and his Army of the West to seize the region. Kearney was a son-in-law of William Clark of the Lewis and Clark expedition. Kearney was ordered to seize the region and he did so, but only after sending a secret emissary ahead from Bent's Fort on the Arkansas to Santa Fe with financial inducements for New Mexico governor Manuel Armijo, who soon skedaddled. This arrangement set the stage for the triumphant entry of the American army into Santa Fe on August 18, 1846, accompanied by some four hundred wagons loaded with merchandise.[11]

Three months later, a detachment of some five hundred men accompanied by a small group of camp followers forced their way into the dusty little adobe village called Tucson, forcing the Mexican commander to flee south to Mission San Xavier without firing a shot. This was the Mormon Battalion led by Capt. Philip St. George Cooke, which had been tasked to build a road across the desert from Santa Fe to California. Cooke is considered "the father of the U.S. cavalry" and was father-in-law to the famous Confederate general J. E. B. Stuart. At the direction of Brigham Young, five companies were recruited under Cooke, with the leadership cadre including Lt. George Stoneman, who later became governor of California. The battalion was mustered into service on July 16, 1846, at Council Bluffs, Iowa, and opened a southern wagon route for travelers through Texas, New Mexico, and Arizona which terminated in San Diego.[12] The battalion fought its only engagement on the San Pedro River in southeastern

Arizona on December 9 when several wild bulls there charged the column, killing several mules. One bull was shot six times before it succumbed to rifle fire.[13]

A Sergeant Tyler recorded that in places along the march, "the men . . . had to pull at long ropes to aid the teams [of horses]. The deep sand alone without any load was enough to wear out both man and beast." On November 18, near a place Tyler described as the "Mimbres," he observed, "no matter where you cast your eye, a most beautiful, grassy plain attracts your vision, stretching out as far you can discern."[14]

The expedition found some four to five hundred inhabitants and two hundred soldiers at the Tucson presidio. The commander, Captain Comaduran, initially refused to surrender but eventually permitted the American column to march though the town and on to the junction of the Gila and Colorado Rivers.[15] When the battalion arrived at the San Diego Mission on January 29, 1847, Captain Cooke observed, "History may search in vain for an equal march of infantry."[16]

A year later, Mexico recognized the annexation of Texas; ceded present-day Arizona, California, and New Mexico; and relinquished parts of present-day Colorado, Nevada, and Utah to the United States in the Treaty of Guadalupe Hidalgo.[17] The United States had offered to purchase much of northern Mexico, including some seaports, for fifty million dollars at the conclusion of the Mexican War but settled for some thirty thousand square miles[18] and slowly established a presence in this vast emptiness. Soon, prospective miners, pioneers, and adventurers began traveling in large numbers across Arizona on the southern route to the California gold rush.

On Christmas Day, 1851, two American surveyors, alongside soldiers occupying Fort Yuma, narrowly survived death at the hands of the Apaches. They were spared when

one of the surveyors was recognized by an Indian girl he
had saved in the desert two years before. The fort had been
established in October 1849 on the California side of the
Colorado River across from present-day Yuma, Arizona.
Fort Defiance was established two years later in northeast
Arizona about twenty-five miles from Gallup, New Mexico.
The Defiance cadre resisted a large-scale Indian attack on
April 30, 1860, only to abandon the place with the com-
mencement of the American Civil War. Fort Buchanan was
established in 1856 south of Tucson, and Fort Mohave three
years later, providing the rest of the scant American military
presence in the Arizona portion of New Mexico Territory.[19]

## An Early Arizona Outlaw

Legend has it that a Dr. Able Lincoln established a ferry
at Yuma Crossing in about 1850 and made some $60,000
($1.5 million today) taking gold prospectors on their way
to California across the Colorado. This soon drew the
unwelcome attention of an outlaw with an eye for profit.
John Joel Glanton was a veteran of the east Texas Regulator-
Moderator War and leader of his own gang of adventurers.
He forced Lincoln to take him in as a partner in the ferry
operations but both Lincoln and the Glanton gang were
supposedly killed by enterprising Yuma Indians competing
with them for ferry customers.[20]

Soon thereafter, rudimentary steamboats began to ply a
route to Fort Yuma. The *General Jessup* began operations
in 1852, hauling as many as fifty tons of freight at the
profitable rate of fifty dollars per ton. A military vessel
described as a "water-borne wheelbarrow" joined the tiny
fleet five years later, setting the stage for Lt. Joseph Ives to
become the first known white man to reach the bottom of
the Grand Canyon.

One year earlier, former naval officer Edward "Ned" Fitzgerald Beale of the U.S. Corps of Topographical Engineers had been directed to build a wagon road through northern Arizona. The year 1857 marked the first stage runs across Arizona, from San Antonio to San Diego. The principal town in the 1850s was Tucson, which had a civil population of about one hundred residents after the Mexican garrison departed in March 1856.[21] American dragoons arrived eighteen months later.

## Confederate Arizona Territory

Much of what we know today as southern Arizona and New Mexico was first organized as a Confederate territory, created in 1861 after federal soldiers fled the area at the beginning of the Civil War. Since strong secessionist sentiment existed in that region at the beginning of hostilities, a secessionist convention was held at Mesilla, New Mexico Territory, on March 16, 1861, and pro-Southern Texas forces took possession of that town on July 25. The "Battle of Mesilla," launched by the small but bold Second Texas Mounted Rifles, prompted federal forces under Maj. Isaac Lynde to flee north. On August 1, Col. John Baylor formally issued a Proclamation to the People of the Territory of Arizona, taking possession of present-day southern Arizona and New Mexico for the Confederacy. Southern legislation implementing these measures was passed in January 1862 and the Confederate territory was officially created by proclamation of Confederate president Jefferson Davis on February 14.

This state of affairs was short lived. The Battle of Glorieta Pass, in northern New Mexico, a two-day engagement in late March, has been described by some historians as the "Gettysburg of the West" even though it involved few troops.[22] At the conclusion of the engagement, Texans led by Maj. Charles L. Pyron and Lt. Col. William Read Scurry departed for Texas via Santa Fe. Although an April 15 engagement known as the Battle of Pichacho Pass or Pichacho Peak was a draw, the eventual demise of Confederate Arizona Territory was readily apparent. Five months after the Davis declaration, Union forces arrived at Mesilla, forcing the Confederate territorial government into a comfortable yet humiliating exile at San Antonio.

Confederate and Union interest in present-day Arizona had been prompted by the need for roads and trails westward to California, as well as the prospect of mineral wealth which turned remote places like Gila City and Tubac—near Tucson—into boom towns in the late 1850s. Pres. Abraham Lincoln signed the Arizona Organic Act, making the land within present-day Arizona a United States territory, on February 24, 1863. Territorial governor John N. Goodwin located the first capital at Fort Whipple primarily because Tucson was perceived as a haven for former secessionists. The first location was succeeded by Prescott (1864), Tucson (1867), Prescott again (1877), and finally Phoenix (1889).

The largest population regions in the first ten years after the American Civil War were Tucson and nearby Tubac, followed by Yuma, La Paz, Ehrenberg, Gila City, Prescott, and Wickenburg.[23] The sparse 1866 population of Arizona Territory consisted of 5,526 whites and Hispanics as well as 25,000 Native Americans.

Despite the small population, lawlessness had prevailed in the new territory for many years. During 1857 and the following year, there were a number of murders at Tucson. Danger and corruption were everywhere. In April 1871, U.S. Marshal Edward Phelps was killed by Mexican bandits. His successor, Isaac Q. Dickason, abandoned his office and died as a bookkeeper in Deadwood, South Dakota, after embezzling twelve thousand dollars in federal funds.[24] On

September 2, 1879, Deputy U.S. Marshals J. H. Adams and Cornelius Finley were murdered by outlaws south of Tucson.[25] Lawmen were not the only ones susceptible to the perils of the West. Gila River ranchers were sometimes compelled in that era to abandon their homes because of Mexican and American outlaws. The John Baker family was massacred in 1871 in the Gila Valley only about a year after a deputy U.S. marshal stationed there was killed in a bar fight over a barmaid.[26] A series of notorious highwaymen, notably including Bill Brazelton, who had arrived in 1877 from California as the owner of a show troupe, also roamed the territory.

## The "Cowboy" Problem

Soon, Mexican authorities alerted American officials about Arizona outlaws selling stolen horses in Mexico. The governor reported early the next year that the cowboy element numbered about one hundred. The first leader, alleged to be Robert Martin, was replaced by Newman H. "Old Man" Clanton, whose sons included Phineas ("Phin"), Joseph Isaac ("Ike"), and William ("Billy"). The cowboy host included Tom and Frank McLaury, John Ringo, and "Curly Bill" Brocius, who has often been identified, or perhaps mis-identified, as William Graham.[27]

In July 1879, cattle stolen in Mexico were reportedly being offered to Americans about fifty miles from the border. Two Pima County deputy sheriffs found stolen stock at Fort San Carlos and offered to pursue the rustlers for a fee.[28]

Rancher Sam Aaron later recalled encountering John Ringo and some seventy others camped among the tall pines of the Chiricahua Mountains. Frank and Tom McLaury eventually provided holding pens for such cattle acquisitions at their new place, established in late 1880, about twenty-five miles east of Tombstone in Sulphur Spring Valley.[29] The McLaury location was four miles south of Soldier's Hole, a crossroads near the White River. Sam Aaron claimed that the rustlers would steal as many as two thousand cattle in Mexico, near Sonora, and then sell them at two to three dollars a head. However, mining rather than ranching became the impetus for Arizona settlement.

## Early Arizona Mining

The first prominent Anglo miner in the San Pedro Valley near Tombstone was Charles DeBrille Poston[30] (b. 1825), a Kentucky native who had first migrated to San Francisco. Poston (Posten) was recruited by a French mining syndicate to prospect in southeastern Arizona. His expedition survived an 1854 shipwreck in the Gulf of California and journeyed to the Santa Cruz Valley south of Tucson, where they found promising silver deposits.[31] Poston eventually returned to California, reported to the syndicate, and then incorporated the Sonora Exploring and Mining Company with Maj. Samuel P. Heintzelman, whom he had met at Fort Yuma.

Life was not easy at the mining operations Poston developed near Tubac, the old presidio which Poston and his men occupied and rehabilitated, but there were certain amenities made possible by the purchase of the Avoca Ranch nearby:

> Supplies to feed the miners . . . were easily obtainable. Wild game—quail, ducks and deer—abounded in the vicinity, so that even a poor hunter could keep the dining table well supplied with meat. Poston hired a German gardener who fenced in and cultivated a field with irrigation water from the Santa Cruz River, thereby providing fresh vegetables. . . . The company's table, open and free of

charge to travelers, became famous for the richness and diversity of its spread. Of this period at Tubac, when Arizona was still a part of New Mexico Territory and civil officials of all types were virtually unknown, Poston later reminisced, "we had no law but love and no occupation but labor. No government, no taxes, no public debt, no politics. It was a perfect state of nature."[32]

Apparently conditions were too perfect. Archbishop Jean Baptiste Lamy of Santa Fe learned of this idyllic state and tasked Fr. Joseph Machebeuf to investigate. Poston had assumed the role of an early day Judge Roy Bean.[33] The mining manager celebrated the rites of marriage, baptized children, granted divorces, and executed criminals, as the *alcalde* (magistrate) of that pueblo. Business was good since Poston charged nothing for marriages and sometimes hired the bridegroom after the nuptials. Father Machebeuf reportedly resolved the sacramental dilemma by blessing the marriages already performed on the assurance that Poston would stop performing the rites of the church.[34]

One of Poston's employees opened a competing mine in 1859. The Brunkow, sometimes whimsically described as the Bronco or Broncho, eventually was considered to be jinxed since the original owner, Frederick Brunkow, and two later proprietors met violent deaths there. Brunkow was a graduate of the school of mines at Freiberg in Saxony. He fled Germany after the Revolution of 1848 and began his Arizona mining career near Tucson with the Sonora Exploring and Mining Company. Brunkow later started the St. Louis Mining Company and selected a spot on the San Pedro River to begin operations. He hired a number of Mexican nationals from Sonora for his operations, as was common. On July 23, 1860, the Mexican employees slaughtered nearly everyone at the mine. This was also common, but the danger had apparently been overlooked in the Brunkow business plan. Only the cook was spared,

supposedly because he was Catholic. Brunkow partner
William M. Williams discovered the massacre of Brunkow;
Williams' own brother, James Williams; and J.C. Moss after
returning from a trip to Fort Buchanan, some fifty miles
away, for supplies. He found Brunkow at the bottom of a
well with a rock drill stabbed into his body.[35]

In spite of such dangers, other adventurers looked
.for opportunities in the region. One Henry Crabb even
attempted to establish a new government in Sonora but
he and his followers were eradicated by military force.
Soon, some Anglos attacked a band of Apaches, prompting
Cochise to begin raids throughout the Santa Cruz Valley,
culminating in yet another destruction of the presidio at
Tubac as Charles DeBrille Poston and his mining partners
fled for their lives.[36]

Milton B. Duffield, a colorful United States marshal in
territorial days, became owner of the Brunkow Mine on
October 23, 1866, by means which are a mystery to this day.
Eventually, Duffield was mortally wounded attempting to
reclaim the ill-fated mine from a competitor; Mr. Joseph T.
Holmes resolved the dispute on June 5, 1874, by emptying
both barrels of a shotgun into Duffield's cranium after
"fair warning." Holmes was convicted of manslaughter but
escaped from prison and was never seen again.[37] Duffield did
not own the mine at the time of his death, or so it seemed,
since his housekeeper, Mrs. Mary E. Vaughn, told the
Tucson citizenry that trespassers were not welcome there
in a July 4, 1874, advertisement in the *Tucson Citizen.* The
Pima County Book of Mines revealed to anyone interested
that Duffield had transferred ownership to Mrs. Vaughn
about a year earlier, perhaps to avoid creditors.

There were some eleven thousand mining claims in
Arizona by 1876, in three principal regions: Mohave
County, the Prescott area, and the Globe-Superior area,
which hosted the Silver King mine.

# A Place Called Tombstone

Some noted in 1879 that outlaws of southern Arizona Territory were protected by Mexican authorities, and about thirty-six stage and mail coach holdups occurred in this era.[38] Much of the crime occurred in the region around Tombstone. The settlement had been started by Pennsylvanian Edward L. "Ed" Schieffelin, who had entered his own mining claim two years before. He later described at length how it all happened[39]:

> In January 1877, I outfitted in San Bernardino, with two mules and all the necessary apparatus for prospecting and left there after outfitting, with twenty-five or thirty dollars in money, going to what is called the Hualapai country, on the borders of the Grand Canyon, not far from Hackberry. While I was there prospecting, a company of Hualapai scouts enlisted to go into the southern part of the Territory scouting for Apaches. I had been there about two months and had not found anything, and thinking that it would be a good opportunity to prospect, to follow the scouting party about through the country and thus be protected from the Indians, I went down with them and arrived at Camp Huachuca about the first of April.

He became acquainted with several of the soldiers and took short trips through the country alone, coming back to the camp. He discovered that he could not prospect while with the soldiers, so he struck out alone.[40]

> Whenever I went into Camp Huachuca for supplies on one of my trips, some of the soldiers would frequently ask me if I found anything. The answer was always the same that I had not found anything yet, but I would strike it one of these days in that country. The Indians at that time were very troublesome, and many settlers were killed previous to and during the year. Several times in reply to my remark

that I would eventually find something in that country, the soldiers said, "Yes, you'll find your tombstone," and repeated that several times. The word lingered in my mind, and when I got into that country where Tombstone is now located, I gave the name to the first location that I made. On the organization of the [mining] district it was called Tombstone from that location.

Soon, he had an opportunity to help a contractor working on the old Brunkow Mine, near the present site of Tombstone. From his vantage point guarding the operation, he could see what were later known as the Tombstone hills and noticed "a number of ledges in the neighborhood, all running in the same direction, about northwest and southeast." Later, he explored the nearby hills and "found some float."[41] What happened next reveals a great deal about how casual mining camp conversations sometimes developed into partnerships:

That night I came into the camp of the two men, who were going into Tucson the next day. . . .One of them, William Griffith . . . proposed to furnish me with provisions and to have such assays made as were necessary, to pay for recording, etc., if I would locate a claim for him at the same time I located one for myself. . . . To this I agreed and told him that one of us should build the monument and the other have the choice of claims; that I would not have any partners, as he knew, from what I told him before, several times while we were at work. This was agreed upon and the two men went the next day into Tucson.

Griffith changed his mind regarding the claim. Instead he made a Desert Act[42] claim with more potential. While Griffith returned to Tombstone, Schieffelin kept himself busy by finding two claims, later called the Tombstone and the Graveyard. Griffith also turned down the opportunity to prospect those mines but eventually helped record the

Tombstone claim, even as Schieffelin faced dim prospects.

> I was now reduced to the last extremity; without
> provisions, almost without clothing, and with but thirty
> cents in money. There was plenty of game at hand, and I
> subsisted on the deer I killed. After a few days, I thought
> my best plan was to hunt up my brother Albert, whom I
> had last heard of working in the Silver King Mine. . . . He
> had some money, and we could have assays made, and
> could obtain supplies. . . .
>
> About that time the company sent a man named
> Richard Gird[43] to the Signal Mine[44] to assay for them,
> and he erected a little office and started his furnace. My
> brother Al was acquainted with Gird. . . . One day Al took
> some of the ore to Gird. . . . After looking at the ore, Gird
> asked where it had come from. Al replied that he did not
> know that I had brought it there from the southern part
> of the Territory. "Well," said Gird, "the best thing you can
> do is to find out where that ore came from, and take me
> with you and start for the place."

Later, Gird assayed samples which ranged in value up
to two thousand dollars per ton, the richest find to that
date in southeast Arizona. The Schieffelin brothers and
Dick Gird departed the Signal Mine on February 14, 1878,
for the Tombstone claim, prompting curiosity and even
some rivals. A site nearby had been called Watervale or
Waterville but shifted about two miles to the southeast to
occupy Goose Flats, an elevated slice of open desert over
the Tough Nut mine. Soon the place was called Tombstone.
Schieffelin also brought in the Lucky Cuss and Tough Nut
mines that year.

Yet another legendary mine of the area was the
Contention, for which a small adjoining hamlet was later
named. The Contention was so called because prospector
Hank Williams claimed it as his own, until Richard Gird
and the Schieffelin brothers pointed out that this was a

joint claim which must be divided as agreed.[45] It was part of the Grand Central claim, which had been established on March 27, 1878.[46] The Contention was sold in May 1878 and yielded $5 million in ore by 1886.

Schieffelin had incorporated the Tough Nut and Corbin Mill and Mining companies by early 1879 and departed on another prospecting venture. When he returned to the Tombstone area in February 1880, he discovered that investors were soon to arrive from Philadelphia. They bought the Schieffelin brothers' interest in the Tough Nut mine for $600,000 ($13 million today). The Tombstone mine, for which the most famous town in the American West had been named, was sold for a few hundred dollars. Although wealthy, Schieffelin died seventeen years later while still prospecting, this time near Canyonville, Oregon.[47]

# Arizona
## Gunfighters

# Chronology of Significant Events

**1540** Coronado began exploration of the Tombstone, Arizona, vicinity but found no evidence of the rich silver deposits he passed.

**1736** Silver was discovered at "Ali-shonak," a "place of the small springs," which possibly was corrupted into the word Arizona.

**1846** The Mormon Battalion entered Tucson en route to California during a road-building expedition.

**1850** New Mexico Territory, which included much of present-day Arizona, was created.

**1857** Stagecoach service across Arizona began.

**1859** The ill-fated Brunkow mine was established southwest of Tombstone near the San Pedro River.

**1861** The short-lived Confederate Territory of Arizona was created by proclamation (February 14).

**1864** Gila City, a mining town established in 1861 near Tombstone, passed into history, leaving only "three chimneys and a coyote."

**1868**  "Old Man" Clanton arrived in Arizona, establishing his family on the Gila River.

**1871**  U.S. Marshal Edward Phelps was killed by bandits (April).

**1877**  Ed Schieffelin began scouting for minerals in the Tombstone area.

Camp Huachuca was founded west of the San Pedro River.

The McLaurys arrived in Arizona.

**1879**  Rustlers began offering stolen Mexican cattle to Arizona ranchers (July).

Tombstone was incorporated in November, and three Earp brothers, James, Wyatt, and Virgil, arrived with their wives early the next month.

**1880**  Buckskin Frank Leslie mortally wounded Mike Killeen in a gunfight over Killeen's wife in Tombstone (June 22).

William Graham (Curly Bill Brocius) accidentally killed Tombstone marshal Fred White in an altercation on October 28. He was later acquitted.

**1881**  A stagecoach originating in Contention, Arizona, carrying at least eighteen thousand dollars in bullion was robbed about eleven miles from Tombstone by Jim Crane, Harry "the Kid" Head, Bill Leonard, and Luther King. Bud Philpot and passenger Peter Roerig were killed during the robbery (March 15). Crane was killed later that year by Mexican soldiers.

Virgil, Morgan, and Wyatt Earp and Doc Holliday engaged and killed brothers Frank and Tom McLaury and Billy Clanton in a gunfight on Fremont Street in Tombstone near the rear entrance to the O.K. Corral (October 26). A coroner's jury conducted an inquest (October 29-30). Judge Wells Spicer began a preliminary examination on November 1 to determine whether the Earp faction members would be bound over for trial on charges of first-degree murder. A month later, Spicer issued a decision determining that the defendants Wyatt Earp, Virgil Earp, Morgan Earp, and Doc Holliday "were fully justified in committing these homicides."

Virgil Earp was ambushed and shotgunned from behind, leaving his left arm useless (December 28).

**1882**   Morgan Earp was ambushed and killed in Tombstone on March 18, 1882.

Frank Stilwell was killed on March 20 in the Tucson train yard, two days after Morgan Earp was killed. Wyatt Earp claimed he killed suspected Clanton factionist Florentino Cruz near Tombstone on March 22 and Curly Bill Brocius at Iron Springs on March 24.

Buckskin Frank Leslie killed Billy "the Kid" Claiborne at the Oriental Saloon in Tombstone (November 14).

**1887**   Jim Roberts and other sheep-grazing Tewksbury factionists held off Tom Tucker and other Graham gunfighters, killing two (August 10).

Andy Blevins (Andy Cooper) killed John Tewksbury and Bill Jacobs in a Pleasant Valley, Arizona, gunfight over grazing rights and then fed the bodies to some hogs (September 2).

Pleasant Valley feudist Andy Blevins (Andy Cooper) was killed at his mother's home near Holbrook, Arizona, by Commodore Perry Owens, who also killed Blevins' brother-in-law Mose Roberts and young Sam Houston Blevins, leaving only John Blevins alive (September 4).

Jim Roberts and Jim Tewksbury held off Graham adherents, mortally wounding Harry Middleton (September 16).

**1895** Will and Bob Christian shot their way out of the Oklahoma City jail, killing two men, before escaping to Arizona Territory (April 27).

**1896** The Christian brothers robbed the International Bank of Nogales, Arizona, then shot their way out of town (August 6).

Will Christian and Bob Hays were ambushed by eight law officers and Hays was killed in the ensuing gunfight.

**1897** Will Christian was mortally wounded in a gunfight with law officers and died later that day (April 28).

**1899** Thomas "Black Jack" Ketchum mortally wounded two miners after a card game dispute at Camp Verde, Arizona (July 2).

Ketchum, Elzy Lay, and G.W. Franks engaged a posse in an all-day gunfight, killing three law officers in Turkey Canyon, New Mexico (July 12).

Black Jack Ketchum was mortally wounded attempting to single-handedly rob a Colorado and Southern train near Folsom, Arizona (August 16).

**1901** Bill Smith and a brother engaged two Arizona Rangers in a gunfight on the Black River in Arizona after a Union Pacific train robbery in Utah. Both Rangers were killed (October). Later that year, Bill Smith gunned down two Douglas policemen in a gunfight.

**1902** Ranger Dayton Graham found and killed Bill Smith.

**1928** Aged Pleasant Valley feudist Jim Roberts killed a bank robber with his old six-shooter at Clarksville, Arizona.

**1930** Law officer Jim East, who was present at the death of Billy the Kid, died at Douglas, Arizona (June 30). Lincoln County War observer Gus Gildea died at Douglas (August 10).

**1956** Burt Mossman, last of the prominent Arizona Rangers, died at Roswell, New Mexico (September 5).

# Outlaw Hideouts, Hangouts, and Locales

**Aurora, Illinois**
Birthplace of Burton Mossman (1867-1956), first captain of the Arizona Rangers.

**Bisbee, Arizona**
The stagecoach operated by "Sandy Bob" Crouch was robbed near here on September 8, 1881.

**Camp Grant, Arizona**
Henry "Billy the Kid" McCarty gambled and stole horses in the area, then mortally wounded Francis P. "Windy" Cahill here on Friday, August 17, 1877.

**Camp Rucker, Arizona**
Army establishment west of Tombstone where the first conflict between the Earps and McLaurys occurred in July 1880.

**Charleston, Arizona**
Henry W. P. Schneider was killed in this mining camp by John "Johnny-Behind-the-Deuce" O'Rourke on January 14, 1881.

M. R. Peel was murdered here by Zwing Hunt and Billy Grounds in March 1882.

### Chiricahua Mountains
A mountain range east of Tombstone frequented by John Ringo, the McLaurys, and other rustlers.

### Clanton Well
A watering hole between Yuma and Phoenix named for rustling patriarch Newman H. "Old Man" Clanton.

### Cochise County, Arizona
Southeast Arizona jurisdiction carved out of Pima County in 1881 with Tombstone as first county seat.

### Contention, Arizona
Named for a nearby mining dispute between the co-owners, this small burg on the San Pedro River was the site of the first Tombstone-area stagecoach robbery, which occurred on February 26, 1881.

### Fourth and Allen, Tombstone, Arizona
Site of the Cosmopolitan hotel, the headquarters of the Earp faction during their feud with the McLaurys and Clantons.

### Dodge City, Kansas
Wyatt Earp became a policeman (assistant marshal) here in April 1876, serving with Bat Masterson.

### Douglas, Arizona
Headquarters of legendary rancher and lawman "Texas John" Slaughter (1841-1922).

### Dragoon Mountains
A mountain range northeast of Tombstone where the Earp party killed cowboy partisan Florentino "Indian Charlie" Cruz in 1882.

## Fairbank, Arizona

A hamlet near the junction of the San Pedro River and Bacocomari Creek. Rustlers Tom and Frank McLaury established a ranch nearby.

Lawman Jeff Milton was seriously wounded here in February 1900, but not before dropping train robber Three-Fingered Jack Dunlap.

## Fifth and Allen, Tombstone, Arizona

Site of Jim Earp's Sampling Room Saloon.

## Florence, Arizona

The "Bandit Queen" Pearl Hart was tried here with Joe Boot in November 1899 for the last stagecoach robbery in Arizona six months earlier. Hart was sentenced to five years in Yuma Territorial Prison, but Boot received a thirty-year sentence, prompting him to escape in 1901, never to be seen again.

## Fort Gibson, Indian Territory

Wyatt Earp and Ed Kennedy were accused of stealing several horses here in May 1871. Earp posted bond and did not return to Indian Territory.

## Fort Huachuca, Arizona

Military outpost established as a camp in 1877 west of Tombstone at the foot of the Huachuca Mountains.

## Fifth and Allen, Tombstone, Arizona

Locale of two prominent watering holes: the Oriental Saloon and the Crystal Palace, later renamed the Golden Eagle Brewery. Bat Masterson was unable to save his friend Charlie Storms from death in a gunfight with Luke Short outside the Oriental on February 25, 1881.

**Fremont Street, Tombstone, Arizona**
Site of the so-called gunfight at the O.K. Corral, which actually occurred in a nearby vacant lot, on October 26, 1881.

**Galeyville, Arizona**
A burg at the foot of the Chiracahua Mountains described in the 1880s as an outlaw refuge. Jim "Jake" Wallace shot Curly Bill Brocius here in 1881.

**Gila City, Arizona**
A mining town north of Tombstone abandoned in 1864.

**Gird Block, Fourth and Fremont, Tombstone, Arizona**
The courtroom at Fourth and Fremont where Justice Wells conducted the Earp-Holliday preliminary hearing within sight of the O.K. Corral gunfight was located here.

**Holbrook, Arizona**
A September 4, 1887, gunfight here during the Pleasant Valley War resulted in the deaths of three men at the hands of Sheriff Commodore Perry Owens.

**Iron Springs, Arizona**
Traditionally designated site of a March 24, 1882, gunfight in the Whetstone Mountains, in which Wyatt Earp claimed he killed Curly Bill Brocius. Recent research indicates that the actual site may have been Cottonwood Springs, about four miles away.

**Lamar, Missouri**
Wyatt Earp served as a constable here in 1869.

**Las Vegas, New Mexico**
On July 19, 1879, John Henry "Doc" Holliday killed his first man, former army scout Mike Gordon, here for shooting up a saloon Holliday ran with John Joshua Webb.

**Liberty, Missouri**
Childhood home of Indiana native John Ringo, whose aunt married into the Younger family of James-Younger gang fame.

**Los Angeles, California**
Wyatt Earp died in a small tourist court bungalow at 4004 West 17th, near present-day Crenshaw and Washington Boulevards, on January 13, 1929.

**Morenci, Arizona**
A town terrorized by Augustin Chacón, known as El Peludo, the Hairy One, in the late 1880s.

**Phoenix, Arizona**
Accused murderers Keller and McCloskey were lynched here in 1878. The second victim jumped high in the air to break his own neck after watching the first victim strangle to death.

**Pleasant Valley**
Region south of the Mogollon Rim in Apache and Navaho Counties where the Pleasant Valley (Tonto Basin) War between the Graham and Tewksbury families raged from 1886 until 1892.

**Pottawatomie County, Oklahoma Territory**
Early stomping grounds of the notorious bank and train robbers Bill and Bob Christian before they moved to the Sulphur Springs Valley in southeastern Arizona.

**Prescott, Arizona**
First Arizona residence of Virgil Earp, who arrived here in 1877. United States marshal for Arizona, Crawley Drake headquartered here. Prescott was the county seat of Yavapai County.

**San Carlos Reservation, Arizona**
Southeastern Arizona Indian reservation established in 1873 which became a major purchaser of beef supplied by rustlers.

**San Pedro Valley**
Site of the 1860 Brunkow mine massacre in which Frederick Brunkow and several others were killed by marauding miners on July 23. Former U.S. marshal Milton B. Duffield was killed in a gunfight with Joseph T. Holmes over ownership of the mine on October 23, 1866.

**San Simon, Arizona**
A station on the Southern Pacific in northwest Cochise County which became a gathering place for cowboys and rustlers such as Curly Bill Brocius.

**Shakespeare, New Mexico**
Western New Mexico mining town which was the eastern terminus of the cattle-rustling circuit roamed by Tombstone-area cattle rustlers.

**Sierra Bonita Ranch, near Willcox, Arizona**
Sulphur Springs Valley was the home of legendary cattleman Henry C. Hooker.

**Skeleton Canyon**
A Peloncillo Mountains locale on the Mexican border where Old Man Clanton and other rustlers killed several Mexican smugglers in early August 1881. Deputy Frank Robson was killed here in August 1896 while pursuing the Christian gang.

**Soldier's Hole, Arizona**
A crossroads east of Tombstone frequented by rustlers and cowboys. The McLaury ranch was four miles to the south.

## Solomonville, Arizona
The bandit Chacón was hanged here November 21, 1902, after killing as many as fifty-two men.

## Sonora, Mexico
Mexican state directly south of the Tombstone region which provided a ready supply of cattle for Tombstone-area rustlers.

## Sulphur Springs Valley
An area northeast of Tombstone which became a reputed haven for rustlers and stagecoach robbers.

## Tombstone, Arizona
A mining town established in 1879 and named for the nearby Ed Schieffelin claim that his companions warned would lead to his early death.

## Tucson, Arizona
Tucson became the county seat of Pima County, the site of several notorious 1857 murders and the 1882 killing of Frank Stilwell by Wyatt Earp. The Southern Pacific reached this place in 1870.

## West Turkey Creek Canyon, Chiricahua Mountains
John Ringo was found dead here on July 14, 1882, of a gunshot wound which may or may not have been self-inflicted.

## Wichita, Kansas
Wyatt Earp's first documented service as a Kansas law officer began in this raucous cow town as early as 1872.

## Willcox, Arizona
Grant Wheeler and Joe George robbed a Southern Pacific

train near here in January 1895. The next month Wheeler was trapped at Mancos, Colorado, and shot himself rather than surrender.

## Young, Arizona
The Perkins store near Young was the scene of the last gunfight of the Pleasant Valley War, in which feudists John Graham and Charles Blevins died.

## Yuma Crossing
Ferry crossing established by Dr. Able Lincoln and frequented by the outlaw John Joel Glanton, who muscled his way in as partner.

# PART I

# Tombstone:
# Bawdy and Rowdy,
# Tender and Tough

# Principal Tombstone Characters

**The Miners**
Charles DeBrille Poston
Edward "Ed" Schieffelen

**The Cattleman**
Henry C. Hooker

**The Cowboys (Rustlers)**
William "Billy the Kid" Claiborne
Newman H. "Old Man" Clanton
Phineas "Phin" Clanton
Joseph Isaac "Ike" Clanton
William "Billy" Clanton
"Old Man" Hughes
Jim Hughes
Robert Findley "Frank" McLaury
Thomas Clark "Tom" McLaury
William R. "Will" McLaury
John Ringo
Curly Bill Brocius

**The Earp "Gang"**
Wyatt Earp
Virgil Earp
Morgan Earp
John Henry "Doc" Holliday

## The Earp Partisans
John Clum, mayor, editor, *Tombstone Epitaph*
Fred Dodge, Wells Fargo undercover agent
Marshall Williams, Wells Fargo resident agent
George Parsons, gentleman miner

## The Gamblers
James, Virgil, Warren, Wyatt, and Morgan Earp
Doc Holliday
Bat Masterson
Luke Short
Charlie Storms
Buckskin Frank Leslie

## The Earp Wives and Courtesans
Alvira Packingham Sullivan "Allie" Earp, wife of Virgil Earp
Nellie Bartlett Ketcham "Bessie" Earp, wife of James Earp
Celia Ann Blaylock "Mattie" Earp, wife of Wyatt Earp
Josephine Sarah Marcus "Josie" ("Sadie") Behan Earp, paramour of John Behan and Wyatt Earp
Louisa Houston Earp, wife of Morgan Earp
Mary Katherine Harony "Big-Nosed Kate Elder," paramour of Doc Holliday

## The Suspected Stage Robbers
Frank Stilwell
Jim Crane
Billy Grounds
Curly Bill Brocius
Doc Holliday
Zwing Hunt

## The "County Ring"
John Behan, sheriff of Cochise County
John Dunbar, stable keeper

Milton Joyce, saloon keeper
Harry Woods, publisher, *Tombstone Nugget*

## The Townsmen
George Goodfellow, surgeon
Milton Joyce, saloon keeper
William M. "Billy" Breakenridge, deputy sheriff
George Parsons, gentleman miner and diarist
Endicott Peabody, minister

## The Coroner and Judges
Henry Matthews, coroner
Wells Spicer, lawyer, justice of the peace
William Stillwell (no apparent relation to Frank), associate
　judge for Arizona
J. H. Lucas, probate judge

## Law Enforcement
Fred White, first Tombstone city marshal
Ben Sippy, second Tombstone city marshal
Virgil Earp, third Tombstone city marshal and deputy U.S.
　marshal
John Behan, first Cochise County sheriff
William M. "Billy" Breakenridge, deputy sheriff
Frank Stilwell, deputy sheriff, suspected stage robber
Crawley P. Dake, Arizona federal marshal
Bob Paul, Pima County sheriff
Jerome L. Ward, second Cochise County sheriff

## The Lawyers
Lyttleton Price, prosecutor
Ben Goodrich, prosecutor
Will McLaury, prosecutor
Thomas Fitch, Earp lawyer
T. J. Drum, Holliday lawyer

## Coroner's Inquest Witnesses
John Behan
R. F. Coleman
Martha King
P. H. Fellehy

## Preliminary Hearing Witnesses
Henry Matthews, coroner
Billy Allen
Martha King
Wes Fuller
Wyatt Earp
Virgil Earp
H. F. Sills
Addie Boland
J. H. Lucas

## The Vendetta Riders
Morgan, Warren, and Wyatt Earp
Doc Holliday
Sherman McMasters
Charlie Smith
Dan Tipton
Turkey Creek Jack Johnson
Texas Jack Vermillion

## The Vendetta Victims
Frank Stilwell
Florentino "Indian Charlie" Cruz
Curly Bill Brocius (?)

## CHAPTER ONE

# Pasteboard and Ivory

History is an argument without end.
—Pieter Geyl, in Napoleon: *For and Against* (1949)

The Tombstone city marshal and his vagabond posse strode down Fremont Street, pausing just long enough for a few words with Sheriff Johnny Behan before brushing past him. They were dressed for town but loaded for bear.

Thus began the famous march towards destiny. Virgil, Wyatt, Morgan and Doc walked slowly down Fremont Street toward the confrontation that would become known as the gunfight at the O.K. Corral. Virgil carried a walking stick in his right hand and a six-gun in his waistband. Wyatt and Morgan were carrying pistols, and Doc was concealing the Wells Fargo shotgun under his undercoat.

As they came within ten feet of the Clantons and McLaurys, Virgil called out, "Boys, throw up your hands, I want your guns." Then something went terribly wrong. Someone fired a shot, and as Ike Clanton put it, "the ball opened." Within thirty seconds, six men had been shot. Billy Clanton and both McLaury brothers were dead or dying; Virgil and Morgan Earp were seriously wounded, and Doc Holliday was slightly hurt. Wyatt was unscathed. So was Ike, the instigator of it all, who had run away when the shooting began.[1]

Forty-seven years later, an old man rested in a small,

51

nondescript Los Angeles tourist cottage, attended by his wife, a kitten, and a doctor. Wyatt Stapp Earp died early on the morning of a bright mid-January day. His last words raised more questions than answers. "Supposing—supposing—" he had said to no one in particular before falling back on a pillow with an exasperated "Oh well."[2]

We can easily suppose what might have happened to that wide spot in the road called Tombstone, Arizona, were it not for Wyatt Earp and a long-ago gunfight whose details and aftermath are vigorously argued by knowledgeable historians to this day. Tombstone—the O.K. Corral—a place and time many only slightly familiar with the American West think they know all about. And yet, there are still many questions. Who started the fight? Did the McLaurys or Clantons try to surrender? Did the Earp brothers and Doc Holliday get away with murder? Why were all these people in the middle of the desert anyway?

One word answers the last question: silver. An early Tombstonian could see the source of most money in the town by looking towards the surrounding hills from Fifth and Toughnut. The Grand Central and Contention Mines, as well as the Toughnut Mine, near the Tombstone water tank, could be seen in the distance, as could the West Side Mine and the Lucky Cuss.

The early life of Tombstone, the most famous place in the American West, was not much different than that of an earlier boomtown called Gila City nearby. Men "hurried to the spot with barrels of whiskey and billiard tables. . . . Traders crowded in with wagonloads of pork and beans; and gamblers came with cards and Monte tables."[3] In 1861, just months after its first residents arrived, Gila City had everything but a church and jail. Three years later, a traveler reported, all that was left of that boomtown was "three chimneys and a coyote."

The silver strikes that began in 1878 assured that

Tombstone would be more, much more than that. And where there were miners, there were gamblers. Among the early Tombstone gambling men were Luke Short and Charlie Storms from Texas, Lou Rickabaugh and Ed Clark from Colorado, and many lesser lights. Deputy Sheriff William Breakenridge considered Bat Masterson, Doc Holliday, and Wyatt, Virgil, Morgan, and Warren Earp "from Kansas and Oklahoma" to be among the most conspicuous gamblers.[4] Attorney Wells Spicer observed in February 1880 that the town boasted "two dance houses, a dozen gambling places, over twenty saloons and more than five hundred gamblers. Still, there is hope, for I know of two bibles in town."[5]

The Crystal Palace and Oriental Saloon sat astride the corner of Fifth and Allen. The Palace was anything but, merely a narrow, false-fronted structure with scarcely a window. The next year the Crystal Palace became the Golden Eagle Brewery, often just called the Eagle. A second story was added to house the offices of Deputy U.S. Marshal Virgil Earp and Dr. George Goodfellow, a man destined to become a prominent West Coast surgeon. The proprietors were the Tribolet brothers of Switzerland. Godfrey Tribolet came to Tombstone with nothing, accumulated enough money to start a new business, and then sent for his brothers, with whom he built a fortune in booze and beef. The brothers became politically prominent and were even involved in futile peace negotiations between the Apache chief Geronimo and Gen. George Crook.[6]

The Oriental Saloon was started by Milton Joyce and William Crownover Parker, the son of a prominent Oakland, California, family. The Oriental opened on Thursday, July 22, 1880, and was described at the time as the "finest one in town."[7] The place was run by Lou Rickabaugh, who eventually hired Wyatt Earp to keep order. The faro dealers at the Oriental would eventually include Morgan Earp, Luke Short, and Buckskin Frank Leslie.[8]

Of course, Tombstone was not inhabited exclusively by gamblers. Mining engineer and Yale graduate John Jay Hammonds, a nephew of legendary Texas Ranger John Coffee Hays, was among the early visitors. Noted surgeon John Goodfellow practiced in the early camp, as did Kentuckian Mark Smith, a lawyer who eventually became the first senator from Arizona. Wyatt Earp claimed many years later that the law enforcement environment in early Tombstone "was not half as bad as Los Angeles" in 1926.[9] Through the early boom years, Tombstone even boasted of appearances by such stage stars as the father of playwright Eugene O'Neill, James O'Neill, who had the misfortune of catching "silver fever" during his visit. One historian noted that James O'Neill

> proved an easy mark in 1880 when he fell into the clutches of a swindler named George M. Ciprico. Himself a sometime amateur actor, Ciprico in 1879 salted a claim in Tombstone known as the Cumberland Mine; then as was the custom, he issued a handsome prospectus offering shares for sale. John E. Owens, an actor with little knowledge of mining, visited the site, failed to detect the swindle, invested in the property, and then persuaded O'Neill and a third actor, Louis Morrison, to buy shares. They invested to the point of ownership, only later to file for bankruptcy after losing their savings. Local wits later dubbed the site "The Actor's Mine."

Nearby Charleston made no such claim of respectability. Deputy Sheriff Breakenridge observed the peacekeeping skills of saloon keeper Jim Burton:

> Charleston had very little law and order, and was . . . well known as a wild and wicked town during 1879 and '80 with a killing there frequently. Jim Burton was justice of the peace, and a saloonkeeper named Jerry Barton was constable. Barton was a powerful man, and it was

reported that he had killed several men with his fist; he was well known as a man-killer, with many notches on his pistol handles. He stuttered badly, and at one time, when he was asked why he killed so many men replied: "Why, m-my tri-tri-trigger finger stut-stutters."[10]

The life and times of early Tombstone were chronicled by William M. "Billy" Breakenridge, an adventurer who arrived there in late 1879, perhaps in November, the very month the new town was incorporated.[11] The Breakenridge autobiography, *Helldorado,* is far from objective but provides one of the most detailed accounts of frontier life available. Breakenridge was born in Watertown, Wisconsin, itself a reputed hotbed of horse thieves, on Christmas Day, 1846. During the second year of the Civil War, Breakenridge[12] worked as a civilian employee of the U.S. Army Quartermasters Department stationed at Rolla, Missouri, freighting supplies to Springfield by mule. He quit that job then traveled to Denver City, Colorado, and met William "Buffalo Bill" Cody at the mouth of the North Platte River.

By the summer of 1864 he had joined the Third Colorado Cavalry at Central City, Colorado, for one hundred days' service in a campaign against Indians following a massacre of the Hungate family about thirty miles from Denver on Cherry Creek. During the pursuit, the expedition received valuable information from Elbridge "Little" Geary , a great-grandson and namesake of a signer of the Declaration of Independence and married to a Cheyenne. According to Geary, a combined force of Cheyenne, Arapaho, and Sioux were assembled at the head of Beaver Creek, some one hundred miles from Denver. When the Indians learned that Geary was an informant, they retaliated by stealing his livestock and the violence escalated.[13]

Breakenridge was present during a late November 1864 army attack on the Cheyenne at Sand Creek, about ten miles north of present-day Chivington, Colorado. He killed one brave he came upon while scouting for a place to treat wounded soldiers. Later, when his sister requested a locket of his hair, a common practice at the time, Breakenridge sent two scalps home. The attack was an out and out massacre of some two hundred mostly friendly Indians, two-thirds of whom were women and children.[14]

Breakenridge also became acquainted with Thomas J. "Bear River Tom" Smith, who was serving as city marshal of Kit Carson, Colorado, then a shipping point for Texas cattle. Breakenridge later adopted Smith's law enforcement methods, which emphasized getting along with everyone as long as possible.[15]

During the American centennial, Breakenridge traveled from La Junta, Colorado, to Prescott, Arizona, with a colonization party organized by outfitting merchants. The party traveled through present-day Trinidad, Colorado; Albuquerque, New Mexico; and Fort Defiance to Sunset Crossing (now St. Joseph), Arizona. Upon arrival, Breakenridge discovered he had been cheated out of his pay but went into business with Sam Hunt, a fellow employee who had obtained a bill of sale on the horses and equipment used in the venture.

Breakenridge observed an unusual lynching in Phoenix two years later. Accused murderers William McCloskey and John Keller were removed from the jail by a local vigilance committee. After the first man strangled to death, his partner jumped off the back of the wagon on which he was standing in order to break his own neck. Meanwhile, the under sheriff, Hi McDonald, stayed behind to shoot a few rounds into the jail ceiling for appearances.[16] Such vigilance committees were hardly unusual in the West. The San Francisco California Committee of Vigilance, formed in 1850, was particularly notable for the ruthlessness with which it disposed of accused criminals. Dodge City and other Kansas cow towns used vigilance as an extrajudicial law enforcement method.[17] "Vigilance" would also become a major influence in Tombstone.

Breakenridge arrived in Tombstone shortly after Christmas 1879. He was there to prospect a claim about 15 miles away, near the Cochise Stronghold.[18] Among the ranchers who resided nearby was Newman H. "Old Man" Clanton, who had lived in Missouri, Texas, and California before arriving in Arizona. His family consisted of five sons and three daughters when he established himself about 1868 on the Gila River in southwestern Arizona, claiming a watering hole between Yuma and Phoenix still known as Clanton Well. Four years later he was ranching near Camp Thomas about 140 miles north of present-day Tombstone, near the San Carlos Indian Reservation, which purchased over three million pounds of beef annually. The general consensus among researchers has been that Old Man Clanton was a rancher, farmer, freighter, and cattle rustler. Eventually he moved to a spot fourteen miles southwest of Tombstone. His sons Phineas (Phin or Fin), Joseph Isaac (Ike), and William Harrison (Billy) associated themselves with the rustling operation.

Robert Findley, Frank McLaury, and Thomas Clark "Tom" McLaury were born in New York State, lived with their parents in Iowa, and arrived in Arizona about 1877, perhaps as cattle drovers. Their older brother Will was a Fort Worth attorney. Frank and Tom established a ranch on Babocomari Creek near its junction with the San Pedro River, near the small hamlet called Fairbank.[19]

Wyatt Stapp Earp arrived in Tombstone in late 1879, the very year a post office was established and the town was formally organized. The streets had been laid out the prior year. Earp later gave this brief account of his arrival:

Wyatt Earp, famously remembered for the shootout at the O.K.
Corral. *(Courtesy Arizona Historical Society, Tucson)*

I have been in Tombstone since December 1, 1879. I came here from Dodge City, Kansas, where, against the protest of businessmen and officials, I resigned from the office of City Marshal, which I held from 1876. I came to Dodge City from Wichita, Kansas. I was on the police force in Wichita, from 1874 until I went to Dodge City.[20]

He was born March 19, 1848, at Monmouth, Warren County, Illinois, and was named for his father's Mexican War company commander. Nicholas Porter Earp (1813-1907) fathered six sons, three of whom served in the Union army during the Civil War. Nicholas moved his family from Missouri to Pella, Iowa, in about 1850, then on to San Bernardino, California, when Wyatt was sixteen. The family returned east to Lamar, Missouri, around 1868. There, Wyatt defeated his half-brother Newton Earp for the town constable post, married in early January 1870, then lost his wife to either childbirth or disease.

He resolved to leave Lamar but had a legal problem to resolve. A litigant charged that Earp had altered an execution writ to extract twenty dollars from him. Wyatt left Lamar before his trial date.[21] Within a few months, he was in trouble again, this time in Indian Territory, to the southwest of Lamar. A Wyatt S. Earp and Ed Kennedy were alleged to have stolen some horses near Fort Gibson, and a grand jury in Arkansas delivered a true bill against them in May 1871. Ed Kennedy was acquitted, but Wyatt S. Earp posted bond. Although he was never seen there again,[22] several months later, he met Ed and Bat Masterson on the Salt Fork of the Arkansas River during a buffalo-hunting expedition.

One tradition relates that by August 1871, Wyatt was a law officer in Ellsworth, Kansas, where he had a confrontation with Texas shootist Ben Thompson. Although documentation is nonexistent, the story circulated for years.[23] He then surfaced at Wichita, a wide-open cow town started in 1872 on the Arkansas River opposite a sin city called Delano. Contemporary documents indicate he became a deputy city marshal on April 21, 1875, but apparently had served as a law officer the prior year, according to newspaper reports of the time. One tale relates that Wyatt led townspeople who confronted a Texas cowboy contingent coming from the Delano side of the bridge and backed down Mannen Clements, a cousin of John Wesley Hardin. Although Wyatt had some success in Wichita, he ended his stint as a policeman there under a dark cloud. After an altercation with city marshal candidate Bill Smith on April 2, 1876, Wyatt and his brothers became the target of vagrancy charges proferred by the city council, perhaps to discourage the Earps from becoming troublemakers.

That month, Wyatt Earp was appointed to serve as policeman with Bat Masterson in Dodge City, Kansas, which catered to the buffalo-hunting trade.[24] During the next four years there, Wyatt served as an assistant city marshal between gambling excursions into South Dakota and Texas. Wyatt met John Henry "Doc" Holliday and Mary Katherine "Kate" Harony, sometimes called Kate Elder, on one such Texas trip, possibly in the fall of 1877 at Fort Griffin while Wyatt was pursuing rustler Dave Rudabaugh.[25]

Wyatt and Bat were not universally admired in Dodge. Some wags of the time described them as "the Fighting Pimps" because of their affinities for prostitutes and other women of questionable morality. Wyatt Earp balanced this specialty with service as church deacon.[26]

Although an experienced law officer,[27] Earp was not in any serious gunplay until July 26, 1878, when a cowboy named George Hoy galloped at full speed down the Dodge City streets towards the Comique Theater, then fired three rounds into the building. Wyatt responded immediately with gunfire that shattered Hoy's arm. He died August 21.[28]

Most historians agree that Wyatt, James, and Virgil Earp

probably arrived together at Tombstone on December 1, 1879, with bags, baggage, three wives, and nary a marriage license among them.[29] Years later, Wyatt explained his reasons for leaving Kansas in a newspaper interview: "In 1879 Dodge City had begun to lose much of the snap which had given it a charm to men of restless blood and I decided to move to Tombstone, which was just building a reputation." Wyatt claimed that he became a deputy U.S. marshal at Prescott on his way there, which was an apparent invention. He estimated that in the early years, the Tombstone population was ten to twelve hundred, including some three hundred cattle thieves, stage robbers, murderers, and brigands.[30]

James Cooksey Earp, known as "Jim," the firstborn of his siblings, was about forty years old that December of 1879. He had enlisted in the Union army at the beginning of the Civil War and was seriously wounded and disabled at Fredericktown, Missouri. He worked as a bartender and professional gambler in many of the towns where Wyatt Earp lived.

Virgil Walter Earp was two years younger than James, also served in the Union army, and worked in Council Bluffs, Iowa, as a stagecoach driver after the war. His domestic life was exotic, to say the least. He eloped at a young age with Ellen Rysdam of Lamar, Missouri. Ellen assumed he died in the Civil War, married another man, then moved to Kansas City and later Oregon, taking with her a daughter whom Virgil met only years later.[31] When he arrived at Prescott, Arizona, in about 1877, Virgil was accompanied by a second wife, Alvira "Allie" Sullivan Earp. Virgil had several occupations in Prescott, including driving a mail wagon, working as a night watchman, and some service as a constable. Arizona Territory's U.S. marshal Crawley Dake appointed Virgil Earp a deputy U.S. Marshal on November 27, 1879, but the office was non-salaried and largely honorific.[32]

Morgan Earp, age twenty-eight, arrived in Tombstone on December 7 and so closely resembled Wyatt that Wells Fargo agent Fred Dodge had some difficulty telling them apart.[33] Morgan, too, had been born in Pella, Iowa, moved to California with his parents, and then moved back east sometime around 1870. Some stories place Wyatt and Morgan together in a gunfight with Wyatt's former in-laws that year in Lamar, Missouri.[34] Years later, Wyatt also claimed that Morgan had served as marshal of Butte, Montana. More certainly, we know that Morgan had joined his brother in Wichita, Kansas, in time to be the target of 1875 vagrancy charges after Wyatt left the police force there.

Only seventy miles away from Tombstone, the Southern Pacific reached Tucson on March 20. The officials were greeted by Charles DeBrille Poston, "the father of Arizona." No one seemed to notice when frontiersman, Indian fighter, and former Texas Ranger William Oury lamented during a welcoming speech that his way of life was over.[35] Many Tombstonians hoped for a railroad of their own, but though the Arizona and Mexico Railroad and Telegraph was organized in April 1880 to run a railroad line through Tombstone into Mexico, it was never successful. Since Tombstone had no railroad and never would, from time to time, Kinnear's Tombstone and Tucson Express stagecoach would race through the streets for effect, coming to a stop in front of the Cosmopolitan Hotel. Two new citizens of note evidently arrived with such a flourish in May 1880.

James Reilly announced in the May 13 issue of the *Tombstone Nugget* that he had opened his legal practice, specializing in collections. Born about 1830 in Ireland, Reilly had served in an army regiment stationed in Texas and worked as a freighter before buying a newspaper which he moved from Yuma to Phoenix before finally settling in Tombstone.

The day before Reilly announced his law practice in

the *Nugget,* one J. Marcus checked into the Cosmopolitan Hotel. This most certainly was Josephine Sarah Marcus. She described herself years later as a Brooklyn native who migrated to San Francisco with her family at age seven, in the late 1860s. She was the daughter of a prosperous Jewish merchant but decided upon a theatrical career early in life. She was in Tombstone to be with Sheriff John Behan, who had met her in San Francisco and with whom she shortly made domestic arrangements.[36]

Taking advantage of the increasing traffic to the region, Wyatt Earp began working as a stagecoach messenger for Wells Fargo. When he became a Pima County deputy sheriff in mid-July 1880 he relinquished the stagecoach job to his brother Morgan. Yet Wyatt was really there for another reason altogether, as he explained while giving a deposition forty-seven years later in Los Angeles. "I intended to start a stage line when I first started out from Dodge City, but when I got there [Tombstone] I found there was [*sic*] two stage lines and so I finally sold my outfit to one of the companies, to a man named Kinnear. But I intended to start this stage line when I went there." After confirming that he worked as a deputy sheriff and marshal, he also recalled, "I dealt awhile in *pasteboard and ivory.*" He was a faro dealer.[37] Wyatt worked as a dealer from time to time at the Oriental Saloon, which Milt Joyce (Joice) opened on July 21, 1880, according to a newspaper report the next day in the *Tombstone Epitaph.* Earp acquired a one-quarter interest in the gambling department of the Oriental Saloon that October for providing security.[38]

Wyatt was not alone in mining the miners more than the mines. The Earps soon began dealing in mining claims, as did many Tombstonians, starting with a prospect sponsored by Robert "Uncle Bob" Winders, a Fort Worth saloon owner. Soon they sold a claim to Harry Finaty of Dodge City and a six-thousand-dollar lease to a San Francisco investor.[39]

Much of the Tombstone citizenry dealt in mine claims while working far removed from the dirty, gritty work of prospecting, an approach that was replicated a few decades later in oil boom towns.

The Earp brothers also made new friends such as Marshal Williams, the Tombstone agent of Wells Fargo, and Fred Dodge, who arrived the same month as the Earps. Dodge was a special agent of Wells Fargo working undercover, initially as a gambler. Among the most consequential, long-term relationships Earp established that year was one with John Clum, a pivotal Tombstonian who edited the *Epitaph,* a leading newspaper in the boomtown. Clum was born in New York State, attended Rutgers College, then went west in the Army Signal Corps. He organized the San Carlos, the first Apache Indian reservation in 1874, and then served several years as agent.[40]

William M. Breakenridge later noted in passing that at least initially, "the outlaws, stage robbers and certain of the gamblers were good friends." He recalled that the Clantons ranched above Charleston on the San Pedro River. He described nearby Galeyville as a "refuge for all outlaws," which sported some eleven saloons. According to Breakenridge, in the early 1880s, cattle rustlers moved stolen Mexican herds through the Guadalupe and Skeleton Canyons and the San Simon Valley to the Galeyville area. John Ringo and Curly Bill Brocius were prominent leaders among the rustlers, who brought stolen herds to the Clanton place. "The McLaurys looked after all the stock brought up from Mexico through Agua Prieta, where Douglas now stands, into the Sulphur Spring Valley." He also described Frank Stilwell, Jim Crane, Harry Head, Billy Grounds, Pete Spencer (Spence), Zwing Hunt, and Billy Leonard as "stage robbers, hold-up men and other outlaws" that made these places a refuge.[41]

Traditional stories relate that John Peters Ringo was

born in Ringoes, New Jersey, or perhaps Missouri, where, a myth states, he attended William Jewell College. More probably, he was born on May 3, 1850, in Greenfork, Wayne County, Indiana, to Martin Ringo and Mary Peters Ringo and received only a rudimentary education. The family moved to Liberty, Missouri, where some members of the Ringo clan already lived. John Ringo's aunt, Augusta Peters, married Col. Coleman Younger, uncle and namesake of the notorious train and bank robber Thomas Coleman "Cole" Younger. According to the journal of Mary Peters Ringo, the year 1864 found Martin Ringo, his wife, and five children in a wagon train headed west. Martin was killed in a gun accident along the way on July 30, leaving Mary to take the young family on to San Jose, California, where they arrived that October. John Ringo reputedly left California in 1869, perhaps joining some of his father's kinsmen who had settled in Texas.

About six years later, Texas newspaper accounts indicate that John associated with Scott Cooley in the "Hoodoo War," a Mason County range conflict. Cooley's interest in the feud was pure revenge. Tim Williamson, his former employer and mentor, had been killed by German factionist Peter Bader with the collaboration of former Mason County deputy sheriff John Worley (Worhle). Cooley, Ringo, and other associates found, killed, and scalped Worley at Mason, Texas, in 1875. Ringo apparently participated in two more Mason County War killings, those of a hireling named Cheyney and Charley Bader, who had been mistaken for his brother Peter Bader, the presumed murderer of Tim Williamson. The Bader killing landed Ringo in the Travis County, Texas, jail in 1877. Fellow inmates included Bill Taylor, John Wesley Hardin, and Mannen Clements, participants all to one degree or another in the infamous Sutton-Taylor Feud.

Ringo reportedly escaped and then briefly served as a

Loyal Valley, Texas, constable before seeking his fortune
in New Mexico. His first publicly reported introduction
to Arizona society about two years later was less than
promising. Ringo took offense when saloon denizen Louis
Hancock refused to accept a proffered drink, then pummeled
and shot him, leaving poor Hancock seriously wounded on
December 14, 1879.

Ringo associated himself with the "cowboy" faction—
Arizona outlaws selling stolen horses in Mexico and bringing
stolen cattle into Arizona—along with Curly Bill Brocius,
another man of mystery. Stories now largely discounted
say Curly Bill started life in Missouri as a different bad
man, William Graham. More certainly, Brocius punched
cattle in Texas and then drifted through New Mexico into
Arizona. There he and Ringo, contemporaries believed, led
the cowboy element, whose primary targets were Mexican
ranchers and smugglers.[42]

During this period, "The rustlers generally roamed between Charleston on the San Pedro and distant Shakespeare, a bleak little mining town in western New Mexico.
The landscape they occupied was rough and mountainous."
Yet the region included "canyons and extensive valleys that
afford the finest sort of range for cattle."[43] Their favorite
haunt the year after the Earps arrived was Galeyville, which
Breakenridge described as yet another focus of outlawry
in southeast Arizona: "Galeyville was a small mining town
with a smelter, and employed some thirty or forty men in
the mine and smelter. It was here where some sixty or more
rustlers, who were engaged in stealing cattle in Mexico, and
bringing them across the line into New Mexico and Arizona
in large herds, made their headquarters; they knew no law
but their own."

Breakenridge further described the criminal opportunities available: "There was no port of entry between El Paso
and Nogales, and the only Mexican custom house, outside

of these places, was on the San Pedro River where it flows from Mexico into the United States. Cattle were cheap and plentiful in Mexico, there were few line riders [cowboys watching the herds] and it was very easy for smugglers to get across the line from both directions." The economic cycle was completed by "Mexicans [who] smuggled Mexican silver into the United States to buy goods, and then smuggled the goods into Mexico, as the duty on merchandise was very high and so was the export duty on silver."[44]

Yet another opportunity was presented by American cattle ranchers in the area who needed stock and did not ask many questions. Their source of supply was a rustlers' ring that operated out of Galeyville. There were lots of cattle to be stolen in Mexico then driven through Skeleton or Guadalupe Canyons and up through the San Simon Valley. The rustlers, being good businessmen, had scattered corrals along the route anyplace there was water, and there they branded the stolen beef and drove them on for sale to the ranchers of the valleys.

The rustling was bad enough; worse was the considerable bloodshed that was part of the price. Since the cowboys had no compunction about shooting Mexicans, much violence accompanied these raids before they returned to Galeyville to drink up the profits.

They also robbed Mexican smugglers bringing in silver across the border as a lucrative sideline in which they traded for goods to be taken back to Mexico. There was little expense since the smugglers avoided government duties on both sides of the border. As for the cowboy ambushes, Billy Breakenridge was probably right in saying that most of the time they killed the smugglers.

Curly Bill Brocius and John Ringo were the acknowledged leaders of the Galeyville mob. They and their followers lived well on their misguided deeds for a time, but trouble was coming.[45]

Wyatt Earp investigated the July 1880 theft of some mules from nearby Camp Rucker.[46] He recalled the incident in November 1881 during court testimony:

> The difficulty which resulted in the death of William Clanton and Tom McLaury originated last spring. . . . A little over a year ago, I followed Frank and Tom McLaury and two other parties who had stolen six Government mules from Camp Rucker—myself, Virgil, and Morgan Earp, Marshal Williams, Captain Hurst,[47] and four soldiers. We traced the mules to McLaury's ranch.
>
> They had branded the mules DS changing the US to DS. After we arrived at McLaury's ranch, Captain Hurst came to us boys and told us he had made a compromise. By so doing he would get his mules back. We insisted on following them up. Hurst prevailed upon us to go back to Tombstone, so we came back. Hurst told us, two or three weeks afterward, that they would not give up the mules to him after we went, saying that they only wanted to get us away so they could stand the soldiers off. Captain Hurst cautioned me and my brothers Virgil and Morgan to look out for these men, that they had made some hard threats against our lives.[48]

The 1928 memoirs of Deputy Sheriff Billy Breakenridge quoted this narrative but related a second version of events. According to "old-timers," Curly Bill, Zwing Hunt, and Billy Grounds "stole the mules and ran them down into the Sulphur Spring Valley near the McLaury Ranch." The trio sold the mules to a freighter, who in turn used them to fulfill a government contract at Camp Rucker, from which the livestock had been stolen.

On July 30, 1880, Captain Hurst published a notice in the *Tombstone Epitaph* offering a reward for the return of the livestock. The notice stated that the mules had been secreted with the assistance of the McLaurys at or near their ranch fifteen days earlier. Six days later, Frank McLaury responded in the *Tombstone Weekly Nugget,* calling Hurst "a coward, a vagabond, a rascal and a malicious liar."

Even so, signs of growing Tombstone prosperity were everywhere, even as potential danger lurked in the nearby hills. Telegraph operations began in July 1880 and local telephone service was available early the next year.[49] The Mimbres Apache leader Victorio escaped from the San Carlos Indian Reservation and had to be recaptured, while dirt-floored saloons and hotels were being replaced by permanent structures back in town. Soon, Tombstone boasted four theaters and the Can Can restaurant, which one enthusiast compared favorably to Delmonico's of New York. Still there were some limitations to all this progress. The nearest train station was Benson, some twenty miles away, and water piped in from the Dragoon Mountains was only available intermittently.[50] The growing population was attended by several physicians then, yet tragedies still occurred. Diarist George Parsons recorded the death of Mary Clum from complications of childbirth.[51] Soon, the Tombstone medical community would be tending other needs.

George Parsons recorded on July 30 that Tombstone had been attracting a hard element, and that there were petty criminals and small-time gamblers associating with the cowboys. A peculiarly notable incident of violence occurred the month before. Handsome, square-jawed "Buckskin" Frank Leslie was a Tombstone bartender with a strong side interest in the ladies. His flirtations took a fatal turn on June 22, 1880, as described by Deputy Sheriff Breakenridge. That day Leslie "attended a dance at the opera house, and walked home with Mrs. Killeen, the Commercial House housekeeper, who had separated from her husband. While they were sitting on the front porch of the hotel above the street, her husband, Mike Killeen, also a bartender, came out onto the porch, and after a few words, either Leslie or his associate George Perine shot and killed Killeen. Leslie

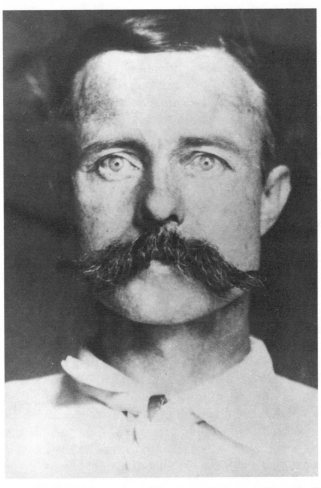

Buckskin Frank Leslie. (*Courtesy Arizona Historical Society, Tucson*)

was discharged by the first judge who examined the case and soon married the widow."[52]

Before he died, Killeen said that he was shot by Leslie associate George Perine, not Leslie. On June 27, Parsons observed that there was some talk of vigilantes "going for Frank Leslie if Killeen were to die."[53] Perine was arrested on August 14. Three days later Perine appeared before Justice of the Peace James Reilly, who had arrived in town only three months before. Perine appeared with attorney Harry Jones. This was a problem. Justice Reilly had warned Harry Jones not to come back after an argument the previous day regarding Reilly's deciding before he assumed the bench a case in which he had an interest. When Deputy Sheriff Wyatt Earp declined to remove Jones from the courtroom, Reilly proceeded to do so himself. After the resulting fracas, both Harry Jones and the judge faced criminal charges.[54] Eventually, George Perine was arrested, but he was cleared by a grand jury in Tucson.[55]

The only Earp stalwart not in Tombstone yet was John Henry "Doc" Holliday. Years later, Wyatt told the *San Francisco Examiner* that he met Doc Holliday and Big Nose Kate (Kate Elder) at Fort Griffin in 1877 while Earp was assistant city marshal of Dodge City, Kansas, in pursuit of cattle thieves.[56] He also claimed that Holliday saved him from an ambush at the hands of an unnamed assailant who was preparing to shoot Earp when Holliday dropped him.

John Henry Holliday was the son of a Griffin, Georgia, businessman. Educated in dentistry in the early 1870s, he moved to Dallas, Texas, for health reasons and initially practiced his profession with success. A series of difficulties, coupled with his own propensities and his senior partner's disdain for Holliday's gambling habits, led him to turn his hobby into an occupation. Doc followed the gambling circuit, which then included Texas stops at Denison, Fort Griffin, and San Angelo. Still, as the years went by he continued to practice dentistry from time to time.

Holliday established a reputation as a fearless gunfighter, an asset in his new occupation. His first gunfight of record in Dallas pitted Holliday against a saloonkeeper in a dispute over card handling. Although shots rang out, neither man suffered any injury. Doc was in at least two more gunfights, these at Las Vegas, New Mexico, the year before he arrived at Tombstone. On July 19, 1879, Holliday killed former army scout Mike Gordon with a single round after Gordon shot up a saloon in which Holliday was a partner. Gordon's former paramour had refused to quit her saloon job and join him, prompting the gunplay. Almost a year later, in June, bartender Charlie White was seriously wounded by Holliday. Months earlier, Holliday and White had clashed in Dodge City, forcing White into a rapid exodus. When Holliday heard White was in Las Vegas, he sought him out, and a gunfight quickly erupted. After White crumpled behind the bar, Doc left him for dead. White, however, did not die and made a full recovery.[57]

Holliday arrived in Tombstone in September 1880.[58] A Captain Malgan had been killed in the streets on Wednesday, August 25, and Parsons reacted for many: "Things are getting to a pretty pass. The death toll since I came here, I mean violent deaths—shootings and poisonings—foots up fearfully large. I have not recorded all. This last shooter will probably be hung if caught by the boys. Something must be done. Lynch law is very effective at times in a community like this."[59]

The level of violence in Tombstone was about to rise again.

CHAPTER TWO

# Whispers in the Moonlight

About one month after Doc Holliday arrived, the city marshal was killed attempting to arrest a leading member of the rustler element. The December 27, 1880, *Arizona Daily Citizen* summarized Deputy Sheriff Wyatt Earp's testimony about the October 28 shooting of City Marshal Fred White. At about 12:30 A.M., Wyatt heard three or four shots on Sixth Street, near the later site of the Bird Cage Theater. Wyatt saw Curly Bill Brocius struggling with Marshal White and tried to help by throwing his arms around Curly Bill just as a pistol which White tried to jerk out of Curly Bill's hand discharged.

Wyatt testified that his brother Virgil then helped disarm Curly Bill. Another witness, James K. Johnson, testified that Brocius did not remove the pistol from its scabbard until White asked for it. Judge Joseph Neugass eventually dismissed the charges against Brocius due to Earp's testimony and the deathbed statement of Fred White to the effect that the discharge of the weapon had been accidental.[1] A great deal of confusion surrounded the details of this incident, even at the time. Doc Holliday claimed later in a *Denver Republican* article published May 22, 1882, that he arrested Curly Bill himself after the shooting.[2]

Irrespective of the details, the Fred White killing was a turning point in town attitudes towards the cowboy element. Still, not everyone admired the Earps. Cowboy factionist Melvin Jones characterized the Earps as "the tin horn gambler" element that was "forever trying to get to be deputy sheriff or constable or deputy anything so they could have the authority to carry a six shooter."[3] Soon the demands of Tombstone citizens provided an opportunity for Wyatt Earp to do just that.

## Cochise County

In early January 1881, Cochise County was carved out of Pima County with Tombstone as the county seat. Curiously, Gov. John C. Fremont, a Republican, appointed Democrat John Behan as the first sheriff. Behan was a Democratic resident deputy sheriff of Pima County residing in Tombstone when appointed. Even though he was a Democrat, his partner in a Tombstone livery stable was John Dunbar, a very close personal friend of Republican senator James G. Blaine of Maine.[4]

Years earlier, Behan served two terms as sheriff of Yavapai County, whose county seat was and is Prescott.[5] Since Wyatt had recently been a lawman in rough and ready Dodge City, Kansas, and a Pima County deputy sheriff until November 1880, he was strong competition, at least in theory. Yet Behan ultimately received the appointment as sheriff in February 1881 and was elected to the position in 1882.[6] Behan later recalled telling Wyatt that if he (Behan) were appointed, he would make Wyatt his under sheriff. Wyatt on the other hand readily told Behan that he could not reciprocate. Wyatt planned to appoint one of his brothers as deputy.[7]

One of Behan's first duties was to take former Tombstone city marshal James Burnett to Tucson for a jail sentence for brawling with Doc Holliday and Milton Joyce at the Oriental Saloon.[8]

Looking back fifteen years later, during a *San Francisco*

*Examiner* interview, Wyatt considered, "The principal factor in all that happened [the McLaury-Earp dispute] was Sheriff Johnny Behan, my political rival and personal enemy."[9] William M. Breakenridge also attributed later difficulties between Sheriff Behan and Wyatt Earp to this appointment.[10] Behan apparently agreed. He claimed shortly after he was appointed that Wyatt had interfered with efforts to find Ike Clanton, whom he was attempting to serve with a subpoena relating to the November 1880 election.[11]

And Wyatt had other adversaries. He described his initial difficulties with Ike Clanton as being over the theft of a horse that he attempted to recover the same night that Behan was trying to serve the ranch owner:

> Myself and Doc Holliday happened to go to Charleston the night that Behan happened to go down to subpoena Ike Clanton. We went there for the purpose of getting a horse that had been stolen from us a few days after I came to Tombstone. I had heard several times that the Clantons had him. When I got there that night I was told by a friend of mine that the man that carried the dispatch from Charleston to Ike Clanton's ranch had my horse. At this time I did not know where Ike Clanton's ranch was. A short time afterward, I was in the Huachucas, locating some water rights. I had started home to Tombstone, and had got within twelve or fifteen miles of Charleston when I met a man named McMasters. He told me if I would hurry up I would find my horse in Charleston. I drove to Charleston, and saw my horse going through the streets toward the corral. I put up for the night at another corral. I went to Barnett's office, to get out papers to recover the horse. He was not at home. . . .

Wyatt telegraphed his brother James from Charleston requesting the legal paperwork required to claim the horse.[12] This was when he met Billy Clanton for the first time.

Ike Clanton. *(Courtesy Arizona Historical Society, Tucson)*

While I was in town, waiting for the papers, Billy Clanton found out I was there. He went and tried to take the horse out of the corral. I told him that he could not take him out, that it was my horse. After the papers came he gave up the horse without the papers being served, and asked me 'if I had any more horses to lose.' I told him I would keep them in the stable after this, and not give him a chance to steal them.[13]

An incident soon thereafter illustrates life and death among the cattle-rustling element. John Ringo, Curly Bill Brocius, "Old Man" Hughes, and his son Jim Hughes sold a large herd of cattle with dubious ownership to the supply contractor at the San Carlos Reservation to feed Apache Indians and their guards living there. They returned to Fort Thomas on the Gila River to begin a poker game which ran several days at Jack O'Neil's saloon. "Dick Lloyd, a Texas cowboy employed by J.B. Collins at the Bear Spring Ranch, was in the habit of coming to Fort Thomas every few months and getting on a rip-roaring drunk. After a few drinks he would get on his horse and with a Texas cowboy's 'Whoopee!' dash through the streets on a run firing his pistol into the air. He was considered quarrelsome when he was drinking," Breakenridge recalled. But Lloyd was only getting started:

On the second day of the poker game, he came into the fort and at once started drinking. The gang of rustlers that were playing cards did not like him, and I guess he soon found out that they did not want him around, for he left O'Neal's saloon [and] went to one kept by Ed Mann. Mann and he got very drunk. They soon got into a quarrel, and staggered out of the saloon and into the street. Mann gave Lloyd a push and he nearly fell down, and Dick cautioned him not to do it again. Mann gave him another shove and this time he [Lloyd] did fall, but it was on account of his drunken condition. Lloyd drew his pistol and took a shot at Mann, but Mann dodged and the bullet caught him just across the back of the neck. He fell as if he were dead, but the shot just creased him and knocked him out.

Lloyd got on his feet and, after looking at Mann, whom he thought he had killed, started to run for his horse which was tied to a tree close by. He was so drunk he fell down several times before he reached it. Placing his six-shooter back in the scabbard, he drew his rifle from the saddle and with another loud "Whoopee!" yelled: "Here is where Dick Lloyd is away for Texas."

But he was not. Lloyd's next stop was a store next to the saloon, where he shot up some tinware as the owner dropped to the floor. Breakenridge reported that "Dick rode in at one door and out of another." Lloyd now moved "toward O'Neil's saloon, but, when meeting a man he knew, threw down on him and ordered him to go to the store and get him some cartridges and to be quick about it." Lloyd's end was no surprise:

The idea struck him that he had better get himself a better horse than the one he had, so riding into the corral back of O'Neil's saloon, he dismounted and, pointing his gun at Johnny Boyle who was in charge of the corral, he ordered him to take the saddle off his horse and place it on a fine horse standing there belonging to Joe Hill. He then mounted the Hill horse, and rode into O'Neil's saloon. As he entered the door, it was supposed that everyone at the poker table took a shot at him.

He fell from the horse riddled with bullets, one of which went through the horn of the saddle. The horse, badly scared, ran off into the brush, with Joe Hill after it, but was soon returned to the corral, and Hill returned to the poker party.

Lloyd was lying dead on the floor all crumpled up and they left him there until the coroner took charge of the body. The poker game continued, and the players started a "kitty" from their jackpots to buy a suit of clothes for Lloyd to be buried in and to pay for funeral expenses. They also hired a couple of Mexicans to dig a grave up on a little hill near by. Next morning, the poker game stopped just long enough for the funeral. The cowboys, all mounted, rode behind the corpse, which, wrapped, in a blanket, they lowered into the grave with their lariats.

The carousers placed about a dozen empty bottles at the head of the grave, fired a salute over it, and returned to their poker game.[14]

## Curly Bill's Prayer Meeting

Charleston, about ten miles to the southwest of Tombstone, was hardly more civil. On Sunday, January 9, 1881, the cowboys conducted a prayer service at Charleston. Parsons recorded the event in his diary the next day,[15] but Breakenridge described the details years later:

> The few law-abiding citizens in Charleston had a small adobe building which they used for a church. One Sunday evening when they were gathered there for their evening service, Curly Bill and a bunch of cowboys came to town, and some of them suggested that they attend church for a change. They agreed, and armed as usual, all trooped into the church. The good people, fearing trouble, began to leave, and soon the place was empty except for the gang. The preacher started to leave also, but he was told that they came to hear him preach and intended no harm. So he remained and preached them a sermon, hitting them as hard as possible. They asked him to line out a hymn, and they all sang. Then they asked him to pass the hat and take up a collection, and they filled his hat with Mexican Dollars.[16]

Although the cowboys supposedly donated the largest gift the church had ever received, Curly Bill was arrested the next day for disturbing the peace.

## The Killing of Henry Schneider

The month Cochise County was organized, Henry "W.P." Schneider, chief engineer of the Tombstone Mining and Milling Company, was shot to death by John O'Rourke, called "Johnny-Behind-the-Deuce," after an exchange of insults in Charleston.[17] One version of the lunchtime dispute on January 14, 1881, relates that O'Rourke interrupted a Schneider conversation, only to be told, "I was not talking to you," prompting O'Rourke to shoot Schneider later without further conversation.[18]

O'Rourke was nearly lynched getting out of town, but as diarist George Parsons reported, "The officers sought to protect him and swore in deputies, themselves gambling men [the deputies that is] to help. Many of the miners armed themselves and tried to get at the murderer. Several times . . . rushes were made and rifles leveled, causing Mr. Stanley and me to get behind the most available shelter. Terrible excitement, but the officers got through finally and out of town with their man bound for Tucson."[19] Lawmen Ben Sippy, George McKelvey, and Virgil Earp quieted the mob and then took O'Rourke to Tombstone in a light spring wagon.[20]

That evening, a Tombstone vigilance committee was formed to deal with problems created by the cowboy faction, according to Parsons, who wrote, "This man [O'Rourke] should have been killed in his tracks. Too much of this kind of business is going on. I believe in killing such men as one would kill a wild animal. The law must be carried out by citizens, or should be, when it fails in its performance as it has lately done."[21]

There were other fireworks that month. The year had opened with a political battle between town-site owners James S. Clark and his partner John P. Gray, who backed Democrat mayoral candidate Mark P. Shaffer and the Republicans, whose candidate John P. Clum was elected on January 4.[22] In a general city election that day, Virgil Earp lost his second bid to become city marshal to Ben Sippy after being defeated by Sippy in a special election on November 13, 1880, following the death of City Marshal Fred White.[23]

Also in January, James Earp opened the Sampling Room on Allen Street, and Warren Earp, age twenty-five, arrived from California.[24] Warren was easily distinguishable from his look-alike brothers and gambled for a living. He could usually be found at the Oriental Saloon in the months to come. Occasionally, when Virgil became Tombstone marshal, he would be deputized for posse work.

## Bat Masterson

Early in February, Bat Masterson arrived in Tombstone at the invitation of his friend Wyatt Earp. Their respect was mutual. Writing twenty-seven years later, Bat said that Earp was "absolutely destitute of fear."[25]

Bartholomew (he later changed his first name to William Barclay) Masterson was one of seven children born to Thomas and Catherine Masterson. "Bat," as he would become known, was born on November 26, 1853, and baptized as "Bertholowmiew" in the parish of St. George, Henryville, county of Iberville, province of Quebec, Canada. His baptismal name was later anglicized to Bartholomew. Scholars debate the origin of his nickname to this day. Some say his parents called him "Bat" as a contraction of Bartholomew, while others attribute the name to his use of a cane to subdue street rowdies while a law officer in Wichita. When Bat was about fourteen, his large family migrated south and settled on a claim at Sedgwick near Wichita, Kansas. Bat and an older brother left the family farm, taking work on the Atchison, Topeka and Santa Fe Railroad but Bat left that job and was soon hunting buffalo on the Western prairie. He was in the company of about a dozen other such hunters on July 27, 1874, at Adobe Walls in the Texas panhandle when the party was attacked by Quanah Parker and a large contingent of Indian warriors. Bat shortly quit buffalo hunting and then joined Gen. Nelson A. Miles as a scout.

There are gaps in Masterson's whereabouts between his October 1874 discharge and his return to Dodge City, Kansas, in 1877, but Masterson was definitely involved in a shooting at Mobeetie, Texas, on January 24, 1876. Officially the death of Sergeant King of the Fourth Cavalry was caused by a shot fired by "a citizen" at the Lady Gay Saloon. Although several variations of the incident exist, most historians accept that Bat Masterson killed King in a saloon gunfight over the affections of one Molly Brennan. King apparently killed the lady accidentally during the fracas. Then in Dodge City, Kansas, on September 25, 1877, Masterson shot several times at A.C. Jackson, who was shooting up the town. Bat missed the unruly cowboy but shot the horse dead.

Masterson opened a saloon in Dodge City in 1877 but got himself summarily pistol-whipped by the city marshal while aiding a jail break. Nevertheless, he was elected Ford County sheriff in November of that year. Two years after his election and shortly after his appointment as deputy U.S. marshal, Bat became an Atchison, Topeka and Santa Fe Railroad detective, joining in the company's dispute with the Denver and Rio Grande Railroad over rail passage rights through Raton Pass, New Mexico, and Royal Gorge,

Colorado. Masterson then traveled through Colorado, New Mexico, and Nebraska before reuniting with old friends Luke Short and Wyatt Earp and his brothers in February 1881 at the Oriental Saloon, where he became a faro dealer.

On February 25, Masterson tried to prevent a gunfight, but could not save his old friend Charlie Storms. Twenty-six years later, Bat remembered the incident vividly:

> One morning I went into the Oriental gambling house, where Luke [Short] was working, just in time to keep him from killing a gambler named Charlie Storms . . . one of the best known gamblers in the entire West. [Storms] had, on several occasions successfully defended himself in pistol fights with "gunfighters."
>
> Charlie Storms and I were very close friends,—as much as Short and I were—and for that reason I did care to see him get into what I knew would be a very serious difficulty. Storms did not know Short . . . [and] had sized him up as an insignificant-looking fellow, whom he would slap in the face without expecting a return.
>
> Both men were about to pull their pistols when I jumped between them and grabbed Storms at the same time requesting Luke not to shoot,—a request I knew he would respect if it was possible without endangering his own life too much. I had no trouble getting Storms out of the house, as he knew me to be his friend. When Storms and I reached the street I advised him to go to his room and take a sleep, for I then learned for the first time that he had been up all night, and had been quarreling with other persons.
>
> He asked me to accompany him to his room, which I did, and after seeing him safely to his apartment, where I supposed he could go to bed, I returned to where Short was. I was just explaining to Luke that Storms was *a very decent sort of man,* when, lo and behold! there he stood before us. Without saying a word he took hold of Luke's arm and pulled him off the sidewalk, where he had been

standing, at the same time pulling his pistol, a Colt's cut-off .45 calibre, single action; but like the Leadvillian, he was too slow, although he succeeded in getting his pistol out. Luke stuck the muzzle of his pistol against Storm's heart and pulled the trigger. The bullet tore his heart asunder, and as he was falling, Luke shot him again. Storms was dead when he hit the ground. Luke was given a preliminary hearing before a magistrate and exonerated.[26]

While gambling preoccupied many who lived in Tombstone, cattle rustling in Mexico to supply the San Carlos Reservation and local ranchers continued apace. Soon, the Mexican government had complained to the United States secretary of state about cattle thefts, which had begun three years earlier.[27]

Meanwhile conflict of another sort was brewing. Wyatt Earp attributed much of the later Tombstone troubles to recriminations over a series of stage robberies. Wyatt himself had been hired to ride as an express guard and once nearly killed several Mexicans mistaken for road agents. The worst came later, after Wyatt and his brother Morgan had moved on to other ventures. The first stagecoach robbery in the Tombstone area recorded by diarist George Parsons was a modest caper on February 26 in which $135 was stolen from a Wells Fargo stage near Contention, with no harm to the passengers.[28] Within two weeks, all of that would change.

## The Murder of Bud Philpot

Bob Paul, an express guard who later became United States marshal for Arizona, provided the information used in a *Denver Republican* article five days after a dramatic March 15, 1881, robbery near Contention which proved fatal.

The coach was full of passengers inside and on the

outside were the driver [Bud Philpot], one passenger
and Paul, who was guarding a treasure box containing
18,000 in gold. The coach was pulling out of a gulley
when a band of concealed Rustlers fired from a clump of
bushes only five feet distant.[29] The outside passenger fell
back mortally wounded and the driver shot through the
head, fell forward between the wheel horses, frightening
them so they dashed madly off. The Rustlers fired into
the coach from the left side, upon which side Paul was
sitting, but, strange to say, he was not hurt. The concealed
robbers fired sixteen shots in all as the coach passed by.
The driver carried the lines with him as he fell, and Paul
was left helpless on the top of the coach with a dying
man beside him, and four frontier ponies plowing madly
forward to certain death a mile ahead, where the road
crossed a chasm on an insecure, narrow and unprotected
bridge. Paul knew of this place, which was approached
by a sudden turn, and very difficult of passage, even by
a skillful driver, but he did not lose his head. He put on
the brake and tried to soothe the horses by calling to
them, but without avail. The brake did not seem to make
the slightest difference in the speed of the coach and the
situation began to look hopeless when the coach plunged
into the last gully before reaching the fatal bridge. In the
midst of the noise and whirl, Paul heard a voice calling
from behind, and looking down saw an inside passenger
standing on the step. The passenger was a fashionably
dressed young man just from the Far East and unused to
scenes of danger, but he was full of grit and cool as ice.

"Put on the brake on the next rise" he said, "and check
them a little while I jump off and head them if I can."

Paul obeyed, and when the team struck a sand hill he
set his teeth and broke [applied the brake] with all his
force. The coach slowed up almost imperceptibly, and
with a half dozen bounds the young dandy had the leaders
by the head, and in another instant bunched them and
stopped the coach right on the edge of the chasm, into
which the frightened passengers looked with a shudder.

When the horses had stopped, it was discovered that in
addition to the driver, Bud Philpot, Peter Roerig, a young
passenger riding atop the coach, was killed by a potshot
from one of the robbers.[30]

Two separate and independent posses pursued the
suspects, while more genteel Tombstone citizenry led by
Mayor John Clum shadowed suspicious-looking characters
around town. A posse consisting of Sheriff Behan, Masterson,
Williams, Holliday, and Morgan, Virgil, and Wyatt Earp
tracked the bandits to the Len Redfield ranch. Suspect
Luther King, about whom little was known at the time,
promptly confessed, implicating Bill Leonard, Harry Head,
and Jim Crane, all members of the cowboy element.[31]

The March 19, 1881, *Tombstone Nugget* reported
what happened once King was confined and claimed that
a prominent Earp factionist had been involved in the
robbery:

> The man arrested at Redfield's ranch charged with
> being implicated in the Bud Philpot murder escaped from
> the sheriff's office by quietly stepping out the back door
> while Harry Jones, Esq., was drawing up a bill of sale for
> the horse the prisoner was disposing of to John Dunbar.
> Under-Sheriff Harry Woods and Dunbar were present. He
> had been absent a few minutes before he was missed.
> A confederate on the outside had a horse in readiness
> for him. It was a well planned job by outsiders to get
> him away. He was an important witness against Holliday
> [whom later rumors would claim was a participant in the
> robbery].[32]

The posse then divided. The first posse, consisting of
Sheriff Behan, Deputy Breakenridge, and Frank Leslie,
received information that the suspects were in Cloverdale,
New Mexico. During the pursuit, they stayed at the ranch of
Joe Hill, himself under suspicion as a close associate of the

Clanton-McLaury faction.[33] The second posse, consisting of Deputy U.S. Marshal Virgil Earp, his brothers Wyatt and Morgan, and Bob Paul also pursued the bandits.[34]

The *Epitaph* asked its readers on March 22, "What action if any did the Coroner take looking to an investigation of the human arm found on the street the other day? It surely demanded some attention." Apparently the authorities thought otherwise for that same day, diarist George Parsons recorded that "another party started out today for [the] robbers—just three or four men but amongst them two of the best trailers." Frank Leslie and Deputy William Breakenridge were highly regarded trackers in their time.[35]

Later observers have noted how Tombstone sentiment divided at this point. Power was concentrated in a "county ring," according to some. This consisted of Sheriff Behan; his business partner John Dunbar and his important Republican connections; Milt Joyce, owner of the Oriental Saloon; and Harry Woods, owner of the *Nugget.* The county ring was thought to have cowboy allies. "The Earps and their friends from this point onward would argue that stagecoach robberies were simply a new and ugly extension of the cowboy problem, a situation exacerbated by county law enforcers' friendliness with the likes of Curly Bill. They asserted that Len Redfield [later a rider with an outlaw gang] and his brother Hank were rustler associates and that Behan and Breakenridge were giving the cowboy element every break, letting King confer with the Redfields before being taken in."[36]

Earp considered the March 15 stage robbery incident to be the prologue "to the bitter and bloody feud that is the central, somber episode of my thirty years on the frontier."[37] One modern researcher agreed, seeing this event as "a cataclysmic moment in which Tombstone would be split open by mistrust and whispers in the moonlight."[38]

Breakenridge illuminated one aspect of the controversy in his memoirs:

> It got to be a common rumor that Doc Holliday, the gambler, was with these men when they tried to rob the stage; that it was he that fired the shots that killed Bud Philpot, the stage driver, and the passenger [Peter Roerig] who was riding on top of the stage; that he was drunk at the time and the others could not restrain him, and that he returned to Tombstone, while the others fled to the San Jose Mountains near where Naco now stands.[39]

Others saw the Contention robbery and those that followed as a natural extension of the gambling element's enterprises. These theorists fell into two schools. Some claimed that the gambling faction committed the robberies themselves and then blamed the Clantons.[40] Others saw an unholy alliance between the Earp and cowboy factions. These theorists contended Wyatt and Doc "were at the head of a gang with Ike Clanton and a bunch of cowboys to do stage holdups just below the town of Contention whenever they were tipped off and the valuables would be thrown out with nobody hurt."[41] Ike Clanton later charged that the Virgil Earp quest for Bill Leonard was a concocted diversion designed to enable the gang's escape to New Mexico.[42] Yet another variation attributed to cowboy ally James Hancock was that Wells Fargo agent Marshall Williams and the Earps simply kept the money shipments originating in Tombstone, sending an empty strongbox for conspirators to rob "as a blind" so that their associates could not simply betray them and ride away with the loot. Rancher John Pleasant Gray of the town-site faction even claimed in his memoirs that the Contention stage robbery had been planned by the Earps.[43]

Some of the Earp associations did little to dispel these

rumors. Their friend Marshall Williams was later characterized by his fellow Earp factionists as a crook who was
tipping off Leonard,[44] and suspicious rumors of a fourth
highwayman promptly fell upon Doc Holliday. A telegraph
worker stringing line between Charleston and Tombstone
claimed he observed the dentist riding towards Tombstone
on a rented horse the witness was familiar with and then
saw "two to three men [on] horseback about one-fourth of
a mile farther up the hill."[45] Worse yet, Holliday was also
an acquaintance of Bill Leonard, one of the stage robbers
named by Luther King. Holliday knew Leonard from earlier
days in Las Cruces, New Mexico, where Leonard had been
charged with assault then reportedly became a rustler. Even
so, Tombstone town-site magnate John Pleasant Gray later
remembered Leonard as a cut above the other rustlers in
intellect and education. Leonard was reportedly a jeweler
from New York who had arrived in Las Vegas, New Mexico,
by June 1879.[46]

One unlikely source of suspicion against the Earps in
later years was Allie Earp, who supposedly once claimed
that the Earps kept disguises for use in stage robberies,
although she renounced *The Earps of Tombstone,* a book
manuscript allegedly based on her recollections and written
by Frank Waters.[47]

Doc Holliday's paramour Kate Harony made similarly
questionable allegations in later years.[48] About four months
after the Contention robbery, an arrest warrant was sworn
out for Doc Holliday in the murder of Bud Philpot and
the attempted stage robbery.[49] Modern researchers have
suggested that the affidavit Kate provided in support of the
arrest warrant was revenge for one of the many domestic
squabbles between her and Holliday. Judge Wells Spicer
promptly dropped the charges as requested by the district
attorney.[50]

## The Deputy Sheriff and the Outlaw

Deputy Sheriff William Breakenridge first encountered Curly Bill Brocius, the killer of Marshal Fred White, in the spring of 1881. After serving a summons on a merchant in San Simon, then a station on the Southern Pacific, he went into one of the watering holes frequented by the local outlaws. His account is colorful and perhaps even true.

> I went [to San Simon] by train, and while waiting for a return train, I went into a saloon kept by a man they called "Shorty." There was a gang of cowboys and rustlers in there playing cards, and Curly Bill were lying on a card table. I had never seen him before. He was fully six feet tall, with black curly hair, freckled face, and well built. Shorty brought in a bucket of water and filling a tin cup, said, "Here's how, boys" and lifted the cup to drink from it.
>
> Curly, who had raised up on his elbow, shot the cup out of his hand, saying, "Don't drink that Shorty, it's poison." The bullet went through the wall of the boarding house.

Breakenridge also assessed and collected taxes on behalf of the sheriff, whose office, in his estimation, was worth $40,000 a year ($881,000 today) due to the 10 percent fee on collected taxes the county board of supervisors allowed him. After collecting taxes in Tombstone, Breakenridge took on the challenge of collecting in the valley and mountains east of Tombstone:

> There had never been any taxes collected in this part of the county, even when it was Pima County, and nearly all the property was personal. There were but few ranches that had any title. There a great many teams hauling lumber from the Chiricahua sawmills to Bisbee and Tombstone mines, and for building purposes in the different town sites. I was told by many that I would have no success, but I started out to try.

Breakenridge claimed in his 1928 memoirs that he was in constant danger from Indian attack in this area. After collecting taxes elsewhere in the county, Breakenridge tried a novel approach in the Galeyville area. "As soon as I reached Galeyville, I hunted up a Mr. Turner, the banker for the rustlers, and asked him to introduce me to Curly Bill," he describes.

> He took me to Babcock's saloon and corral where Curly was, then Turner called him out and introduced me to him. I told him who I was and what I was, and said that I wanted to hire him to go with me as a deputy assessor and help me collect the taxes, as I was afraid I might be held up and my tax money taken from me ify I went alone.
>
> The idea of my asking the chief of all the cattle rustlers in that part of the country to help me collect taxes from them struck him as a good joke. He thought it over for a few moments and then, laughing, said, "Yes, and we will make everyone of those blank, blank cow thieves pay his taxes."
>
> Next day we started and he led me into a lot of blind canyons and hiding places where the rustlers had a lot of stolen Mexican cattle, and introduced me something like this:
>
> "Boys, this is the county assessor, and I am his deputy. We [are] all good, law-abiding citizens and we cannot run the county unless we pay our taxes."
>
> He knew about how many cattle they each had, and if they demurred, or claimed they had no money, he made them give me an order on their banker, Turner. Curly had many a hearty laugh about it. He told them that if any of them should get arrested, it would be a good thing for them to show that they were taxpayers to the county.[51]

Breakenridge noted in his memoirs that Sheriff Behan also maintained good relationships with the cowboy element as a means to collect taxes. Josephine Sarah Marcus Earp remembered, or was said to have remembered, such things years later:

> Johnny entertained all of the Rustlers except Old Man Clanton at our house at one time or another, for political motives. He was always having a little poker-get-together. In addition, Johnny was forever standing in our backyard, out of my hearing, having confidential talks with one or another of the gang. After their business became widely known, the Rustler crowds were no longer invited to come around.[52]

According to one researcher, Behan was not alone in cultivating relations with the rustlers. Wyatt Earp similarly befriended the cowboys.[53]

Breakenridge himself was particularly fond of Curly Bill. In fact, he spoke well of the rustlers from whom he collected about one thousand dollars that spring. He characterized Curly Bill as a great shot who taught him a thing or two about making arrests.

> He was a remarkable shot with a pistol, and would hit a rabbit every time when it was running thirty or forty yards away. He whirled his pistol on his forefinger, and cocked it as it came up. He told me never to let a man give me his pistol butt end toward me, and showed my why. He handed me his gun that way, and as I reached to take it he whirled it on his finger, and it was cocked, staring me in the face, and ready to shoot. His advice was that if I disarmed anyone to make him throw his pistol down.[54]

Deputy Sheriff Breakenridge soon met a Curly Bill associate with whom Brocius shared rustler leadership responsibility in the Galeyville area:

> [John] Ringo was a mysterious man. He had a college education[55], but was reserved and morose. He drank

heavily as if to drown his troubles; he was a perfect gentleman when sober, but inclined to be quarrelsome when drinking. He was a good shot and afraid of nothing, and had great authority with the rustling element. Although he was the leader on their trips to Mexico after cattle and in their raids against the smugglers, he generally kept by himself after they returned to Galeyville. He read a great deal and had a small collection of standard books in his cabin.[56]

Breakenridge once had to serve a warrant on Ringo for robbing a poker game in a Galeyville saloon. Ringo had lost about one hundred dollars then asked his fellow players for an advance on his watch, but they refused and simply closed out the game. Ringo retrieved his horse then reentered the saloon and robbed two other poker games still in progress. Breakenridge was told to anticipate possible trouble and take a posse.

I had met Ringo frequently on my trips to Galeyville and was very well acquainted with him and we had many pleasant visits. I was advised to take a posse with me, as they thought he was sure to resist arrest, but I said that if I could not get him alone, it would take a troop of soldiers to get him, as he had fifty or sixty followers who would stay with him. Because I was certain that I could arrest him alone, I refused to go if they wanted me to take a posse.

Mounting my saddle horse . . . I started over the mountain for Galeyville. I reached there before Ringo was up, and knocked on the door of his room. He came to the door with his six-shooter in his hand. He invited me in, and I told him I had a warrant for him for holding up the poker game.

"What," he said, "are you going to arrest me for that? Why that was all settled."

He dressed and we went to breakfast together, and he

asked me not to say anything about it, as he did not want any of the boys to know he was under arrest. He said that he would have to wait until Turner, their banker, came in that afternoon, to get some money, and if I would head back to Prue's ranch, he would meet me there in the morning. I considered his word as good as his bond, so I went back to the ranch, and next morning, Ringo was there for breakfast. He had come in the night and rather than disturb us he had slept in the haystack.

We rode into Tombstone that day, and Ringo told me enough about his family for me to know that they were not aware he was an outlaw.[57] We were both heavily armed, for the Indians were out and we had to be on the alert all the time. On reaching the town [Tombstone] we put up our horses, and as it was about dark we first got supper at a restaurant and then went to the jail. I asked the jailer, who I knew had an extra room, to let Ringo keep his arms and sleep in his house across the street from the jail, and I would be down early next morning and help him get his bond.[58]

The next day, according to Breakenridge, Ringo's attorney represented that Judge Stillwell had approved his bond and Ringo rode away after Breakenridge brought the prisoner his horse. Breakenridge strongly implies that the good judge had a change of heart after a visit from the local vigilance committee which had been organized to bring law and order to Tombstone. That evening, Judge Stillwell was shocked to learn that Ringo had been released, then gave an arrest warrant to two members of a newly formed vigilance committee. The posse rode to Charleston, where they were promptly disarmed and held by local cowboys while Ringo rode back to Tombstone of his own volition. Eventually, the original poker game robbery charges against Ringo were dismissed for lack of witnesses.[59]

## The Contention Mine Horse Theft

Breakenridge once traveled to the McLaury ranch in search of a prized horse. The steed had been taken from E.B. Gage, general manager of the Contention Mine, by Sherman McMasters. Sheriff Behan had no luck finding the horse until Breakenridge got a tip.

One afternoon, Ike Clanton met me on the street and told me that if I wanted the Contention horse to get to McLaury's Ranch before dark and I should find him there. Ike passed on with no further information. I had just come in from a hard trip and my horse was tired, so, going to a livery stable, I hired a pony to make the trip.

I did not arrive at the ranch until after dark, as the pony was very slow and lazy.

As I rode up, I saw that there was a large crowd of cowboys there, and the place in front of the house was covered with water from an irrigating ditch. Not wanting to come on them unawares, I holloed [*sic*] and asked if it was safe to ride through the water. Frank McLaury came to the door. When I told him who I was, he asked me in, and upon entering I found Curly Bill and some ten or twelve rustlers there with him. They were nearly all strangers to me. I went out with Frank to put up my horse in the corral, and told him what I was there for.

I said "Frank, I am not the only one who knows that the horse is here. Half of Tombstone knows it. You are posing as honest ranchmen. It is well known that you are harboring rustlers and outlaws and dealing in stolen cattle, and you dare not let me go back without the horse. You are under suspicion, and if I go back without the horse and tell that you would not give it up, you will have to quit ranching here and join the rest of the rustlers."

He thought it over and said the horse was not there at the time, but would be there before morning; he would not tell me who stole it. He asked me to remain overnight

and we entered the house. It was crowded, and Curly
and some of the others divided blankets with me and I
slept on the floor with them all night. I was up at daylight
and the horse was in the corral. Several parties came in
during the night, but I did not know who they were.

As I started for the corral to catch up the horse, Frank
said he would catch it for me. On our way to the corral he
told me I was alright and safe while I was at the ranch, but
the fellow who had the horse was sore about my taking
him, and he and his gang intended to hold me up after I
left the ranch and take the horse away from me.[60]

Breakenridge claimed some cowboys took a few shots at
him on the way back to Tombstone. Later, he discussed the
incident with Billy Clanton and John Ringo. "They knew all
about my getting the horse, and laughed and said, 'You had
better look out or you will get caught the next time.'"

The conflicts between Tombstone residents and the
cowboy element would soon become much more serious.

CHAPTER THREE

# Desperate Men and a Desperate Encounter

Bat Masterson departed Tombstone in early April 1881, less than a month after the Bud Philpot murder, even as hordes of new residents began to arrive with the completion of the second transcontinental railroad line at Deming, New Mexico. He celebrated his return to Dodge City on April 16 by engaging two of his brother's enemies in a dramatic yet bloodless gunfight known as the "battle of the plaza." Masterson would play no other role in the Tombstone troubles.[1]

The next month, Deputy Sheriff Breakenridge arrested one Jim (Jake) Wallace, a drifter who had wandered into Arizona from Las Vegas, New Mexico. Wallace had threatened Galeysville's Constable Goodman, who had been too inquisitive about the horse Wallace rode in on. Sometime later, Wallace also threatened Breakenridge, who disarmed him with an unusual and risky technique:

> As I passed the saloon where the cowboys were, somebody told Wallace I was a deputy sheriff from Tombstone. As I came back on my way to the Wilkins store he was on the saloon porch. Evidentially expecting to have some fun, he called me to the porch and asked if I was after that horse.
>
> I told him "No, I am riding a better horse than that."
>
> He started to draw his gun, but I was too quick for him and grasped his hand, at the same time, placing my gun against his stomach, I told him to drop his own weapon, which he did. Stepping up on the porch I took his gun,

but knowing that he could get another, I thought it best to run a bluff on him. I handed the gun back to him and told him he was making a fool of himself, and to put it back in his scabbard. Then, I turned my back on him and walked into the saloon. I asked the crowd to have a drink and went on to the store where I was taking the inventory.

What Breakenridge claimed happened next defies modern thinking but accurately portrays relationships that sometimes developed on the American frontier.

A lot of the boys saw the occurrence and told Curly [Bill Brocius] about it. Curly, who was about half drunk, took Wallace to task for trying to pick a fuss with the officers, and every time he looked out the door and saw the horse with the white face he threatened to shoot it, but the others talked him out of it.

Later . . . Wallace . . . told me that Curly was very angry with him and told him he had to apologize to me. He wanted me to go the saloon with him so he could square himself with Curly. I went with him and he apologized, and I thought everything was all right, but Curly, who was still drinking, wanted to have a row with Wallace and still threatened to shoot the horse.

After more drinking and conversation between Wallace and Brocius, things took a more serious turn:

Wallace left Babcock's saloon, and soon afterward Curly came out and stepped off the porch. Just as he was getting on his horse, Wallace stepped up behind [Brocius] and shot him. The bullet hit him in the cheek and knocked out a tooth, coming out through his neck without cutting an artery.[2]

The May 16, 1881, *Arizona Weekly Star* reported Curly Bill was not expected to live. The *Star* dramatized the ambush by claiming that Curly Bill had followed Wallace out of a saloon after an argument. In fact, Breakenridge found Wallace and took him to the local justice of the peace, who promptly discharged the prisoner on his plea of self-defense. Breakenridge bought the prisoner supper and loaned him ten dollars which Wallace later repaid. Breakenridge recorded that Wallace was later killed in Roswell, New Mexico. Curly Bill convalesced for two weeks and "was well as ever."[3]

Virgil Earp became acting city marshal after Ben Sippy's June 6, 1881, resignation following a conflict with the city council over the release of some prisoners and a brief absence from his duties.[4] Meanwhile, Jim Crane, Harry Head, and Bill Leonard, suspects all in the Bud Philpot murder three months earlier, hid that summer in New Mexico. The June 23, 1881, *Arizona Weekly Star* reported that Bill Leonard later confessed to the robbery as he lay dying from gunshot wounds inflicted during a gunfight while trying to rob the Haslett Brothers Store. Specifically, Leonard said he "wished someone would shoot him in the heart and put him out of his misery, as he had two big holes in his belly that he got when he tried to rob the stage at Tombstone." The Breakenridge memoirs relate that Head, Leonard, and Crane were killed in Eureka (now Hachita), New Mexico, on June 22, 1881, while trying to rob the Hasletts,[5] but in fact, Crane survived. Jim Crane and other associates later killed the Haslett brothers about twenty-six miles outside of Eureka in revenge for the deaths of Head and Leonard.

That same day, the first major fire at Tombstone started at the Arcade Saloon when a whiskey barrel burst into flames. Sixty-six businesses with a combined total value between $175,000 and $300,000 burned to the ground.

Wyatt Earp had other flames of his own to worry about that day. Although Josephine Sarah Marcus had confirmed transmission of twenty-five dollars sent to San Francisco as

"Josie Behan" eleven days before, she had already coupled with Wyatt, whose common-law wife, Celia Ann "Mattie" Blaylock, was none the wiser.

Newly appointed deputy sheriff Frank Leslie encountered the outlaw Jim Crane at the Las Animas Ranch owned by John Pleasant Gray that July. Although Leslie had a warrant for Crane in his pocket, the trio lunched together as Crane cradled a rifle in his lap pointed at Leslie. Later, Leslie departed without comment.[6]

According to Breakenridge, in early August 1881, Old Man Clanton, Brocius, and others ambushed and killed Mexican smuggler Miguel Garcia with two to eight others in Skeleton Canyon in the Peloncillo Mountains, yielding some four thousand dollars in silver, mescal, horses, and cattle. This state of affairs was not overlooked by surviving smugglers. Outlaw elder statesman Old Man Clanton, Billy Land, and Dick Gray were killed in Guadalupe Canyon on or about August 13.[7] The attackers were identified as Mexican soldiers. Some Americans were unsympathetic towards the Guadalupe Canyon victims. Diarist George Parsons opined four days later that the killing was in retaliation for the earlier ambush of the Mexican pack train and was "perfectly justifiable." According to Parsons, the Jim Crane who participated in the March 15, 1881, Contention stage robbery was among the dead. Parsons remarked that he was "glad they killed him, as for the others, if [they] were not guilty of cattle business, [they had] no business to be found in such company."

Acting Governor John Gosper, who had roomed with Doc Holliday in a Prescott boardinghouse some months earlier, arrived in Tombstone in early September to investigate conditions. He found Virgil Earp and Sheriff Behan all too eager to blame each other for the lawlessness attributed to "the power of the cowboys."[8] Gosper's proposed solution was extrajudicial. He recommended that the Tombstone business community renew the earlier vigilantism used to deal with Johnny O'Rourke. Soon the Citizens' Safety Committee was formed.

## The Sandy Bob Stage Robbery

Another stage robbery occurred at 11 P.M. on September 8 between Tombstone and Bisbee. The stage operated by Charles "Sandy Bob" Crouch departed Tombstone with twenty-five hundred dollars in a Wells Fargo safety box but no guard for the trip to Bisbee, a copper mining community near the Mexican border. After taking the safety box as well as six hundred dollars from an unlucky passenger, one of the two bandits pressed his luck further and searched a driver's pockets for money, which he called "sugar." Later, this caught the attention of the authorities. Deputy Sheriff Frank Stilwell, who had worked as a stage driver, teamster, and miner before arriving in Tombstone, used that expression all the time to describe money.[9] One of the robbers wore high-heeled boots, much like the boots favored by Stilwell. The day after the robbery, Frank Stilwell had a Bisbee shoemaker replace his high heels with lower ones.[10]

The stage arrived back in Tombstone at 9:30 A.M. the next day. A posse consisting of Deputy Breakenridge and Wyatt and Morgan Earp immediately left for Bisbee.[11]

> We went to the place where they held up the stage [Breakenridge describes], and we were able to get a good view of the tracks of both men and horses. We had no difficulty in following the horse tracks toward Bisbee until they were obliterated by a drove of cattle passing over them.
>
> On our arrival in Bisbee, where we would spend the night, we interviewed several of the passengers. They told us that the smaller of the two robbers did most of the

talking, and asked each one if he had any sugar. This was a well known expression of Frank Stilwell's, who always called money "sugar." We learned also that Stilwell had his high heels taken from his boots and low heels put on in place of them. The shoemaker gave us the ones he had taken off and they fitted the tracks at the scene of the hold-up. Pete Spence [Spencer] and Frank Stilwell had come into Bisbee together and were still there.

Soon, the rest of the posse, consisting of Deputy Sheriff Neagle, Fred Dodge, and Marshal William, arrived.[12] Stilwell and Spencer were returned to Tombstone on a state arrest warrant for robbery and a federal warrant for robbing the mail and express. They each posted a seven-thousand-dollar bond with the assistance of Ike Clanton.[13] Spencer was a Texan who lived near Virgil and Allie Earp back in Tombstone. He dealt in mining claims, as did many Tombstonians, and had recently married a young Hispanic girl.

Breakenridge describes this as a defining moment of conflict "between the two gangs."[14] He recalled in his memoirs that Virgil Earp claimed the McLaurys had threatened to kill "everyone who had a hand in arresting Stilwell and Spence[r]" and advised Breakenridge to "shoot them the first time I met them or they would get me sure." Wyatt Earp later said that Frank McLaury scolded Morgan for the arrests.[15] Deputy Breakenridge laughed off the threat and asserted that a few days later Tom McLaury denied that he had any interest in protecting Spencer or Stilwell. He also states in his memoirs that he never knew of any warrants being issued for the McLaurys or Clantons.

At the same time he was denying rumors concerning McLaury and the Sandy Bob robbers, Breakenridge was quick to report speculation in Tombstone about ties between the Earps and area desperadoes. Sherman McMasters and Pony Deal were suspects in a recent stage holdup near

Globe, Arizona. Deal had been arrested in Tucson, but Breakenridge writes that

> McMasters came to Tombstone, Virgil Earp recognized him, and wired Paul [a Wells Fargo detective and Pima County sheriff] asking if McMasters was wanted. But before he got an answer, McMasters left town, and it was reported that it was he who stole a valuable horse from the Contention Mine. The horse belonged to E.B. Gage, general manager of the mine, and he was anxious to get it back. It was rumored that Earp told McMasters to leave, and, as he joined the Earp party later, it looked as if it might be so.[16]

## The Reward-Sharing Arrangement

Wyatt reported in November 1881 court testimony that he offered Ike Clanton and Frank McLaury all the reward money if they would "put me on the track" of William "Bill" Leonard, Harry "the Kid" Head, and James "Slim Jim" Crane, suspects in the Bud Philpot murder. This exchange later morphed into one of the main causes of the famed O.K. Corral gunfight which took the lives of three men. According to Wyatt, Wells Fargo agent Marshall Williams confirmed in June 1881 that a thirty-six-hundred-dollar reward would be paid for the robbers dead or alive. Joe Hill, an associate of the Clantons and McLaurys, then traveled to Eureka, New Mexico, looking for the trio but reported back that he missed them by one day.[17]

Wyatt claimed also that numerous Tombstone residents now warned the Earps that Ike Clanton, the two McLaurys, Joe Hill, and John "Ringhold" (Ringo) were threatening to kill them:

> I knew all those men were desperate and dangerous men; that they were connected with outlaws, cattle thieves, robbers and murderers; I knew of the McLowrys

[McLaurys] stealing six government mules and also cattle, and when the owners went after them—finding his stock on the McLowry boy's ranch—that he was drove off, and told that if he ever said anything about it they kill him [*sic*], and he kept his mouth shut until several days ago.[18]

Deputy Breakenridge was assigned to round up jurymen and witnesses for the fall term of the Cochise County Court at Tombstone. While doing so, he approached the San Simon Cienega Ranch. McLaury associate Joe Hill warned everyone there, and the prospective jurors ran for the hills, providing the basis for a cartoon sketch which later appeared in the *Police Gazette.*[19]

Of course, horse theft was a serious yet frequent occurrence in that part of the West, according to Breakenridge, who related,

One day a cowboy from New Mexico came into Tombstone riding a splendid horse. He put up at the O.K. Corral, said he was broke, and offered to sell the horse for about half what it was worth. He soon found a purchaser, and after he received his money, the buyer asked him, "What about the title?"

The cowboy replied, "the title is perfectly good as long as you go west with him, but don't take him east; it is not so good in that direction."[20]

Events took a more deadly turn on October 2 at Cedar Springs, about fifteen miles northwest of Grant's Pass, when Apaches under Geronimo killed five teamsters. Four days later, Breakenridge found another victim of the same attack. Before the last body was found, a posse consisting of Sheriff Behan, Breakenridge, George Parsons, John P. Clum, and others had left Tombstone and moved towards Antelope Springs then tracked the Indians towards the McLaury ranch in the Sulphur Spring Valley.[21] En route to the McLaury ranch, on October 5, the posse stopped at the ranch of a Mr. Frink (Frinck), who had lost all but one of his horses to the Apaches. The ranch house was so small that some of the posse had to sleep sitting up while a heavy rain obliterated the Apache tracks overnight. Breakenridge and Frink were able to recover the trail while the rest of the posse awaited them at the mouth of the Horseshoe Pass in the Swisshelm Mountains, known today as Leslie Canyon. However, when the two trackers returned to Horseshoe Pass, the posse was gone. While Breakenridge rode after them towards the McLaury place, the rancher devised a plan of his own: "Mr. Frick, seeing that we were not returning, again took up the trail, and by a short cut through the hills got to a point between the Indians and the squaws. Then he rushed in and cut off nearly all the stolen stock and stampeded them back into the valley. The Indians did not even follow him, but hurried on for Old Mexico."[22]

The posse breakfasted at the McLaury ranch on October 6. There they encountered Curly Bill Brocius, who had killed Marshal White, but shook hands all around anyway. Only five days earlier Parsons had recounted in his diary how he took a roundabout route to avoid cowboys, explaining to posterity, "Be it understood in this journal cowboy is a rustler at times and rustler is a synonym for desperado—bandit, outlaw and horse thief."[23]

Meanwhile, another stage robbery had occurred on October 8, near Charleston. The bandits took eight hundred dollars but cheerfully refunded five dollars in expense money to each passenger.[24]

Deputy Sheriff Breakenridge later recalled that on October 23 accused cattle rustler Milt Hicks, an accused murderer named Sharp, and a Charles Thompson, known as "the Yank," made a sensational escape from the Tombstone jail in typical frontier fashion:

The jailer, William Soule, left the jail and went uptown leaving the jail keeper, Charles Mason, on watch. Shortly after his departure, the "trusty" who cleaned up the jail desired to go in where the prisoners were for the purpose of removing some slops. As Mason opened the door and let him in, Sharp caught Mason, and while they were struggling Hicks and Yank ran outside. By the time this Sharp managed to break away from Mason, who was inside, and in an instant he, too, was outside, and with Yank trying to pull the door shut; but they were for a moment prevented by Mason's getting his arm between the door and the jamb. Jerry Barton [the stuttering pugilist was in jail at Tombstone awaiting trial on assault charges] came to the keeper's help and with his wonderful strength prevented Mason's arm from being broken in the door. Finding that he and Barton could not keep the escaping man from closing the door, Mason threw the lock at Sharp, striking him on the cheek and inflicting a deep cut. Yank and Sharp then locked the door and followed Hicks who had already started down Tough Nut Street.

Breakenridge had arrested Milt the morning before at the Grand Hotel, extending his right hand in friendship as he grabbed Hicks' holstered pistol with his left hand. Despite the efforts of a posse that included Sheriff Behan, Breakenridge, City Marshal Virgil Earp, Morgan and Wyatt Earp, and Buckskin Frank Leslie, the escaped prisoners were never seen there again.[25]

Any animosity between Sheriff Behan and Deputy U.S. Marshal Virgil Earp was hard to detect as they pursued the escapees on October 25. Although the rustlers were not found, the two lawmen returned before nightfall.[26]

## Late-Night Troubles

Late that evening, Ike Clanton and Tom McClaury arrived

from Antelope Springs driving a light wagon and leading
a saddle horse.[27] Ike Clanton quarreled with Doc Holliday
at the Alhambra lunch counter, drawing the attention of
Morgan Earp, as reported many years later by Earp adherent
Fred Dodge:

> While Morg and I were sitting in the rear part [of the
> Can Can Lunch and Eating Counter in the Alhambra] Ike
> Clanton come in and set at the lunch counter. It could be
> seen that he had been drinking sufficiently to loosen his
> tongue and make him talkative. Soon after, Doc Holliday
> come in and seeing Ike, he went over to him and said,
> "I hear you are going to kill me, now is your time to go
> to work." Ike Clanton said that he did not have any gun.
> Doc called him a liar. Doc's vocabulary of profanity and
> obscene language was monumental and he worked it
> proficiently in talking to Ike. Morgan was going to take
> me to my room; I was sitting in a chair on the edge of a
> table when these men come in. Morg remarked, "This
> won't do" and stepped over to Doc Holliday and took him
> by the arm and led him away to the door where he met
> Wyatt and Virgil Earp and they took Doc away.[28]

Deputy Sheriff Billy Breakenridge presented an entirely
different version of this incident, which portrayed Morgan
Earp as an instigator rather than a peacemaker:

> Clanton went out of the house [identified as the Eagle
> Brewery] and saw Virgil Earp, the city marshal, on the
> sidewalk just outside the door. Morgan Earp and Holliday
> followed him out and continued to abuse him, although
> they [Virgil and Morgan Earp] were both peace officers.
> They claimed he had been talking about Holliday and the
> Earp party. Ike first got drunk, then went to the corral
> where he had left his team and arms and went to bed.[29]

Apparently he was not inclined to call it a night, however.
That evening, men who would soon be shooting at each

other played a game of all-night poker. Ike Clanton, Tom McLaury, Virgil Earp, and Sheriff Behan finished their game in the wee hours. After the game was finished, Ike asked Virgil to deliver a message to Doc: "The damned son of a bitch has got to fight." Virgil's wife, Allie, encouraged him to deliver the message, commenting that he should just let them kill each other. "Neither of them amounts to much," she quipped.[30]

## An Incident in Harwood's Lumber Yard

Bartender E. F. "Ned" Boyle encountered Ike Clanton on the former's way home from the graveyard shift. "His pistol was in sight," he said, "and I covered it with his coat and advised him to go to bed. He insisted that he wouldn't go to bed; that as soon as the Earps and Holliday showed themselves on the street, the ball opened—that they would have to fight." Boyle did not take the threat as an idle one. He warned Wyatt Earp about the remark before going home to bed. According to Wyatt, Deputy Sheriff Harry Jones soon told Earp that Ike was hunting the brothers with a Winchester and a six-shooter.[31] Virgil Earp said later that a man named Lynch warned him Ike was hunting him and threatened to kill him on sight. Even Doc's paramour, Kate Harony, knew about the danger. She encountered a man carrying a rifle in the Fly Photography Gallery in spite of the city ordinance prohibiting firearms. After the man walked into the Fly boardinghouse dining area, Mrs. Fly told her that Ike Clanton was looking for Doc, who only commented later, "If God will let me live long enough, he will see me."[32]

Now Virgil, Morgan, and Wyatt began searching for Clanton. R. F. Coleman would testify that he saw what happened when the Earps and Holliday finally found

Clanton at the Capitol Saloon near Fourth and Fremont: "I saw [the] city marshal, [Virgil] Earp speak to [Ike], but did not hear what he said. The marshal made a grab and took the rifle out of Clanton's hand. There seemed to be a little scuffle by both of them when Clanton fell. I did not see the marshal strike him but I saw Clanton fall, and they took his revolver from him, and took him to police court."[33]

Ike found himself across the street in the Recorders Court waiting with a bandaged head to answer charges of carrying a concealed weapon after being "buffaloed" by Virgil's six-shooter. R. J. Campbell, clerk of the Cochise County Board of Supervisors, recalled that Wyatt confronted Clanton, saying that Ike had threatened his life two or three times. Wyatt wanted it stopped, Campbell related. "Fight is my racket and all I want is four feet of ground," Ike supposedly replied. Campbell also testified that Morgan offered Ike his own confiscated six-shooter. Wyatt called Ike a cattle thief and said, "If you are anxious to make a fight, I will go anywhere on earth to make a fight with you."[34]

After Clanton paid a twenty-five-dollar fine, Wyatt tangled with Tom McLaury along Fourth Street, according to Apollinar Bauer, a town butcher, who said, "Wyatt raised his left hand or fist-like, and run it into Tom McLaury's face." Wyatt then asked, "Are you heeled or not?" While McLaury backed away Wyatt pulled a six-shooter and struck Tom three or four times on the head and shoulders. "I could kill the son-of-a-bitch." he supposedly muttered.[35]

Moments later, Wyatt encountered Tom and Frank McLaury with William Clanton at the Spangenberg Pioneer Gun and Locksmith Shop, where Frank's horse was standing on the sidewalk with his head in the store.

> I took the horse by the bit [Wyatt later recalled], as I was deputy city marshal, and commenced to back him off the sidewalk; Tom and Frank McLaury and Billy Clanton

came to the door; Billy Clanton laid his hand on his six-shooter; Frank McLaury took hold of the horse's bridle. I said, "You will have to get this horse off the sidewalk." Frank McLaury backed him off on the street. Ike Clanton came up about that time and they all walked into the gunsmith shop. I saw them in the shop changing cartridges into their belts. They came out of the shop and walked along 4th street to the corner of Allen; I followed them as far as the corner of 4th and Allen streets, and they went down Allen Street and over to Dunbar's corral.[36]

Sheriff Behan has traditionally been considered sympathetic to the cowboy faction. During court proceedings, he gave an account of what happened on Fremont Street. He was in the barbershop getting shaved while his barber was talking about the probability of there being a fight between the Earps and the cowboys. The time was about half past one or two o'clock. He noticed a crowd gathering on the corner of Fourth and Allen Streets. The barber quickly finished so that Behan could disarm the parties and he crossed over to Hafford's corner. "[I] saw Marshal [Virgil] Earp standing there and asked him what was the excitement. He said there were a lot of [expletives] in town looking for a fight. He did not mention any names. I said to him, 'You had better disarm the crowd.'" Earp refused, but Behan insisted, "It is your duty as a peace officer to disarm them rather than encourage the fight." Behan then proceeded down the street.

Marshal Earp was at this time standing in Hafford's door. Several people were around him. I don't know who. Morgan Earp and Doc Holliday were then standing out near the middle of the street at Allen and Fourth Streets. I saw none other of the defendants there. Virgil Earp had a shotgun.

I went down Fourth Street to the corner of Fremont and met Frank McLaury holding a horse. I told McLaury that I would have to disarm him, as there was likely to be trouble in town and I proposed to disarm everybody in town that was carrying arms. He said he would not give up his arms, as he did not intend to have any trouble. I told him he would have to give up his gun all the same. I said "Frank, come along with me." We went down to where Ike Clanton and Tom McLaury were standing. I told them they must give up their arms. Billy Clanton was there. When I got down to where Ike was, I found Tom McLaury, Billy Clanton, and Will Claiborne. I said to them, "Boys, you have got to give up your arms."

Frank McLaury demurred; he did not want to give up his arms. Ike told me he did not have any arms. I searched him and found he did not have any arms. Tom McLaury showed me by pulling his coat open that he was not armed. Claiborne said he was not one of the party; he was trying to get them out of town; I said "Boys, you must go to the sheriff's office and leave your arms, and stay there until I get back." I told them I was going to disarm the other party.

Now Behan saw the Earps and Holliday coming down the sidewalk near the post office. He told the Clantons, "Wait here awhile, I will go up and stop them." Behan walked to Bauer's butcher shop and told the Earp party not to go any farther, that "I was down there for the purpose of arresting and disarming the McLaurys and Clantons. They did not heed me. I told them to go back. 'I am sheriff and am not going to allow trouble if I can help it.'" He continued:

They brushed by me and I turned and went with them, begging them not to make any trouble. When they arrived within a few feet of the cowboys [west of the O.K. Corral rear entrance in a side yard], I heard Wyatt Earp say, "you s— of a b——, you have been looking for a fight and you can have it." Some one of them said, "Throw up your hands," and then the fight commenced. Some twenty-five or thirty shots were fired. Billy Clanton said, "Don't shoot, I don't want to fight." Tom McLaury threw open his coat and said, "I have got nothing." Billy Clanton and Frank McLaury were the only ones armed, they had their horses ready, they were leading them, and were leaving town. Their rifles were on their saddles.

They had their hands up when the Earp crowd fired on them. Doc Holliday shot Tom McLaury with a shotgun and killed him instantly. Morgan Earp shot Billy Clanton while their hands were up.[37]

The gunfight actually began in a vacant lot on Fremont Street between Fly's Lodging House and the Harwood house, in a space no more than eighteen feet wide. William A. Harwood, the second mayor of Tombstone, stored lumber

O.K. Corral, Tombstone. (*Courtesy Arizona Historical Society, Tucson*)

for sale here, when available. The McLaurys had come to that place by entering Fremont Street from the rear O.K. Corral entrance. The O.K. Corral itself fronted on Allen Street, sporting a brick entrance with windows that could have easily been seen in New York City or any other major American city of the time.

The gunfight at the O.K. Corral has been described as "the prototypical Western gunfight of all time,"[38] but it was not the most lethal. Two encounters in present-day Oklahoma were much more deadly. A gunfight between tribal lawmen and deputy U.S. marshals in 1872 at Goingsnake Schoolhouse near the Arkansas border resulted in the death of at least ten men.[39] A conflict at Ingalls, in present-day Payne County, Oklahoma, on September 1, 1893, between federal officers and the Doolin Gang resulted in the death of three lawmen and the injury of two bystanders, one of whom later died. All of the outlaws save one rode away.[40]

The next day, diarist George Parsons described the Fremont Street gunfight as "a bad time yesterday when Wyatt, Virgil and Morgan Earp, with Doc Holliday, had a street fight, the two McLaurys and Bill Clanton and Ike, all but the latter being killed . . . Desperate men and a desperate encounter."[41]

And with that, the controversy began.

## CHAPTER FOUR

# Just Innocent Enough

Everyone in the gunfight except Wyatt Earp was killed or wounded. Morgan and Virgil Earp were shot, as was Doc Holliday. Ike Clanton had run away from the fight and sustained no injuries. Billy Clanton and Tom McLaury were taken to a residence near the corner of Fremont and Third to await their deaths. According to Sheriff Behan, Billy asked him to "go away and let me die." After asking Thomas Keefe to "drive the crowd away," Clanton did just that. Tom McLaury died with scarcely a sound just a few minutes before while Frank McLaury had expired at about the same time on a sidewalk across the street from the vacant lot where it all happened.[1] The McLaurys and Clanton were then taken to a back room at the Dexter corral to wait for the undertaker.[2]

The next day, the corpses were exhibited in then-traditional open coffins under a sign which proclaimed in all capital letters: "Murdered in the streets of tombstone."[3] At least three hundred people joined the procession that left from the undertaking premises of Ritter and Eyen at 3:30 P.M. that Thursday.

> The procession headed by a brass band moved down Allen Street and thence to the cemetery. The sidewalks were densely packed for three or four blocks. The body of Clanton was in the first hearse and those of the two McLaury brothers in the second, side by side, and were interred in the same grave. It was a most impressive and saddening sight and such a one as it is to be hoped may never occur again in this community.[4]

In 1932, Josephine Sarah Marcus Earp remembered that day while quoting the reminiscences of Tombstone resident and Wells Fargo operative Fred Dodge. Her own gloss provides insight to that era:

> "The band, the firecrackers and the works" was how Fred put it. "It was the only good thing those boys ever did for Tombstone." I don't mention this with disrespect, for the dead . . . but because some writers like [Breakenridge] have pointed to the size of the funeral as evidence of the popularity of the Rustlers. It wasn't so. A funeral in those times was like a circus; the people weren't primarily mourners but spectators.[5]

An inquest was held Friday, October 28, by Coroner Henry Matthews, a former army surgeon from Virginia, who assembled ten jurors representing a cross-section of the Tombstone business community.[6] His witness list included individuals favorable to the cowboy element and others considered neutral. The lead witness in importance was Sheriff Behan, who oozed benign neutrality but testified that Virgil Earp was spoiling for a fight and wanted to give the cowboys a chance to "begin the ball." Soon, however, Behan dropped a bombshell which had not been published in the local papers:

> When they got to the party of cowboys, they drew their guns and said, "You sons of b——, you have been looking for a fight and you can have it!" Someone of the party, I think Marshal Earp, said "Throw up your hands! We are going to disarm you!"
>
> I heard Billy Clanton say, "Don't shoot me! I don't want to fight," or something to that effect.
>
> Tom McLaury said, "I have got nothing," and threw his coat back to show that he was not armed. This was instantly with the shooting, almost at the same time. The order to throw up their hands and this remark and the shooting were almost simultaneous.

Behan went on to make another significant point before his testimony was concluded that day, a revelation which would influence the whole case against the Earps and Holliday: "I can't say who fired the first shot. It appears to me that it was fired from a nickel-plated pistol [Holliday was known to carry such a weapon]. There were two shots very close together. I know that the nickel-plated pistol was on the side of the Earps. I won't say which one of the Earp crowd fired it."[7] One distinguished legal historian has suggested that this approach "served a strategic purpose, both at the inquest and in the latter criminal prosecution. By making Doc [Holliday] the primary bad guy (or maybe the scapegoat), Behan could avoid making wild accusations against the otherwise upright Earps, while still presenting an account in which Virgil and Wyatt were indirectly responsible for the killings."[8]

Two other witnesses loosely associated with the cowboy element testified in support of Behan's account. Ike Clanton corroborated the Behan version of events, complete with the taunt "You ought to make a fight" and a reference to the nickel-plated pistol supposedly carried by Doc Holliday. Neutral witnesses included R. F. Coleman, a miner who testified that someone in the posse ordered the cowboys to "throw up your hands" or "give up your arms." However, Coleman also testified that Billy Clanton had his hand on a pistol in his scabbard after the firing commenced. Martha King, a housewife who was shopping nearby, related that she heard one of the Earps say, "Let them have it" and Doc Holliday reply, "All right."[9] Perhaps the most damaging testimony came from P. H. Fellehy, a laundryman who claimed he heard something particularly damaging from Virgil Earp: "Those men have made their threats. I will not arrest them, but will kill them on sight."[10] If believed, this would be significant evidence of first-degree murder under Arizona law. However, Fellehy did not testify again and no one corroborated this statement in the inquest or later preliminary hearing.

The verdict issued by Coroner Matthews on October 28 was ambiguous at best. Arizona law required a clear determination whether the homicides were criminal or justified. Instead, Matthews ruled, "William Clanton, Frank and Thomas McLaury, came to their deaths in the town of Tombstone on October 26, 1881 from the effects of pistol and gunshot wounds inflicted by Virgil Earp, Morgan Earp, Wyatt Earp, and one Holliday, commonly called 'Doc' Holliday." The *Nugget* commented, "We might have thought they had been struck by lightning or stung to death by hornets, and we could never have told whether they were in the way of lightning or the lightning was in their way."[11]

The one thing the verdict did not do was exonerate the Earps and Holliday, thus providing an opportunity for Ike Clanton to file first-degree murder charges the next day. Virgil Earp was then temporarily suspended from his duties as chief of police. The diarist George Parsons commented on October 31 that he met Wyatt Earp, who took him to visit his brother Virgil, mentioning that the Earps were getting along well but things "look bad for them all thus far."[12] That day, Judge Wells Spicer, a justice of the peace, began a preliminary hearing in the first-degree murder charges against the Earps and Holliday.

The charges filed by Ike Clanton did not distinguish between the defendants, charging them all with equal culpability. However, as one legal historian has noted,

> From the very beginning then, the prosecution of the Earps and Holliday was a divided venture. Johnny Behan represented what might be called the moderate wing [of the prosecution] providing testimony consistent with a murder case against Holliday and lesser charges against the others. Ike Clanton and [prosecution leader]

Ben Goodrich, however, pressed for capital punishment without discrimination, however sparse the proof of premeditation might be.[13]

Politics became an issue almost as soon as the prosecution began. Nominally, the lead prosecutor was district attorney Lyttleton Price, one of the few Republican office holders in Cochise County. Although a Republican himself, Gov. John C. Fremont had appointed a number of Democrats to important Cochise offices ten months earlier, notably Sheriff John Behan, in order to mollify the largely Democratic population. Just before the Earp-Holliday preliminary hearing began, Price had successfully repelled efforts by Democratic lawyer John Miller to become district attorney himself. For these reasons and perhaps others, Ike Clanton and the cowboy element raised a fund rumored to be ten thousand dollars in order to retain Ben Goodrich as de facto leader of the prosecution team supervised in name by Price.[14] Goodrich was a well-connected Texas-born Democrat who had helped Ike Clanton prepare murder charges against the Earps and Holliday at the conclusion of the coroner's inquest.

The defense team was also formidable. Forty-three-year-old Thomas Fitch was born in New York City but had moved west and become active in Republican politics at an early age. He was elected to the California legislature at age twenty-four, moved on to Nevada, then to Utah. Although he was not a Mormon, he became a trusted confidant of Brigham Young. He began practicing law at Prescott, Arizona, in 1877 and moved to Tombstone during the early days of the silver strike there. Fitch was an old friend and literary associate of Mark Twain's.[15] Doc Holliday was represented separately by T. J. Drum, who followed Fitch's lead in every respect, providing a unified front which became critical as the hearing progressed.

The most important lawyer in the room of course was Judge Wells Spicer. As we have seen, Spicer moved to Tombstone in its infancy. He was born in New York and grew up in Iowa, where he read law under the supervision of an established lawyer and was admitted to the bar in 1853. Spicer arrived in Nevada about sixteen years later after a brief sojourn to Colorado. He then moved to Utah where, in a pattern typical of frontier lawyers in those times, he practiced law, worked as a journalist, and even launched a brief, undistinguished career as a miner.

Life in Salt Lake could be difficult for non-Mormons, but Spicer eventually gained the confidence of church leader Brigham Young. In 1874 he was asked to defend church elder and militia leader John D. Lee in the Mountain Meadows massacre case. Seventeen years earlier, the Fancher party had left Harrison, Arkansas, for California and stopped in Mormon country for a brief rest. The local population was suspicious of their motives, particularly after learning that some members of the party were from Missouri, from which the Mormons had been driven a few years before. Allegedly led by Lee, a party of Mormons dressed as Indians killed over one hundred men, women, and children, sparing only those under the age of six. The first prosecution of John D. Lee, whom Spicer defended, resulted in a hung jury. Lee was convicted in the second trial two years later amidst rumors that the federal prosecution had agreed to exonerate church authorities of complicity with Lee serving as a convenient scapegoat. He was convicted by an all-Mormon jury and executed shortly thereafter as Spicer looked on. One legal historian has speculated that the jaundiced view of prosecutorial intent which compelled Spicer to call himself "the unkilled of Mountain Meadows" predisposed him to look "long and hard" at the evidence against the Earps in the McLaury-Clanton killings.[16]

On the last day of October, Judge Spicer began the

preliminary examination to determine whether Wyatt, Virgil, and Morgan Earp or Doc Holliday should be bound over for a first-degree murder trial.[17] The next day Coroner Matthews reported his inquest findings and was followed by cowboy associate Billy Allen, who insisted that the first shot in the gunfight was from a pistol and the second from a shotgun, although he did not say which side fired first. He did not corroborate testimony in the inquest about one of the Earps commanding, "Let them have it."[18] On November 2, day three of the hearing, Sheriff Behan essentially repeated his inquest testimony which had so badly damaged the Earps. On cross-examination, his earlier statements about the first shot coming from a nickel-plated pistol, which everyone present most certainly knew meant Doc Holliday, were ridiculed and effectively destroyed by defense attorney Thomas Fitch.

The chances of a prosecution dovetailing with Sheriff Behan's focus on Doc Holliday as the most culpable of the four defendants disappeared in the desert wind with the arrival of attorney and eldest McLaury brother Will McLaury from Fort Worth on the evening of November 3. McLaury wanted to hang them all. Earlier, Judge Spicer had granted bail to Wyatt Earp and Holliday in the amount of ten thousand dollars each. He excused Virgil and Morgan Earp from appearing at the preliminary hearing due to the severity of their wounds. McLaury began November 4, his first day on the prosecution's team, by contesting bail for Wyatt and Doc.[19]

Later that day, Martha King repeated her inquest testimony and added something of potential significance. When asked about one of the Earps saying, "Let them have it" and Doc Holliday's response, "All right," she added that she knew exactly what was meant from conversation she heard at the butcher shop: "When I first went in the shop, the parties who keep the shop seemed to be excited and did not want to wait on me. I inquired what was the matter, and they said there was about to be a fight between the Earp boys and the cowboys."[20]

This was followed on Monday, November 7, by the morning testimony of cowboy associate Wes Fuller, who acknowledged he had heard one of the Earps tell the McLaurys and the Clantons, "Throw up your hands" and Clanton's response begging, "Don't shoot me—I don't want to fight" just before the shooting started. Later that day, Wyatt and Doc were remanded to the county lockup for the rest of the hearing, guarded from time to time by friends who feared for their safety.[21]

Tuesday, November 8, brought the appearance of William Harrison "Billy the Kid" Claiborne. His testimony about the gunfight differed little from that of Behan. He claimed he heard Wyatt Earp say, "You son of a b——, you have got to fight," and City Marshal Virgil Earp insist that they throw up their hands. He claimed that all three cowboys had their hands up when the shooting started.[22] He summarized his memory with this account: "Tom McLaury threw open his coat and said, 'I haven't got anything boys, I am disarmed.' And then the shooting started." According to Claiborne, Doc Holliday shot Tom McLaury, Morgan Earp shot Billy Clanton, and Wyatt Earp shot Frank McLaury.

Thus, at the conclusion of day eight, three potential bases of premeditated murder had been introduced, if the witness accounts were to be believed. Behan testified that Virgil Earp spoke of giving the cowboys "a chance to fight"; Martha King heard one of the Earps say, "Let them have it"; and Claiborne testified that the Earp faction rounded the corner into the lot with guns in their hands. Now the prosecution produced their least-compelling witness, Ike Clanton. Most historians consider Clanton's testimony to be a turning point in the defense's case. Many have found little credibility in his account of how he made arrangements with Wyatt Earp to apprehend the men who killed Bud Philpot in the Benson stagecoach robbery. Worse yet, during the course of his testimony, he charged Wyatt Earp with robbery, embezzlement, murder, and other crimes with such a fantastic story that some have suspected he was under the influence of cocaine or other drugs. Yet somehow, Will McLaury was so satisfied with this testimony that he wrote his brother on November 9, "I think we can hang 'em."[23]

The prosecution recalled the coroner that day and also presented three witnesses who testified they saw Wyatt Earp slap Tom McLaury shortly before the gunfight.[24]

Seven days later, on the morning of November 16, Wyatt Earp was allowed to present a written statement in court taking advantage of a unique Arizona law of that time.[25] He described the last few seconds before the most famous gunfight in American history:

> We had walked a few steps further when I saw Behan leave the party and come towards us, every few steps he would look back as if he apprehended danger. I heard Behan say to Virgil Earp, "For God's sake don't go down there or you will get murdered." Virgil replied, "I am going to disarm them"—he, Virgil Earp being in the lead. When I and Morgan came up to Behan he said, "I have disarmed them." When he said this I took my pistol which I had in my hand, under my coat and put it in my overcoat pocket. Behan then passed up the street, and we walked on down. We came up on them close—Frank McLaury, Tom McLaury and Billy Clanton standing all in a row against the east side of the building on the opposite end of the vacant space west of Fly's photographic gallery. Ike Clanton and Billy Claiborne and a man I did not know were standing in the vacant space about halfway between the photograph gallery and the next building west. I saw that Billy Clanton and Frank McLaury and Tom McLaury had their hands by their sides and Frank McLaury's and Billy Clanton's six-shooters were in plain sight. Virgil

said, "Throw up your hands. I have come to disarm you."
Billy Clanton and Frank McLaury had their hands on
their six-shooters.

One commentator reminds us that Sheriff Behan
consistently and repeatedly denied that he told the Earps
the cowboys had been disarmed.[26] Wyatt now came to a
critical part of his testimony, relating that "Virgil said, 'Hold,
I don't mean that; I have come to disarm you.' They—Billy
Clanton and Frank McLaury—commenced to draw their
pistols, at the same time Tom McLaury threw his hand to
his right hip and jumped a horse."

Wyatt now recalled that he had his pistol in his overcoat
pocket where he had placed it when Behan told the Earp
party he had disarmed the McLaurys and Clanton.

> When I saw Billy and Frank draw their pistols I drew
> my pistol. Billy Clanton leveled his pistol at me but I
> did not aim at him. I knew that Frank McLaury had the
> reputation of being a good shot and a dangerous man,
> and I aimed at Frank McLaury.
>
> The first two shots that were fired [were] by Billy
> Clanton and myself; he shot at me, and I shot at Frank
> McLaury. I do not know which shot was first; we fired
> almost together. The fight then became general. After
> about four shots were fired Ike Clanton ran up and grabbed
> my arm. I could see no weapon in his hand and thought
> at the time he had none, and so I said to him, "The fight
> has now commenced, go to fighting or get away."
>
> At the same time I pushed him with my left hand.
> He started and ran down the side of the building
> and disappeared between the lodging house and the
> photographic gallery. My first shot struck Frank McLaury
> in the belly. He staggered off on the sidewalk but first
> fired one shot at me. When we told them to throw up
> their hands Claiborne held up his left hand, and then
> broke and ran. I never saw him afterwards until later

in the afternoon, after the fight. I never drew my pistol or made a motion to shoot until after Billy Clanton and Frank McLaury drew their pistols. If Tom McLaury was unarmed I did not know it. I believe he was armed and that he fired two shots at our party before Holliday, who had the shotgun, fired at and killed him. If he was unarmed there was nothing to the circumstances or in what had been communicated to me, or in his acts or threats, that would have caused me even to suspect his being unarmed.

Wyatt then confirmed that he never fired at Ike Clanton, even after the shooting commenced, repeating that he thought Clanton was unarmed.

Next he addressed what he considered to be a conspiracy against the Earps:

I believed then, and believe now, from the facts I have stated, and the threats I have related, and other threats communicated to me by different persons as having been made by Tom McLaury, Frank McLaury and Isaac Clanton, that these men, last named, had formed a conspiracy to murder my brothers Morgan and Virgil, and Doc Holliday and myself.

Wyatt claimed he would have been legally and morally justified in shooting any of them on sight but did not attempt to do so since he saw no advantage.

When I went as deputy marshal to help disarm them and arrest them, I went as a part of my duty and under the direction of my brother the marshal. I did not intend to fight unless it became necessary in self defense and in performance of official duty.

With this, he addressed his self-defense plea directly: "When Billy Clanton and Frank McLaury drew their pistols I knew it was a fight for life, and I drew and fired in defense of my own life and the lives of my brothers and Doc Holliday."[27]

More than one astute researcher has theorized that testimony indicating that Wyatt and Virgil fired their weapons only after Clanton or Frank McLaury drew theirs was in all probability perjured. In fact, this would be consistent with controversial late-life statements attributed to Josephine Sarah Earp to the effect that "Wyatt and Verge both said what was necessary at the hearing to protect Morgan and Doc [who may have fired the first shots], as well as themselves."[28] Likewise, Wyatt's preliminary hearing testimony that at the beginning of the gunfight his pistol was in his pocket is questioned to this day.[29]

Earp then contradicted the earlier statements of Sheriff Behan and Ike Clanton:

> The testimony of Isaac Clanton that I had anything to do with any stage robbery, or any criminal enterprise, is a tissue of lies from beginning to end. Sheriff Behan made me an offer in this office on Allen Street and in the back room of the cigar store, that if I would withdraw and not try to get appointed sheriff of Cochise county, that we would hire a clerk and divide the profits. I done so; and he never said another word to me afterward in regard to it. The reasons given by him here for not complying with his contract are false.

The Arizona statute, as Spicer interpreted to allow written testimony, effectively shielded Wyatt from cross-examination that might have revealed he was lying when he claimed that he entered the lot with his pistol still in a heavy coat pocket when it was more likely he rounded the corner with his weapon drawn. Historian Steven Lubet has speculated that if Wyatt had been cross-examined and the prosecution had pursued the lesser charge of manslaughter, convictions against the four might have been secured.[30]

Three days later, Virgil Earp testified from his sick bed at the Cosmopolitan Hotel on a Saturday morning. He recalled a heated exchange before the gunfight in which Frank McLaury challenged him: "I'll tell you, it makes no difference what I do, I never will surrender my arms to you. I'd rather die fighting than be strangled [by vigilantes]." Virgil then referred to a surprise witness who was eventually revealed to be H. F. Sills: "There was a man [who] met me on the corner of Fourth and Allen Streets about 2 o'clock in the afternoon of the day of the shooting. He said, 'I just passed the O.K. Corral,' and he said he saw five men all armed and heard one of them say, 'Be sure to get Earp, the marshal.' Another replied and said, 'We will kill them all.'"[31]

After three witnesses provided testimony as to the "dangerousness of the Clantons and McLaurys and their fearsome Cowboy friends," H. F. Sills, a furloughed railroad locomotive engineer, testified that as he was passing the O.K. Corral he heard several men "talking of the trouble they had with Virgil Earp, and they made threats at the time, that on meeting him, they would kill him on sight."[32] One researcher contends there are significant indications that this testimony was perjured and possibly arranged by the Earps, based on Sills' sudden arrival in Tombstone, his inordinate attention to detail, and his claim that he told no one what he saw before giving his testimony.[33]

On November 28, Addie Boland, a dressmaker with no apparent tie to any of the combatants, testified that she watched the gunfight from across Fremont but did not hear any of the discussion because she was inside her shop.

> I first saw five men opposite my house leaning against the small house west of Fly's. They were cowboys. One man was holding a horse. Four men came down the street toward them and a man with a long coat on walked up to the man holding the horse and put a pistol to his stomach,

then stepped back two or three feet, and then the firing became general. That was all I saw. I don't know which party fired first, did not see any of the cowboys throw up their hands. I watched them until the firing commenced, then I got up and went into the back room. It looked to me as if they were all shooting at the same time. I saw no parties fall.

Judge J. H. Lucas testified that he was in his office on the opposite side of the street and about two hundred or three hundred feet from the Fly building. He heard a couple of reports of a gun or a pistol, hesitated a moment, heard a couple of more reports, then started for the door. Then he heard four or five more reports. When he got to the hall door, he looked up and down the street and saw a man he thought was Billy Clanton standing in front of the little house just below Fly's building:

He had his pistol up and I thought he was firing, and for fear of a stray bullet I drew my head in for an instant. I looked again and still saw him standing there with his pistol and I thought fighting. I drew my head in again and still saw him with his pistol. I continued to look at him, then looked to see if anyone else had weapons. I did not see anyone else that I thought had weapons. I think his pistol was discharged twice from the time I thought he was hit till he was down on the ground. About the same time he got to the ground, the firing ceased. I heard some considerable shooting, but could not see any of the parties except Billy Clanton. I am satisfied the shooting came from the other parties besides Billy, though I could not see them.[34]

Breakenridge recalled in his memoirs that "six witnesses swore that the McLaurys and Clanton held up their hands as directed by the Earps, and three swore that they did not see them throw up their hands, four of the witnesses heard the Earp party say that the cowboys would have to fight, and heard Virgil Earp tell the sheriff he would not arrest them, but would kill them on sight."[35] However, as noted previously, P. H. Fellehy was the only witness at the coroner's inquest who testified about Virgil's alleged threat to kill the cowboys "on sight." Fellehy did not testify again and no one corroborated this statement in the inquest or later preliminary hearing.[36]

Judge Wells Spicer focused in his lengthy written opinion issued December 1, 1881, mainly on the testimony of one witness.

Addie Boland, who saw distinctly the approach of the Earps and the beginning of the affray from a point across the street where she could correctly observe all their movements, says she cannot tell which side fired first, that the firing commenced at once from both sides upon the approach of the Earps and that no hands were held up. That she would have seen them if there had been. Judge Lucas states he saw Billy Clanton fired on or in the act of firing several times before he was shot, and he thinks two times afterward. Still asserts that the firing was simultaneous. He cannot tell who fired first. . . .

[Then, Spicer concluded] I cannot resist the firm conviction that the Earps acted wisely, discreetly, and prudently to secure their own self-preservation; they saw at once the dire necessity of *giving the first shot* to save themselves from certain death. They acted: their shots were effective, and this alone saved the Earp party from being slain.

I conclude that the performance of the duty imposed upon me by saying the language of the statute; There being no sufficient cause to believe the within named Wyatt Earp and John Holliday guilty of the offense mentioned within, I order them released.

Some Tombstone citizens were unsatisfied, as Breakenridge noted forty-six years later, quoting an editorial by the pro-cowboy *Tombstone Nugget* opining that "The sentiment of the community was that justice had not been done." Breakenridge then added, "It is my belief that the cowboys were not expecting a fight, as only Billy Clanton and Frank McLaury were armed. They had their pistols on, and their rifles were on their saddles, as they were about to leave town. If they had expected that the Earps were coming to kill them, they could have shot down the whole Earp party before they got within pistol-shooting distance."[37]

After Judge Spicer released them, the Earps went to the Oriental Saloon for a celebration. Milton E. Joyce, who owned the place, was not in a celebratory mood. He insulted them then and there and even confronted the Earps again in another saloon the next day. Later, Holliday shot up the Oriental and shot Joyce in the foot, trying his best to kill him.[38]

The prosecution had elected to seek conviction for first-degree murder, foregoing the opportunity to pursue second-degree murder or manslaughter charges for reasons that have never been fully explained but might not amount to much more than bravado. Had they been convicted of murder or one of the two lesser charges that could have been alleged, the Earp party might have been known to history as outlaws. Instead, since the prosecution charged them with a higher crime than could be proved, the star-crossed Earps were "just innocent enough" to escape conviction.[39]

CHAPTER FIVE

# War and Remembrance

Tombstone was quiet that November as the inquest droned on, but trouble was roiling beneath the surface. After his release, Virgil Earp was so concerned he requested military assistance from Gen. Orlando Willcox to thwart a possible "cowboy invasion."[1] Soon, on November 14, Breakenridge noted, there was yet another killing.

> During the winter of 1881, [Frank] Leslie went to work for Milt Joyce, proprietor of the Oriental Gambling Saloon, tending bar. One day he was serving two men over the bar, when a cowboy named William Claiborne [Claibourn], known as the Kid, came in drunk and started to argue with the two men. Frank ordered him out of the house. Claiborne left and went to the corral and got his rifle, saying he was going to kill Leslie. He stepped behind a fruit stand on the sidewalk near the door of the saloon. Someone went into the saloon and told Leslie that the Kid was out there with a rifle and meant to kill him when he came out. Leslie, taking his pistol in his hand, came out of a side door behind the Kid and spoke to him, and as the Kid turned Leslie shot and killed him.
>
> He stood there with his pistol in his hand until the city marshal came and arrested him. [Breakenridge related that] as the marshal reached for the pistol, Leslie cautioned him to be very careful, as it was very light on the trigger. After carefully letting the hammer down, he handed it to the officer. Leslie was tried and acquitted, as it was claimed he acted in self-defense.[2]

A month later, shots were fired at a stagecoach carrying Mayor John Clum from Tombstone to nearby Benson, raising suspicions of an attempted assassination.

Still, despite the ongoing conflicts, there were good times as well. Tombstone citizens welcomed the opening of the Bird Cage Theater on December 21, 1881.[3] The Bird Cage offered the only entertainment of its kind in town and the place was full every night. Deputy Sheriff Breakenridge watched the place from a vantage point nearby one evening:

> Although no one had been killed there, and Hutchinson [the co-owner] ran it in an orderly manner, we looked for trouble between the two factions to come off at any time.
>
> One dark, rainy night, I was tired and decided to go home, and before doing so took a walk up the street to the corner opposite the Bird Cage, to see if everything was quiet. At McKnight's store, on the corner opposite the theater, as I was hugging close to the building, because of the rain, I ran up against a gun-barrel which was placed against my breast. Looking up, I saw it was Frank Stilwell.
>
> I asked him what he was trying to do, and he said that a certain party had boasted that he was going to get him that night, and that he would not do it if he saw him first. I told him that it was much too late for him to kill anyone that night, that he was in enough trouble already, and to go home. He did as I told him, and I turned back wondering who he was after. About the middle of the block I met Doc Holliday, who roomed a short distance up the street, on his way home. It flashed through my mind that I had inadvertently saved Holliday's life that night.[4]

Frank Stilwell, then about twenty-four, was from the Missouri-Kansas border area. He was a younger brother of

"Comanche Jack" Stilwell, who worked as a scout and later became a deputy U.S. marshal in present-day Oklahoma. He may have drifted through Dodge City, Kansas, before arriving in the Sulphur Spring Valley area near Tombstone, where, as we have seen earlier, he was associated with Pete Spencer, Billy Grounds, Zwing Hunt, and others generally described by their contemporaries as outlaws, rustlers, and stage robbers.[5] In spite of this, Stilwell became a deputy sheriff of Cochise County and served admirably—until he was arrested for robbing the Bisbee stagecoach in September 1881.

Breakenridge may have thwarted Stilwell's assassination attempt on Doc Holliday, but more violence was on the horizon. Virgil Earp was shotgunned outside the Oriental Saloon on Allen Street as he walked towards the Cosmopolitan Hotel on December 28. Diarist George Parsons roomed nearby and recorded his experience:

> Tonight about 11:30, Doc G [Goodwell] had just left and I thought couldn't have crossed the street—when four shots were fired in quick succession from very heavily charged guns, making a terrible noise and I thought were fired under my window, under which I quickly dropped, keeping the [a]dobe wall between me and the outside till the fusillade was over. I immediately thought Doc [Goodwell] had been shot and fired in return, remembering a late episode and knowing how pronounced he was on the Earp-cowboy question. He had crossed through and passed Virgil Earp who crossed to [the] west side of 5th and was fired upon when in range of my window by two or three concealed in the timbers of the new two story adobe going up for the Huachuca Water Co. He did not fall, but recrossed to the Oriental and was taken from there to the Cosmopolitan, being hit with buck shot and badly wounded in [the] left arm, with flesh wound above left thigh.

Parsons had little good to say about law enforcement that night, recalling that even though cries of "There they go! Head them off!" were heard, "the cowardly apathetic guardians of the peace were not inclined to risk themselves and the other brave men, all more or less armed, did nothing."[6] Parsons also reported that after he went to the hospital for medical supplies and returned to the Cosmopolitan Hotel, it was difficult getting through to Virgil's room. However, Earp was in good spirits, telling his wife, "I've got one arm left to hug you with." Once the town began to gossip about the shooting, the cowboy suspects mentioned included Ike Clanton, Frank Stilwell, "Apache" Hank Swilling, and John Ringo.[7]

Scarcely a week later, on January 6, 1882, at about three in the morning, the Tombstone to Bisbee stage was robbed near the Clanton ranch. A mine payroll of about $10,000 ($212,000 today) was taken along with the shotgun of Wells Fargo messenger Charlie Bartholomew. Later, Wyatt Earp claimed that Curly Bill Brocius tried to kill him with this shotgun.[8]

Wyatt Earp was appointed deputy U.S. marshal the same day as the Bisbee stage robbery. Less than a month later, at about the time their friend Marshall Williams skulked out of town owing money to Wells Fargo and others, Virgil and Wyatt tried to submit their resignations as deputy U.S. marshals to U.S. Marshal Crawley Dake. They were bothered by the "harsh criticisms" they had received from certain quarters in Tombstone. Dake, who was then staying at the Grand Hotel in Tombstone,[9] simply ignored the tendered resignation. After this, Wyatt appointed several men to serve as a federal posse in February and March 1882. These individuals included Morgan and Warren Earp, Doc Holliday, Sherman McMasters, "Texas Jack" Vermillion, and "Turkey Creek Jack" Johnson, who headquartered at the Bob Hatch Saloon. Other posse members included Charles Smith and Dan Tipton.[10]

More eastern civility soon arrived in the person of Endicott Peabody, a seminarian from a "wealthy old aristocratic family of Massachusetts." Peabody had been "educated at Cambridge University in England and then, back, in America." He later "abandoned the family banking business to study for the Episcopalian ministry." During a seven-month Tombstone visit, Endicott raised money for a church, then returned to the seminary and eventually became headmaster of the prestigious Groton School. Decades later he conducted services during two inaugurations of his former student, Pres. Franklin Delano Roosevelt.[11]

According to Breakenridge, sometime in early 1882, John Ringo offered to end the Earp-cowboy feud by dueling Doc Holliday. He supposedly confronted Wyatt Earp one day: "Wyatt, let's end this row. It has gone on long enough. Let Holliday and me get out here in the middle of the street and shoot it out. If you get me, the cowboys will go on home and consider the feud ended. If I am the winner, you agree to do the same and it will be over." After the Earps declined the offer, or so the story goes, Ringo was required to turn in his weapons to Sheriff Behan and later picked them up and left town without permission. After two posses failed to bring him back for violating Tombstone's gun ordinances, he presented himself and paid a thirty-dollar fine.[12]

Much more serious business was afoot. The evening of March 18, 1882, was apparently a quiet one—at least for Tombstone—because the next day the diarist George Parsons recorded that he heard the two shots that killed Morgan Earp while he was "playing pool in the Campbell and Hatch Billiard Parlor."[13] Morgan was placed on a sofa in a nearby room, where he soon said that this was the last game of pool he would play, whispered something to Wyatt, and died. Breakenridge recalled that Morgan was killed by a shot fired through the glass top half of a back door.[14]

A curious letter written by Will McLaury, brother of the slain Frank and Tom McLaury, to his father about two years later has caused many to ask whether Virgil and Morgan Earp were shot at his direction since Will had watched the Earp brothers walk away free at the conclusion of their preliminary hearing on murder charges. Will told his father: "My experience out there [in Tombstone] has been very unfortunate to my health and badly injured me as to money matters—and none of the results have been satisfactory. The only result is the death of Morgan and the crippling of Virgil Earp and the death of McMasters."[15] Still, Sherman McMasters was not killed and no direct, convincing evidence connecting Will McLaury to the shootings of Morgan and Virgil Earp has ever surfaced.

One thing is known with some certainty: although there is no evidence that Frank Stilwell shot Morgan Earp, Wyatt killed Stilwell two days later in the train yard at Tucson. As Virgil and Allie set off to accompany Morgan's body to Colton, California, Wyatt, Warren, Doc, McMasters, and Johnson boarded the train with them at Contention and planned to return to Tombstone from the Tucson train station.

One of the earliest accounts of the Stilwell shooting was provided by Virgil Earp in a May 27, 1882, interview with the *San Francisco Examiner*. Virgil did not reveal exactly who killed Stilwell. "It was our boys that killed Stilwell," he related. "Before Stilwell died he confessed he killed Morg, and gave the names of those who were implicated with him." Most researchers believe that the Earp party in Tucson that evening consisted of Wyatt, Warren, Holliday, McMasters, and Johnson.[16]

During a May 14, 1893, interview with the *Denver Republican,* Wyatt related that when he arrived at Tucson,

> a friend of mine told me that Ike Clanton and Frank
> Stilwell were in town and expected me. I thanked him

and set out to find them. I came on them across the railroad track as it was coming to dusk. Both of them began to shoot at me. I had a shotgun.

I ran straight for Stilwell. It was he who killed my brother. What a coward he was! He couldn't shoot when I came near him. He stood there helpless and trembling for his life. As I rushed upon him he put out his hands and clutched at my shotgun. I let go both barrels and he tumbled down dead and mangled at my feet. I started for Clanton then, but he escaped behind a moving train of cars. When the train had passed I could not find him.

Frank Stilwell was killed on March 20 without firing a shot himself. His body had been pierced by both buckshot and pistol or rifle fire.[17] Wyatt later claimed that at this point, the Earps and the rest of their contingent had become fugitives from Cochise County authorities.

Years later, Breakenridge recalled that the Earps suspected Stilwell and two mixed-blood Indians of killing Morgan Earp, but Breakenridge doubted Stilwell had been personally involved since the shooting occurred at about 11 P.M. in Tombstone, and Stilwell was observed far away (for that time) in Tucson the next morning.[18] Breakenridge theorized in his memoirs that Ike Clanton was at the station when the Earps arrived on March 20 and warned Stilwell.[19] He also speculated that Stilwell was probably looking for an opportunity to shoot the Earp party but they found him first in the train yard.[20] One source reports that witnesses saw four men shooting at Stilwell.[21]

The Earp party hopped a freight train to Contention, a small burg northwest of Tucson, and from there a stage to Tombstone. On March 21, according to a late-life recollection of a telegraph operator in Tombstone, the telegraph office manager warned the Earps that a warrant from Sheriff Bob Paul of Pima County had been wired to Cochise County sheriff Behan.[22] Sheriff Behan received the telegraph at 8

P.M., while the Earps were preparing to leave town. The Epitaph reported on March 22 what happened next:

> Sheriff Behan was standing in the office of the Cosmopolitan Hotel when Wyatt Earp and the others comprising the party came into the office from the rear entrance, each one having a rifle in his hands, in the ordinary manner of carrying a gun, and passed through the room to the street. As Wyatt advanced to the front and approached Sheriff Behan, the sheriff said to him, "Wyatt, I want to see you." Wyatt replied, "You can't see me; you have seen me once to [sic] often," or words to that effect. He passed out into the street and said, "I will see Paul," [referring to Pima County sheriff Bob Paul] and then the party passed on down the street.[23]

Wyatt Earp, Doc Holliday, Sherman McMasters, Texas Jack Vermillion, Turkey Creek Jack Johnson, Charlie Smith, and one Tipton then departed Tombstone armed and ready for action.[24]

The morning of March 22, just after sunrise, they rode into a wood-cutting camp operated by Pete Spencer looking for two individuals whom they suspected of complicity with Frank Stilwell in the death of Morgan Earp. One of the men was elsewhere, but Florentino "Indian Charlie" Cruz was working on a hill near the camp. Soon after the Earp party arrived, the workers in the camp heard several gunshots. Later, they discovered Cruz dead.[25]

The next move was among the most controversial killings in the Old West, if it took place at all. Years later, Wyatt Earp described a gunfight on March 24 at a place the *Tombstone Epitaph* named as Mescal Springs, but it is described in most of the literature and here as Iron Springs. However, recent evidence suggests that the gunfight might have occurred at a place called Cottonwood Springs.[26] Some fourteen years later, in an 1896 *San Francisco Examiner* interview, Wyatt recalled approaching a certain spring, whatever it was named:

> As we got near the place, I had a presentiment that something was wrong, and unlimbered my shotgun. Sure enough, cowboys sprang from the bank where the spring was and began firing at us. I jumped off my horse to return the fire, thinking my men would do the same, but they retreated. One of the cowboys, who was trying to pump some lead into me with a Winchester was a fellow named Curly Bill, a stage-robber whom I had been after for eight months, and for whom I had a warrant in my pocket. I fired both barrels of my gun into him, blowing him all to pieces. With that the others jumped into a clump of willows and kept on firing, so I retreated, keeping behind my horse. He was a high-strung beast, and the firing frightened him so that whenever I tried to get my Winchester from the saddle he would rear up and keep it out of my reach. When I had backed out about a hundred yards I started to mount. Now, it was a hot day, and I had loosened my cartridge belt two or three holes. When I tried to get astride I found that it had fallen down over my thighs, keeping my legs together. While I was perched up thus, trying to pull my belt higher with one hand, the horn of the saddle was shot off. However, I got away all right, and just then my men rallied. But I did not care to go back at the rustlers, so we sought out another water hole for camp. The skirt of my overcoat was shot to pieces on both sides, but not a bullet touched me.[27]

Wyatt Earp related an earlier version of this story to the *Denver Republican* on May 14, 1893. The story of how he approached the place was very similar to the detailed narrative above, but his earlier telling had more detail about his confrontation with Curly Bill and subsequent escape:

I was surprised when I looked around to see them [Earp's companions] disappearing in a cloud of dust as fast as their horses could carry them. My horse reared and tugged at the bridle in such wild fashion that I could not regain the saddle, I reckoned that my time had come. But if I was to die, I proposed that Curly Bill at least should die with me.

He churned several shots at me from his Winchester, but he fired rapidly and his shots went wide. I threw my shotgun to my shoulder and fixing a bead directly on his heart, turned loose both barrels. His chest was torn open by the big charge of buckshot. He yelled like a demon when he went down.

His death struck a panic into the rest. They turned and ran for their lives and took shelter behind a clump of willows beyond the spring. I knew it would be useless for me to stand there in the open and fight eight men who were screened from my view; I backed away, using my horse's body as a bulwark against the flying lead, and firing as I withdrew. When I had got a hundred yards or so away, I mounted. But I swore then that that cowardly crowd should not make me run and I walked my horse half a mile further, with Winchester bullets singing all the way thick around my ears.

When I joined my companions, Holliday came up to me and caught me gently by the arm, "I'll help you from your horse, Wyatt," he said, "You must be shot to pieces." "No," I answered, "I am not touched."[28]

The fight at Iron Springs has not been substantiated to the satisfaction of all historians.[29] Deputy Breakenridge also noted in his 1928 memoirs that the death of Curly Bill in this incident was far from certain.

A reliable merchant and rancher living at Safford told me about two weeks after the Earp party reported killing Curly Bill, Curly himself came to his home and said he had just got back from Old Mexico; that he was leaving the country [area] and going to Wyoming where he was going to get work and try to lead a decent life, as he was tired of being on the dodge all the time. The merchant gave him a good saddle horse to ride away on. A Mr. Vaughn, now living in Tombstone, told me that ten years later Curly Bill came through Benson on the train bound for Texas, and stopped off long enough to visit the postmaster, whom he had known in his early days in Arizona.

A more dubious source, accused bank robber Alex Arnold, claimed at the time that Curly Bill was not even at the spring, but in "Old Mexico," according to Breakenridge:

> Just a short time before the [gunfight at the spring] a couple of cowboys named Pink Truly and Alex Arnold, whose true name was supposed to be Bill Alexander, were accused of robbing a store in Charleston. They got away, but Pink Truly was soon arrested for the robbery, and at his trial a number of his cowboy friends proved their usual alibi for him. They all swore that he was at their ranch the night of the robbery playing poker with them, that it was an all night game and that Truly never left the house that night. So he was acquitted and the matter dropped.
>
> Arnold, however, had gone into hiding at Mescal Spring with two cowboys. As soon as Pink was free, he took some provisions out to the spring where they were hiding, and was there when the Earp party rode up. Both Truly and Arnold told the following story about the fight as soon as they returned to Tombstone: They stated that Curly Bill was not there; that he had been in Mexico for the past two months. As the Earp party rode up to the spring the four cowboys took refuge behind an embankment, and all except Wyatt of the Earp party turned and rode away. Wyatt, however, rode up rather close to them and dismounted, and with bridle rein over his arm stepped in front of his horse, raised his rifle and fired at them. They

returned the fire. Alex Arnold reported that Earp was wearing a white shirt which made a splendid target. He was only a short distance away and drew a fine bead on Wyatt and fired. Earp turned partly around and staggered back to his horse which he mounted and rode away after the others of his party. Both Arnold and Truly claimed that Wyatt Earp had a steel vest on under his shirt which deflected the bullet. They also stated they shot the horn off Earp's saddle and killed Texas Jack's horse, and that Jack got on behind one of the men and rode away.[30]

Yet Wells Fargo undercover agent Fred Dodge firmly believed Curly Bill was dead. Dodge wrote Wyatt Earp biographer Stuart Lake on October 8, 1928, substantiating the death of Curly Bill. Dodge related that he was personally told by Johnny Barnes, a cowboy factionist involved in the fight at Iron Springs, that Curly Bill was killed in this incident. Dodge related in the same letter that Ike Clanton confirmed Curly Bill's death although the basis of Clanton's knowledge was not disclosed.[31]

This concluded the so-called vendetta ride in which Wyatt, Warren Earp, Doc Holliday, Sherman McMasters, and Turkey Creek Jack Johnson sought revenge against the cowboy faction for Virgil's injuries and the death of Morgan Earp. The Earp faction killed Frank Stilwell, Florentino Cruz, and perhaps Bill Brocius.[32] Fourteen years later, Wyatt told the *San Francisco Examiner* that they "withstood more than one attack from outlaws who had been implicated in the death of one brother and the disablement of another—attacks which resulted fatally to some of my enemies and left me without a scratch."[33]

On March 25, Earp and his crew camped about six miles north of Tombstone with Doc Holliday and one or two faithful comrades. The group included Charlie Smith, who sometimes wrote stories for the *Epitaph,* identifying himself as "one of them." The group traveled the next day to Summit

Station and then on to Henderson's ranch, where Deputy Sheriff Hereford hid from them as an accommodation to Henderson, who did not want his sick wife made worse by a gunfight. According to Breakenridge, Hereford listened from hiding to a conversation about the fight at Iron Springs and later reported "that he could see plainly that Earp's overcoat had a bullet hole through each side of the front of it and he heard them [Wyatt's companions] say 'The steel saved you this time.'"[34] While this seems a minor concern today, Wyatt Earp was incensed at such a suggestion and emphasized how uncomfortable such protection would be in the desert.[35]

Sheriff Behan and a posse began chasing the Earp party on March 22 and were still in pursuit five days later, according to diarist George Parsons.[36] But the Behan effort was in difficulty. Breakenridge noted that it took "a couple of days" after the Frank Stilwell killing on March 20 for Sheriff Behan to assemble a posse since "horses were scarce, and the chase was likely to be a long one." Behan was very careful in selecting his posse, which consisted mostly of rustlers. Breakenridge was first told that he was to go along but eventually was asked to stay in Tombstone and loan his horse to the rustler John Ringo, who had left his rifle at a ranch close to the town and who with several others of the cowboys and rustlers made up the posse. Behan took this crew because he believed that if the Earp faction were found, they would fight. Somehow, Sheriff Behan met with little success.

> The posse followed the Earp party to near Fort Grant and the Hooker ranch. Henry Clay Hooker, who had suffered severely from the rustlers staking his cattle, was friendly with the Earps, and when Behan came with a posse composed mostly of rustlers and cowboys, with John Ringo and Finn [Phineas Clanton] and Ike Clanton among them, he would give them no help or information.

At the fort, Behan tried to get Indian scouts to follow the trail, but the commanding officer would not let him have them, and he had to return without finding the Earp party. They got out of the country, and so far as I know, none of them returned. They went on to Colorado, and Bob Paul, the sheriff of Pima County, where the crime was committed, got extradition papers for them and went there after them, but the Governor of Colorado would not honor them.[37]

## The Death of Billy Grounds

While Sheriff Behan and his rustlers were pursuing the Earps, Deputy Breakenridge raised his own posse to pursue two young Texas hard cases.[38] Billy Grounds had been named Arthur Boucher when he was born in central Texas twenty short years before that Cochise County posse began to search for him. Difficulties long forgotten in his hometown of Dripping Springs sent him west to Arizona, where he met John Ringo, and he eventually moved to Tombstone. Later, Grounds moved on to nearby Charleston. Zwing Hunt was reportedly a Kopprel, Texas, native and as was often said of troublemakers during those times, "born of a good family." Zwing worked for the Chiricahua Cattle Company but resigned his lumber-hauling position to pursue other interests, mainly cattle rustling. According to Breakenridge, these two were partners during the pursuit. Soon Hunt and Grounds supposedly expanded their scope of operations by ambushing and killing a party of Mexican silver smugglers, thus leading generations of disappointed treasure hunters to try their luck in Skeleton Canyon near Tombstone.[39]

Whatever the truth of these stories, it became known that in the fall of 1881 some thirty head of cattle were stolen from the Persley and Woolf Sulphur Spring ranch.

Woolf came to Tombstone and got a John Doe warrant
[recalled Breakenridge in 1929], and I went with him to
try and trace the stock. We followed them to Charleston
and found them in a corral where they had been sold to
a butcher, and one head killed. The thieves had not been
gone over an hour. The man who bought them turned
them back over to Woolf and paid him for the one killed.
From the description given of the men who sold the stock
we were satisfied that they were Hunt and Grounds and
they were indicted for grand larceny, but never arrested,
as they left the country for a time and went to Mexico.[40]

Maybe so. Whether Grounds and Hunt had skedaddled
for Mexico or not, Breakenridge recalled that Tombstone
Mining Company official M. R. Peel was murdered the next
spring in Charleston. The intruders arrived with rifles,
opened the office door, and shot Peel without saying a word,
disappearing into the darkness. Since Peel had no known
enemies, Breakenridge assumed that the shooting had been
accidental.

[The] next day or two, men came out of the hills to
a ranch near Lewis Spring and asked for something to
eat. They claimed they had nothing to eat for the past
twenty-four hours. They were fed, and soon a company
of soldiers came past looking for Indians. The men were
badly scared and did not go out until the soldiers had left.
They slept there the rest of the day and at night went
away. Hunt and Grounds were suspected of doing the
killing. A few days later word was received at the Sheriff's
office that they were at the Chandler Ranch about nine
miles [east] of Tombstone.

Hunt and Grounds arrived at the Chandler ranch on
March 25, 1882, and attempted a shakedown, according to
Breakenridge. They told the hired man that his boss owed

them some money and sent him into Tombstone to collect. Instead, the man went straight to the sheriff's office. Deputy Sheriff Breakenridge raised a posse to make the capture. He recalled the details in his memoirs:

We reached the ranch just before daylight, and, after tying our horses a distance from the house, crept up. I stationed Young and Gillespie at the back door behind a pile of wood, and told them to lie quiet until daylight. Knowing the habits of cowboys, I said they would come outside at daylight to look for their horses. If Young and Gillespie would then cover them with their guns they would surrender. Allen and I would guard the front door. I took the front of the house, as there were both a door and a window there, and only a door on the rear side. Allen and I started for the front of the house, and just as we got there heard Gillespie knock on the door. When asked who was there, he answered, "It is me, the Sheriff." The men inside opened the door and shot him dead and shot Young through the thigh. Neither Young nor Gillespie ever got a chance to fire a shot.

Just then, the front door opened and Bull Lewis came running out, crying "Don't shoot, I am innocent." A shot came out from the front door and creased Allen across the neck. It knocked him senseless. I heard someone step toward the door from the inside, and I grabbed Allen by his collar and dragged him under the bank of the dry creek in front of the house. The bank was about a foot high. I jumped behind a small tree just as someone fired from the front door, the bullet hitting a tree. The person who fired it stepped to the door to fire the second shot. I fired one barrel of my shotgun, loaded with buckshot, into the opening. Just as I fired I remembered an old adage to aim low in the dark and I pulled down thinking I would hit him in the stomach. But I hit him in the head and heard him strike the floor. In the meantime, Allen had come to, and Hunt came around the back of the house, calling "Billy, Billy."

Allen and I both fired at him, Allen with a rifle, and I with a pistol, and he disappeared. He was only about fifty yards from us and we both thought he was shot. It was not daylight yet. Young, who had got about thirty yards from the house, holloed that he was shot, and I ran to him and helped him to another house about a hundred yards from where we were. Allen lay behind the creek bank and he guarded the front door so that no one could come out and take a shot at me. All the shots were fired inside of two minutes.[41]

Although Billy Grounds' feet could be seen protruding from the back door, Zwing was unaccounted for. Breakenridge pursued him along a creek, heard some rustling in the weeds, and ordered, "Throw up your hands." And he did. Afterwards, Breakenridge asked why Hunt did not open fire when he heard the deputy coming down the creek. The outlaw said that he was dying of thirst (due to a gunshot through his left lung) and knew he would not get a drink unless he surrendered.

Breakenridge also wondered why Gillespie would chance asking Grounds and Hunt to surrender and soon discovered his motive: "I learned . . . that Gillespie was an aspirant for the Sheriff's office at the next election, and that he thought I was too cautious or afraid, and that he could go in and make the arrest alone and get the credit for it."

There was a second miscalculation that morning. "Hunt told me that they thought it was the Earp party after them, and if he had known who it was, he would never have made a fight." Billy Grounds died later that evening at the hospital in Tombstone. Dr. George E. Goodfellow performed an autopsy, which Breakenridge studiously avoided.[42]

## The Flight of Wyatt Earp

On the very day Billy Grounds was killed resisting arrest,

the Earp faction was on the move. The afternoon of Monday, March 27, found them at the Sierra Bonita Ranch operated by Henry Clay Hooker, who furnished supplies and fresh horses for a 7 P.M. departure.[43] Behan arrived about twelve hours later, and Hooker was barely civil once he saw the posse consisted mostly of rustlers. He refused to provide Behan any information at all. Charlie Smith claimed in a report to the *Epitaph* that later that morning the posse rode right past them at Eureka Springs, north of Fort Grant. Years later, in a *San Francisco Examiner* interview published on August 2, 1896, Wyatt claimed that the posse was only a bluff since Earp had sent word to Behan explaining exactly where he could be found. Sheriff Behan returned to Tombstone empty handed on the afternoon of Thursday, March 31.

While the Tombstone citizenry debated the controversial death of Curly Bill at Iron Springs, Earp and his crew trekked through the desert to Silver City, New Mexico, and arrived there on April 8. Henry "Billy the Kid" McCarty had lived here as a boy only eight years before the Earps arrived and had been killed at Fort Sumner, New Mexico, the prior July. The Earp party came here for anonymity and a rest before traveling east to catch a train. The sale of their horses at bargain prices before departing on the Fort Cummings stage aroused some suspicion, but most of Silver City was none the wiser.[44] April 18 found them in Albuquerque, even as charges against Pete Spencer in the Morgan Earp murder were being dismissed back in Tombstone for lack of evidence.

Tombstone had now captured nationwide bad publicity. Pres. Chester Arthur proposed an amendment of the Posse Comitatus Act to permit military intervention against Arizona outlaws. The bill languished in Congress long enough to prompt a presidential proclamation on May 3 threatening to impose martial law on southeastern Arizona and declaring a state of rebellion,[45] although John Pleasant Gray and other Tombstonians thought Arthur overstated the rustler threat.

That same week, the Earp party arrived at Trinidad, Colorado, and disbanded. Holliday had a falling-out with the Earps and left for Denver. Wyatt and Warren Earp departed for Gunnison, some 150 miles from Denver, while the rest reportedly returned to New Mexico.[46]

Doc Holliday was arrested on May 15 in Denver by Perry Mallan (Mallon, Mallen), who was described in a May 17, 1882, *Denver Tribune* article as a deputy sheriff of Los Angeles, California, but his office has not been proven. Holliday was held in the Denver jail on murder charges arising from the death of Frank Stilwell. The same article related the Doc Holliday version of the Tombstone difficulties although he was not directly quoted. Holliday opined that the events in Tombstone arose from both political and personal differences and claimed that Sheriff Behan took the part of the lawless element, which he described as cowboys. Wyatt Earp on the other hand, according to Holliday, sided with the United States marshal to suppress lawlessness. Holliday went on to say (erroneously) that Curly Bill had killed "the Marshal of El Paso and a son of General Benjamin F. Butler during a stagecoach robbery." Holliday explained that the Earp faction had resolved to rout the cowboys and that "Troubles grew until the fight on the street . . . took place." The *Tribune* article also related that according to Mallan, Holliday had killed one Harry White in a St. George, Utah, gambling hall some seven years prior to the interview.[47]

Holliday was again interviewed in an article which appeared five days later in the *Denver Republican*. The reporter described him as "a slender man, not more than five feet six inches tall and would weigh perhaps 150 pounds. His face is thin and his hair is sprinkled heavily with gray. His features are well formed and there is nothing remarkable in them, save a well-defined look of determination from his eyes. . . . The first thing noticeable about him in conversation was his soft voice and modest manners." In this article Holliday did not describe his Arizona opponents as cowboys at all but as

> a gang of murderers, stage robbers and thieves from the Eastern States. The proper name for them is Rustlers. They ran the country down there and so terrorized the country that no man dared say anything against them. Trouble first arose with them by the killing of Marshal White by Curly Bill. Marshal White fell into my arms when he was shot and I arrested Curly Bill. The trouble then is familiar to all.

During the same interview, Holliday incorrectly claimed that the cowboys were part of the "Fort Griffin Gang" and that Sheriff Behan instigated the assassination of Morgan Earp and later deputized "the rustlers." He also claimed that Frank Stilwell was seen running with Pete Spencer from the spot where Morgan Earp was assassinated. He acknowledged the death of Frank Stilwell "near Tucson" but claimed no role. He did admit that he was present when Curly Bill was allegedly killed, stating that eight rustlers, including Pete Spencer and Pony Deal, were there. He described the gunfight as having occurred at about 3 P.M. at a spring located in a hollow.

Pima County sheriff Bob Paul arrived on May 22 expecting to find the Earps and Holliday in the jail but found that only Holliday had been arrested. He applied to the Colorado governor for extradition, which was denied three days later. Meanwhile, Doc Holliday was released from the Denver jail on May 24 on a writ of habeas corpus and transported to Pueblo, Colorado, to face charges that he swindled a local man out of about one hundred dollars. One researcher has suggested that the Pueblo charges were filed to avoid

Holliday's return to Tombstone on the murder charges there, perhaps at the instigation of Bat Masterson. In any event, Doc pled guilty to the Pueblo charges, was fined, and was released in July.[48]

While Doc was facing minor charges in Pueblo, Warren Earp was interviewed by the Gunnison, Colorado, *Daily News-Democrat* for an article published June 4, 1882. The reporter described Warren as "a young man of twenty-eight to thirty, weighing about 160 pounds with clear blue eyes, brown hair and a mustache" but "not a man to fool with." After falsely claiming that the Colorado governor had refused to permit their extradition to Arizona, Warren focused on the problems in Tombstone with more than a bit of Earp spin as Wyatt looked on:

> This whole trouble grew out of the efforts of the "Rustlers" to run the town. Wyatt was United States marshal, and my brother Virgil was town marshal of Tombstone. My other brother, Morgan, was a policeman under him. If we had left the offices alone we could have made a barrel of money. Wyatt had the finest saloon and gambling house in Tombstone. The bar alone cost him three thousand dollars, and he was doing a rattling business. But the citizens prevailed upon him to take the office of deputy sheriff and United States Marshal. He used to be marshal of Dodge City, Kansas and anybody from there can tell you what kind of Marshal he made.
>
> The first trouble began with Ike Clanton. He made a "gun play" and my brother Virgil disarmed and fined him. As soon as he got out he got his brother Billy and Tom and Frank McLaury[49] and Billy the Kid[50], and they swore they would kill us. The boys went out to disarm them and they tried to stand 'em off. The fight lasted about half a minute, and Billy Clanton and Tom and Frank McLaury were killed. Virgil was shot through the shoulders, but he is now recovering. After that they killed my brother Morgan by shooting him through a window while he was

playing pool. There were five men in the crowd, Frank
Stilwell, Pete Spencer, "Curley Bill" and two half-breeds.
Stillwell, "Curley Bill" and one of the half-breeds named
Florantine [sic] have since been killed. That makes six of
the gang that have gone under.

During his own interview that day in Gunnison, Wyatt
vowed that he would return and run for sheriff, but he never
saw Tombstone again.

Doc Holliday gave his own version of the famous gunfight
to the *Gunnison News-Democrat* fourteen days later. After
relating his earlier life as a Methodist dentist in Dallas, Doc
related that he lived in Denver during 1875 and 1876. Then
he told yet another version of the Fremont Street gunfight
in Tombstone:

> Bill Earp [Virgil] was city marshal of Tombstone. Morg
> Earp was a special policeman. Wyatt Earp was a deputy
> U.S. Marshal. One day six of the cowboys came into town
> and proposed to run it. The Earps were informed of their
> doings, and they invited me over to where the cowboys
> were. One of the Earps said, "Throw up your hands; we
> have come to disarm you." Instead of putting up their
> paws they put up their revolvers and began firing. Three
> of them were killed on the spot and two of the Earps
> wounded. I received a slight wound on the hip, which
> caused me some inconvenience for a few days.

## The Mysterious Death of John Ringo

John Ringo was found dead on July 14 across Turkey
Creek from the mouth of Morse's Canyon. The July 18,
1882, *Tombstone Epitaph* expressed little doubt about
what had happened:

The circumstances of the case hardly leave any room for

doubt as to his self-destruction. He was about 200 feet from water, and was acquainted with every inch of the country, so that it was almost impossible to lose himself. He was found in a clump of oaks, springing from the same stem, but diverging outward as to leave an open space in the center. On the top of the main stem and between the spreading boughs, was a large stone, and on this pedestal he was found sitting, with his body leaning backward and resting on a tree. There was a large bullet hole beneath his right eye and a small part of his scalp was missing.

Despite this and a coroner's jury verdict of suicide, a number of his contemporaries have been suspected of murdering John Ringo. These include Doc Holliday, Buckskin Frank Leslie, and Michael "Johnny" O'Rourke, known as "Johnny-Behind-the-Deuce." The most intriguing of all the suspects is Wyatt Earp, who said in a May 14, 1893, interview with the *Denver Republican* that during the vendetta, "I never succeeded in finding Ringo. He got out of the country and was killed by somebody else." Nonetheless, two different authors who prepared manuscripts which Wyatt reviewed but ultimately disapproved included a story to the effect that he killed Ringo before leaving Arizona.[51] Finally, Josephine Sarah Marcus Earp claimed in her oft-criticized and doubted autobiography edited by Glenn G. Boyer that Wyatt and Doc returned to Arizona, saying, "Ringo was smart. In the end, Wyatt caught him on the run and dispatched him with a fast rifle shot, admittedly a lucky one, since it hit the last of the Rustler leaders square in the head."[52] Unlikely as this version of events may be, the death of John Ringo by his own hand or otherwise meant the end of the vendetta.

None of this meant an end to crime in southeastern Arizona. "Don't mutilate my body or shoot me full of holes," croaked vain, shoeless, and shirtless John Heath (Heith) on February 22, 1884, just before facing eternity at the end of a Tombstone telegraph pole. His early origins are a mystery, but by 1880 he was in Dallas attracting the unwelcome attention of police suspicious of his possible roles in certain burglaries and horse thefts. Unfazed, he partnered with colorful whore Georgia Morgan to start a bordello. Later, they expanded into saloon operations. Reasons now unknown prompted John's departure for Bisbee, Arizona, where he founded a dance hall and pursued other interests, fitting quite well into the young community from all appearances.

Although the Tombstone-area mines had begun to close in May of the previous year due to low silver prices, something else was wrong. Underground water seepage in the mines had been controlled in the early days, but the flooding had recently reemerged.[53] Nevertheless, mining was still a mainstay of the greater Bisbee area in those days. Since the town did not have a bank, the Copper Queen Mine payroll was managed by the Goldwater and Castenada Store. On payday, Saturday, December 8, 1883, five young men appeared for the disbursement. Unfortunately, none of them was employed by the Copper Queen. "Big Dan" Dowd, "Red" Sample, James "Tex" Howard, William Delaney, and Daniel "Yorkie" Kelly were there to steal the payroll but arrived before the money did. After treating themselves to six hundred dollars in petty cash from the safe, the quintet stepped into the streets and was fired upon by concerned citizen James Krigbaum. Responding with suppressing fire, the gang missed Krigbaum but killed two noncombatants, including Annie Roberts, who was with child.

An enraged posse led by the newly elected sheriff of Cochise Country, Republican Jerome Ward, and his predecessor, John H. Behan, included young Mr. Heath among its numbers. Luben Pardu, a small rancher who operated nearby, claimed he had recently seen the five killers accompanied by an additional suspect. Then Pardu dropped a bombshell. The apparent gang leader was riding with the posse. John Heath protested his innocence and even asked later for a separate trial, which he received. Once captured, his five confederates were convicted on February 19 of first-degree murder and sentenced to be hanged. Two days later, Heath was found guilty of second-degree murder and sentenced to life in prison. However, the sentence was commuted to a single day by a disgruntled Tombstone crowd, which lynched him on February 22. The five killers were legally hanged together in Tombstone on March 28, 1884.[54]

About five months later, the August 20 *Leadville (CO) Daily Democrat* reported that Doc Holliday shot one Billy Allen, perhaps his old nemesis from Tombstone, who was described as an ex-policeman and bartender. Apparently, Doc owed Allen five dollars and had refused to pay. Holliday was bound over for trial but acquitted on March 28, 1885.[55]

## Wyatt Earp Remembers Tombstone

Much of the notoriety of the Fremont Street gunfight is attributable to the stories Wyatt Earp told years after leaving Tombstone. In a series of 1896 *San Francisco Examiner* articles, Earp expanded upon his 1881 testimony. In particular, he elaborated on his story about the reward money arrangement with Ike Clanton. Wyatt said that Wells Fargo agent Marshall Williams had apparently guessed that Ike was Wyatt's source of information about the robberies and pumped Clanton for details. Clanton complained to Wyatt Earp and later to Holliday, whom in reality knew nothing at all about the proposal. According to Wyatt's *Examiner* interview, Ike was concerned that his cowboy confederates would learn that he was an informant: "Clanton knew he had to kill us or be killed."[56] Ike telegraphed Charleston, Earp alleged, bringing Billy Clanton, the McLaurys, and Billy Clayton (actually Billy Claiborne). Wyatt also claimed in these articles that the four eventually sent word to the Earps to come to the lot on Fremont Street because "if we did not come down there and fight, they would way-lay and kill us." Then Wyatt revisited the gunfight at Harwood's lumberyard, claiming the McLaurys and Clanton fired first.

This account, written some twenty-five years after the event, contained numerous factual errors. The Clantons never sent any warnings to the Earp faction although intermediaries relayed threats they had heard. Billy Claiborne, rather than Billy Clanton, ran from the gunfight, which probably took some thirty seconds rather than a minute. Ike Clanton had no gun and did no shooting in the lot itself or from any nearby building. If Earp saw anything, it might have been Billy Allen firing from the east side of a nearby building.[57]

Preliminary questions put to Wyatt Earp during the course of a 1926 Los Angeles deposition in a then-famous probate case gives yet another view of early Tombstone. Earp discounted the violent reputation Tombstone had acquired in later years and recounted his recollections of those times.[58] He recalled the death of J. T. Waters, who was shot four times and mortally wounded by E. L. Bradshaw on July 24, 1880, after Waters struck Bradshaw for ridiculing a new red shirt Waters was wearing. Wyatt delved into other long-ago matters including the death of Mike Killeen, supposed to have been killed by Buckskin Frank Leslie exactly one month after J. T. Waters died in his tacky red shirt. Earp testified that Mike Killeen was not killed by Buckskin Frank Leslie—a contention consistent with Mike's "deathbed statement" as published in the August 24, 1880, edition of the *Tombstone Epitaph*. Mike said that Leslie's friend George Perine had done the shooting, although at the time, a jury found Perine innocent.

When questioned about how amenable Tombstone had been to law, order, and morality some forty-six years earlier, Earp had quipped, "It was not half as bad as Los Angeles." This regard for Tombstone was a sentiment he shared with his old nemesis Billy Breakenridge, who recalled in memoirs published two years later, in 1928,

> Tombstone has a reputation as a wild and wicked city with a man for breakfast every morning. This is all a mistake. Tombstone was an orderly town, with very little crime. The large majority of the inhabitants were law abiding. Yes, there were a few tough outlaws there, but they mostly confined their quarreling and shooting to themselves. Even though there were a few killings, as happened in all frontier towns, practically none of the law-abiding citizens were ever killed.[59]

During his 1926 cross-examination, Wyatt was questioned about Sheriff Behan, whom he described as being with an opposing faction:

> This fellow Behan, he intended to run for sheriff and he knew that I did, and if I do say it myself I was a pretty strong man for the position. He knew that he had to do me some way and he done everything in the world that he could against me. He stood in with this tough element, the cowboys[60] and stage robbers and others, because they were pretty strong and he wanted their vote.

## Tombstone Epilogue

Judge Wells Spicer found himself deeply in debt by 1886. Despite his work as a defense lawyer following the Mountain Meadows massacre and as the deciding judge who exonerated the Earps after the Tombstone gunfight notoriety of October 1881, his law practice slowly dwindled to nothing. Although he was involved in two of the most significant cases in the history of the American West, he became despondent and simply drifted into the Sonora desert, never to be heard from again.[61]

Despite his fighting spirit, in the end, Doc Holliday was no match for the tuberculosis that had lingered within him for many years. On November 8, 1887, at a hotel in Glenwood Springs, Colorado, Doc's luck ran out. All of his worldly possessions were shipped to his childhood friend and cousin, Sister Mary Melanie, a Sister of Mercy living in Georgia. Years later, their mutual kinswoman Margaret Mitchell used the good sister as her model for the impossibly sweet character Melanie in *Gone with the Wind*. Among the few valuable possessions delivered to Sister Melanie was an expensive stickpin from which the diamond had long since been removed.[62]

Ike Clanton was killed by correspondence school detective J. V. Brighton in 1887 while resisting arrest on cattle rustling charges. His brother Phin meekly surrendered and went to prison.[63]

The next year Wyatt's second wife, Celia Ann "Mattie" Blaylock Earp (his first wife died in Lamar, Missouri), died at Pinal, Arizona, telling one acquaintance that Wyatt had wrecked her life and she did not wish to live.[64]

Although he was wealthy, Edward L. "Ed" Schieffelin died alone at age forty-nine in May 1897 in a modest prospector's cabin in Oregon. He was surrounded by high-grade gold samples.[65] Soon thereafter, he was buried near Tombstone with a pick, shovel, and canteen. The founder of Tombstone rests there today beneath an outsized monument.

Texas Jack Vermillion became a Virginia preacher. His old saddle partner Sherman McMasters worked for the United States Army during the Spanish American War.[66]

Warren Earp returned to Arizona where he drove a stagecoach between Globe and Willcox and worked as a bartender. He was shot and killed while in his cups at Willcox in 1900 after challenging his longtime nemesis Johnny Boyett to a gunfight. Warren died with only a penknife in his hand.[67]

Virgil Earp left Arizona in March 1882 for Colton, California, where he recovered from the wounds sustained in his attempted assassination. Four years later, he opened a detective agency in Colton, returned to Arizona briefly to prospect, then became Colton city marshal before prospecting in numerous locales throughout the West. He died while serving as deputy sheriff of Esmeralda County, Nevada, in October 1905.[68]

Former sheriff John H. Behan went on to become a prison superintendent and an employee of the Southern Pacific Railroad before his 1912 death in Tucson.[69]

Bat Masterson stayed only briefly in Tombstone, departed for Dodge City, then went on to Colorado before joining the so-called Dodge City Peace Commission with Wyatt Earp and others in 1883. He gambled and worked as a sports official throughout the West, then moved to New York City in 1902. He became a sportswriter and died on October 25, 1921, while writing an article.[70] Within a few years, Newton and James Earp had died peacefully in California.

After the 1882 vendetta ride, Wyatt stayed in Colorado briefly then moved from one mining camp to another, taking time to participate in the bloodless, overblown Dodge City War of 1883 as a member of the Peace Commission famously gathered and photographed that year. Now joined by Josie, he wandered throughout the West. He wrote a highly sanitized version of his early days for the *San Francisco Examiner*. A few months later, on December 2, 1896, he suffered a reversal of fortune from an unexpected quarter—the boxing game. He agreed at the last minute to referee a San Francisco bout between Bob Fitzsimmons and Tom Sharkey for $10,000 ($246,000 today) and a shot at heavyweight champion Jim Corbett. The crowd was not impressed by his display of a pistol to establish his bona fides and even more displeased when he declared Tom Sharkey the winner in a controversial decision which promptly earned him a fine for carrying a concealed weapon.[71] After prospering briefly in the Alaska gold rush, Josie and Wyatt began yet another cycle of prospecting part of each year while spending the warmer months in Los Angeles. He cooperated with several authors, none of whose work he endorsed before his death in January 1929. Among the mourners were Tombstone diarist George Parsons, John Clum, and two movie stars, William S. Hart and Tom Mix.[72]

That same year, Tombstone lost the Cochise County courthouse to Bisbee but gained potential tourist traffic with the first Helldorado celebration, which launched the gunfight at the O.K. Corral myth.[73]

John Clum, the fourth mayor of Tombstone and editor of the *Epitaph,* survived Wyatt by three years. He had prospected in Alaska and retired in the Los Angeles area. Clum served as a pallbearer at Wyatt Earp's 1929 funeral and wrote a lengthy article about early Tombstone for the *Arizona Historical Quarterly* before his death in 1932.[74]

The diarist George Parsons also left Tombstone for Southern California, where he was active in the Episcopal Church and the Y.M.C.A. and was a founding member of the local chamber of commerce. Beyond this, Parsons was largely responsible for San Pedro's becoming the center of Los Angeles maritime operations instead of Santa Monica. The "father of the deep harbor" died January 3, 1933.[75]

Fred Dodge worked many years as a Wells Fargo operative, wrote his memoirs, and died December 16, 1938, at his ranch near Boerne, Texas. His memoirs were published thirty-one years later.[76] The controversial and often-challenged recollections of Josephine Sarah Marcus Earp as edited and compiled by Glenn G. Boyer were published in 1976, thirty-two years after her death.[77]

Doc Holliday's paramour, Mary Katherine Harony, known to her contemporaries in the West as Kate Elder, stayed in Colorado and married George M. Cummings in March 1890. She left her alcoholic husband nine years later, worked as a domestic, and died in the Arizona Pioneers Home at Prescott in November 1940.[78]

And so, by 1944, the year of Josie's death, virtually all of the important players in the early years of Tombstone were gone, their deaths for the most part peaceful and predictable. All, that is, except Buckskin Frank Leslie.

Leslie had a respectable record as a deputy sheriff back in Tombstone, but trouble began to find him on a regular basis beginning in the summer of 1880, when he began courting May Killeen, who had separated from her husband. On the evening of June 22 either Frank or his associate killed Mike Killeen in a scuffle which started when the unhappy husband found May and Frank spooning on the porch of the Cosmopolitan Hotel. Frank married the bereaved widow one week later.

Leslie then killed William F. "Billy the Kid" Claiborne on November 14, 1882, outside the Oriental Saloon in Tombstone following an argument.[79] Within five years of the Claiborne killing, Leslie's wife divorced him, in part, so the story goes, for using her in target practice, thus earning May the Tombstone sobriquet "silhouette girl."[80]

Frank Leslie was operating a ranch owned by Mike Joyce in July 1889, assisted in the enterprise by a new paramour, Mollie Williams Bradshaw, a former Bird Cage Theater entertainer whose husband and reputed pimp E. L. Bradshaw had been killed and dumped in an alley by persons unknown. Leslie also employed James Neal as a ranch hand.[81] On the evening of July 10, Leslie quarreled with Mollie in a drunken rage and then shot her before turning the pistol on Neal, who was wounded but escaped to a nearby ranch. After being shot, poor Mollie ran from the front porch to the back door and then fell dead. Leslie was arrested for murder, convicted, and entered Yuma Penitentiary to serve a ten-year sentence. He was pardoned in 1896 due to exemplary work as the prison doctor's assistant or, according to some accounts, as the prison druggist.[82] One researcher related that the next year Leslie married a woman with whom he had corresponded while in prison.[83]

Breakenridge claimed in his memoirs that he arranged temporary employment for Leslie with the Southern Pacific railroad assisting a geologist searching for coal deposits in Mexico. Leslie disappeared without a trace from an Oakland, California, pool hall in 1925, carrying his pay and a pistol stolen from his employer, never to be seen or heard from again.[84]

# PART II

# Bovines and Bleaters:
# The Pleasant Valley War

Tom Tucker (right) and Billy Wilson, ca. 1880. The latter would be lynched during the heat of the Pleasant Valley War. *(Courtesy Arizona Historical Society, Tucson)*

## CHAPTER SIX

# Can't We All Just Get Along?

No one was more surprised to be alive than rain-soaked half-conscious Thomas "Tom" Tucker. He and five of his compatriots had just endured a shootout at the Wilson ranch in the Tonto Basin of Arizona. He took a rifle ball to the chest and was left for dead. They were five against seven but the seven were barricaded inside a house and began firing on the mounted men without warning. Revived by the rain, Tucker dragged himself for hours over craggy terrain, leaving behind two of his number dead. Another of the group was wounded but managed to gallop to safety, as did a fifth man who raced away untouched.[1]

Toward nightfall Tucker again succumbed to blood loss and dehydration. He lay along a ridge with one thought in mind: he was to die here. Sometime in the night a second cloudburst poured into the valley. As water rushed around the semiconscious Tucker, he was roused from his stupor. He knew he had but one chance to stay alive. He would have to summon courage and strength not before known to him and continue his desperate crawl over rock and cacti toward survival itself. The pain in his chest disrupted normal breathing. Again he took up the sluggish and agonizing contest with death. By the time he managed to reach the Sigsby Ranch the next day, blow flies and maggots had already begun feeding on the rotting flesh of his wounds.[2]

That incident at the Wilson ranch on August 9, 1887, took place between two barricaded brothers, James and Ed

Tewksbury—sometime sheepmen—against the horsemen, loose associates of the Graham family, who were staunch cattlemen. For many in Arizona it was the spark that ignited the blaze that would forever be known as the Pleasant Valley War. The animosity between these two parties originated in a falling-out between factions of an outlaw gang rather than in a conflict between sheepmen and cattlemen as has been often assumed. While sheep did play a role in this bloodiest of all of Arizona's range wars—one that lasted for more than five years—the longstanding contempt between cattlemen and sheepmen started before embattled herdsmen of the bovine and bleater persuasions in Texas and New Mexico locked horns.

Since the Spanish introduced sheep to the vast territory under their control in North America in the late 1500s, sheep herders have had a tough time of it even though they managed the dominant livestock. The Spanish North American holdings included present-day Texas, New Mexico, and Arizona. Herds were under constant threat of attack and summary destruction by various factions. Indians, Mexican raiders, Anglo outlaws, and even the French took delight in conducting merciless raids on flocks. Many of those who perpetrated the raids apparently did so to prevent the defoliation of the grasslands by the large flocks. Sheep were known for their buzz-saw-like grazing which left in its wake a vast wasteland. That fact alone set many a horse and cattle operator's jaw angrily against the munching mutton. So it was no great surprise that by the mid- to late 1800s an accepted intolerance of the woolies was widespread throughout the Southwest.

The renowned Texas pioneer cattle impresario Charles Goodnight[3] was particularly intolerant toward the bleaters and their keepers. In 1876, Goodnight established a cattle operation in the Texas panhandle some distance west of present-day Amarillo. But Goodnight eyed more suitable lands for his ranching domain. He chose an area encompassing the Palo Duro Canyon to the southeast. Any warring Indians who had previously inhabited the canyon were gone, leaving just one obstacle in the way of Goodnight's empire building: the weapons of grass destruction—sheep.[4]

Goodnight brokered a deal with the flocks' owners that if they stayed out of the Palo Duro Canyon he would leave the Canadian River valley to them. The deal had legs, so to speak, and all appeared amicable between the cattleman and sheepmen. That is until a Mexican sheepherder apparently unaware of the cozy deal wandered into the Palo Duro Canyon with his flock. The herder was quickly educated on the finer points of the peace treaty while being worked over with the coiled lariat of Goodnight's brother-in-law, Leigh Dyer.

Goodnight's men had experienced similar defiance the year before, in 1875, while staking grazing land in New Mexico. When a large flock was discovered encroaching on the Goodnight range along the Canadian River, cowboy Dave McCormick and another hired hand were sent to instruct the intruders to leave. The sheepmen failed to heed the warning and instead were observed the next day building a winter settlement. This embarrassed and infuriated McCormick, who with another cowboy whooped, hollered, and generally worked the flock into frenzy. They then stampeded the confused and agitated animals into the Canadian River, drowning most of them.

However, sheepmen gave little ground; in fact they wound up with most of it. From the mid-1870s to the late 1880s, it was sheep, not cattle, that dominated the panhandle landscape along the Canadian River. Many new settlements consisting of sheepherders and their families dotted the terrain. Dry goods stores and the occasional saloon sprang up. Each was uniquely qualified to provide for the needs and wants of the Mexican sheepmen and visiting Anglo cowboys alike. And as long as both factions limited their endeavors to eating, drinking, and dancing together things went along just fine. But when some in the cattle business sought to expand their herds on land already occupied by sheep, things turned dangerous.

In central Texas, San Saba County night riders attacked the pens of the Ramsey brothers on January 12, 1880. The hired sheepherder, a man named Colvin who probably feared retribution if he dared interfere, remained out of sight. The cowboys entered the Ramsey pens and cut the throats of 240 sheep. Not satisfied with their night's work the marauders then scattered the remaining 1,100 sheep across the range.[5]

At the very center of Texas lay the most heated of the sheep-cattle conflicts. In just a few short years, from the mid-1870s into the 1890s, most of the hostilities between the two factions took place in the central counties of Hamilton, Nolan, Brown, Coleman, Tom Green, Schleicher, San Saba, and Llano. In the far northwest section of the panhandle, Potter, Oldham, and Hartley Counties saw related activity. One reason the conflicts festered in central Texas was the lush native grass growing there. Buffalo grass is considered the only truly native grass in Texas. It is a persistent, drought-resistant grass which grows from northern Mexico through central Texas and as far west as El Paso. It continues its swath through the panhandle and stretches north into lower Canada. Buffalo grass requires very little of nature. In fact it thrives when left to its own devices. It likes neither cultivation nor heavy irrigation. It grows best in hard, undisturbed clay-based soil and prefers no more than thirty inches of rain a year. A lot of central Texas provided these conditions and a lot of Buffalo grass claimed central Texas.

It was a herdsman's paradise. Many a cattle trail was established following Buffalo grass. The Goodnight-Loving Trail followed the grassy plain from south of San Antonio to just south of San Angelo, where Goodnight turned his herds due west into New Mexico. Buffalo grass stretched before his herds all the way to the eastern edge of New Mexico before the herds turned north toward Cheyenne, Wyoming.

Cattlemen and sheepmen alike found these grassy plains to be a lifeline for livestock and neither was willing to give up a single acre without complaint. These complaints often became physical and even fatal. Since the introduction of sheep into Nolan County in 1876, tensions between cattlemen and sheepmen had intensified in fervor and escalated in number. Incidentally, it was sheep, not cattle that first grazed that area of central Texas.

Texas luminaries readily accepted the wave of antipathy for sheep held by fellow cattlemen. The man who would found Sonora, Texas, Charles G. Adams, once recalled, "At that time no cattleman had any reputation who had not punctured one or two sheepmen."[6] Adams and a senior partner in a joint cattle operation were once jailed for shooting a sheepman. The victim was struck in the leg by the bullet, prompting other cattlemen in the area to grouse that the pair had poor marksmanship. Adams and his partner were later released.

Years later, once he discovered water and established a working well, Adams formally declared Sonora a viable town. The *San Angelo Standard Times* remarked that Adams' finding water at a depth of only 180 feet depth in the area was "worth thousands of dollars in this section."[7] In 1879, Adams christened the town Sonora, in honor of a servant whose family had its roots in Sonora, Mexico.[8]

To further complicate matters for flock owners, the Texas legislators bent a sympathetic ear to cattlemen by bringing to an end sheepmen's right to free-range grazing on March 9, 1881.[9] The new law mandated that sheep could no longer be grazed on property not belonging to that individual sheepman without consent from the property owner. This presented more than an inconvenience to the sheepherders as they were now forced to either purchase or lease grazing land, a near impossibility for herds on the move to market or railheads. It also meant that sheep farms would have to fence their pastures to prevent herds from wandering onto open lands, whether privately or state owned.

Two years later, during the April 1883 session, another law requiring all sheep to be inspected for disease before they could be moved from one county to another was passed.[10] All of these conditions came at great personal expense to sheep owners. Cattlemen, on the other hand, were not included in the new state laws and continued to enjoy the convenience and financial freedom of open-range grazing at the generosity of a seemingly biased legislature. Despite having the upper hand, by the grace of the 17th and 18th sessions of the Texas Legislature, cattlemen persisted in committing acts of intimidation against sheepmen.

When a drought struck the country in 1883, tempers rose with the heat. Attacks on sheepmen and their flocks were rampant. Cattlemen were determined to hold any land where their herds traditionally grazed, whether it belonged to them or not. The need for grass and water preempted any claims of land ownership in the eyes of the cattlemen. A spate of violence spread across the Texas plains with hundreds of sheep being clubbed to death by angry cowboys. Numerous sheep ranchers and their herders were beaten or shot. It seemed nothing short of abandoning property and leaving the country could stop the hostility.

But the sheepmen were not to be so easily cowed. Acting in concert with the laws of 1881 limiting flock mobility, the sheep rancher decided that if he could not move his flocks freely over open range as did the cattleman, he would prevent the cattleman from entering his property. Barbed wire was introduced all across Texas. Now the open-range cattle herds were barred by barbs from intruding on sheep pastures. Seeing the benefit of this, some cattle ranches copied the practice.

None of the open-range faction saw this as anything unusual. They reacted as they had against open-range sheep: with aggression. The open-range cowboys primarily burned fence posts or, if they were made of rock, knocked them over. In some cases the marauders painstakingly cut each strand of wire between each and every post. In one case, that of Tom Green County sheep rancher Charles B. Metcalfe, cowboys apparently with nothing better to do cut four miles of his fence.[11] With an almost Puritanical work ethic Metcalfe rebuilt the damaged fence. Once his work was completed he set out for San Angelo, where he knew he would find the man behind the crime. Metcalfe was able to secure a pact from the offending cattleman to leave his property unmolested in the future. The sheepman's power of détente was enhanced by the shotgun he carried to the conference.

In an unrelated incident, a Coleman County sheep rancher suffered regular attacks on his fences. He repaired them as they occurred. At one point during the run of intimidation the sheepman found a wooden coffin on his property with a penned threat reading: "This will be your end if you keep fencing." The sheepman, C. W. Mahoney, shrugged off the incident and used the pine box as a watering trough for his horses.

Less humorous was the financial burden the repeated depredations were having on the whole of Texas's economy. Because fence-cutting diverted ranchers of sheep and cattle alike from tending to the business of raising and selling livestock to being armed guards and fence repairmen, sales were down. With the reduction of sales came a reduction in tax valuations to the tune of nearly $30 million, a sum the state could ill afford to lose. The legislature convened a special session and in January 1884, the rampant fence cutting became a felony, and a punishment of one to five years' imprisonment would be imposed on any violator.[12] Parties on all sides could now be held responsible for their actions and in many cases snarled warnings replaced fence cutting.

As a result enmities abated as did incidents of fence cutting. Still, there were some cases where the new law failed to bulletproof the law-abiding. Believing the new fence-cutting law would protect them, one sheep rancher and his herdsmen approached an established and well-defended deadline of a cattle rancher in Tom Green County. Cowboys rode out to remind the sheepmen of the perimeter, which existed at the river's edge, but the flock's owner ignored the warnings. He brazenly continued to cross the river and the arbitrarily created boundary. The cowboys rode back to their camp, where they enlisted help, then returned with a vengeance. Over their heads they wore burlap sacks with eyeholes cut out. The raiders killed the owner of the flock and one of his herders although a second herder somehow escaped. They proceeded to callously slaughter two thousand of the rancher's nine thousand sheep. The rest were left wandering the plains.

In a few incidents no less dramatic, pointed rifle barrels were replaced with pointed conversations and tragedy was avoided. But the mayhem beatings and killings nevertheless continued and sheep herders suffered the worst of it. The killing of sheepmen became such regular work in Texas that cattlemen eventually ceded the job to a professional. They hired Jim Miller, a Texan known throughout much of the Southwest as Killin' Jim. Miller was a professional assassin who made good on his contract to kill sheepherders at a rate of $150 each. The call for Miller's talents was not limited to Texas; he also found employment in New Mexico and Oklahoma.[13]

Miller was a dapper assassin who was always dressed to kill, sporting a full-length black coat, wide-brimmed black hat, white shirt, and bow tie. He was so adorned when he was lynched at Ada, Oklahoma, in 1909 for the contracted killing of a locally prominent businessman. He and his three employers were hanged together in the same livery stable. The otherwise abandoned stable housed just one horse, whose bare back was used as a makeshift gallows platform from which the accused were launched into eternity.

In time, cattlemen accepted a new reality: sheep ranching was becoming an ensconced way of life in the Lone Star State. Tempers flared on occasion and sheepmen continued to meet with harassment and hazing but rarely did that result in any serious consequence. Once in 1893, a sheep rancher was even dropped into a dry well for "safekeeping" until his herd left the area and he paid a five-hundred-dollar bond. With the passage of time an uneasy truce emerged. Isolated sheep clubbing and like behavior was reported from time to time, but not to the degree of the decade past. The majority of cattlemen realized the woolies were here to stay. They reluctantly began to lift their once heavy-handed control from the Texas grasslands. The truce between cattlemen and sheepmen had been signed in blood. Nearly thirty-two hundred sheep were slain in raids and by some counts almost two dozen men, mostly sheepmen, lost their lives.[14]

Over in New Mexico Territory, one sheriff also served as vice president of the cattlemen's association.[15] The symbol of his allegiance to cattlemen's protected grazing rights was the badge on his chest even as the area where Lincoln County sits comprised the greatest concentration of sheep in the territory. The northern section of New Mexico was inhabited by more than four million woolies in 1884, but political might was with the cattlemen: they were large-landed outfits whereas the sheepmen tended to be more transient in nature. Because cattlemen owned land, homes, livestock, and equipment they likely paid a disproportionate share of territorial taxes than did the wandering sheepman whose holdings usually, but not always, consisted of his flock, sheepdogs, a couple of horses, and a wagon. The sheepmen therefore contributed less to the territory's coffers, making their political capital almost nil. And, as in Texas, the political might of the cattle interests was most effective at keeping sheepmen and their wandering flocks from grazing on public lands. In New Mexico laws were enacted which were meant to keep "homeless" flocks on the move by requiring them to travel a minimum of six miles each day. Crafty herdsmen obeyed the letter of the law by trailing their sheep three miles in one direction and then trailing them back the same three miles to the point of origin, fulfilling the six-mile requirement without having made any real forward progress.

In spite of the pro-cattle politicos, sheepmen had a staunch ally in the New Mexico territorial governor, Edmund Gibson Ross. A Republican until he changed parties in 1872, Ross believed the control of land by a contingent of large open-range cattle operators behaving like overlords discouraged the emigration of Easterners and thwarted economic growth. His stand favoring the small rancher (sheep or cattle) and the homesteader put him at odds with the powerful members of his own party on occasion, but he continued to support legislation aimed at leveling the "grazing" fields.[16]

Still, his efforts were not always sufficient to curb the violence suffered by sheepmen and their herders and flocks. In 1884, cowboys swarmed the Lincoln County camp of Arcadio Sais, killing his herd of seven hundred. One year later two sheepmen lost their lives to such raids. One of the victims, Ricardo Jacques, was shot and killed by cowboys who traveled from Durango, Colorado, for the purpose.[17]

Local authorities were less than diligent in investigating the complaints of sheepmen. The local courts behaved no better, allowing gun-toting sympathizers inside the courtroom. The armed cowboys openly intimidated testifying sheepmen and their witnesses, which resulted in acquittals of the accused in nearly all cases.

And still, New Mexico governor Ross continued his campaign for parity between cattlemen and sheepmen. Seeing a population trend of states such as Texas and California, whose exponential growth eclipsed that of New Mexico, he called for reconciliation among the hostile factions. In 1880, Texas registered a population of nearly 1.6 million while California's growth had spurted to more than 800,000. New Mexico trailed at number forty-four in population among states and territories in 1880, with 110,565 souls calling it home. Arizona, incidentally, experienced the best known range wars between sheep and cattle interests in the 1880s yet boasted a paltry population of only 40,440.[18]

Ross was a man of considerable influence long before his appointment as New Mexico's territorial governor by Pres. Grover Cleveland in 1885. His business acumen led to his preeminent standing throughout communities across the nation and lent his words an air of authority. When he spoke his intended audience paid attention. The Ohio-born activist moved to Topeka, Kansas, in 1856, where the former Republican spearheaded the Free State initiative. Apparently finding time on his hands, Ross published two newspapers and became a member of the Kansas state constitutional convention from 1859-1861. He was also instrumental in the commercial success of a railroad company during that time. He enlisted in the Union army in 1862 as a private and left the service with the rank of major just three years later. He served in the United States Senate until 1871. His most noteworthy contribution may have been casting the decisive vote to prevent the impeachment of Pres. Andrew Johnson in 1868.[19]

Ross moved to Albuquerque, New Mexico, in 1882 and in 1885 became its territorial governor. This was the man few dared to openly challenge when he called for the two obstinate factions to cease their atrocities. Admonishing cattlemen specifically in a speech, Ross said, "People are worth more to a state than steers . . . for with people comes capital and the spirit of commercial adventure, development, prosperity, and greatness."[20] Under his leadership tensions between the cowboys and the mutton-men cooled to an edgy peace. Edmund Ross retired from politics after his term as governor of New Mexico. He died in Albuquerque on May 8, 1907.[21]

From Texas to New Mexico, Arizona to Idaho, and all the way to the Pacific Northwest, conflicts among cattlemen and sheepmen were a constant part of pioneering life. Coalitions were formed on both sides with the seemingly impossible goal of lessening hostilities. These efforts rendered minimal success. In time those same coalitions were transformed into bodies of armed men whose purpose was to provide protection or retribution, whichever seemed to fit a given situation. And so it was back in the summer of 1887, in the then lush, green, and grassy valley of the Tonto Basin in eastern Arizona when a bullet slammed into Tom Tucker's chest, providing the spark that became the blaze known as the Pleasant Valley War.

## CHAPTER SEVEN

# Goats and Gun Smoke

"I thought that Pleasant Valley was probably a peaceable Mormon settlement, and if necessary I might be able to get all the help and accommodations that I might need," Winslow, Arizona constable Joe T. McKinney recalled of seeing a sign board proclaiming, "Pleasant Valley 25 miles" on August 7 or 8, 1887, just one or two nights before the first shots of the Pleasant Valley War were fired.

When John D. Tewksbury moved into the Tonto Basin in the Pleasant Valley area of eastern Arizona in about 1879, he brought a second wife, a toddler named Walter, and three grown sons from his first marriage. He settled the brood on a farm on Cherry Creek and began with a few head of cattle and feral hogs which rooted the area. John's three older sons, John, Edwin, and James, were conceived somewhere in California with John's first wife. She was a Native American of the Pitt or Digger tribe of the Eel River, where John spent time panning for gold. When she died John brought his sons to Globe, Arizona, where he met and married a widow named Lydia Crigler Shutes. Her name has variously been listed as Shoulter or Shultze. Together the couple bore three more offspring: Walter, Parker, and an unidentified daughter.[1]

Since no actual family history for the early Tewksburys exists, John's claims at the time of his arrival in Arizona are almost impossible to substantiate. He purportedly told any who asked that he came to California via a tall-sail ship which rounded Cape Horn from his native Massachusetts.

What is known for certain of John Tewksbury and his clan is chronicled after his move to Arizona and is linked with the Graham brothers, and one James Stinson, who employed members of both families.

Stinson was a visionary of moderate talent who owned quite a bit of land on which he ran his cattle operation. A large portion of the Stinson Ranch nestled in east-central Arizona, on the Mogollon Rim and in the White Mountains. Those ridges formed an almost endless barrier against the elements, creating a semiarid climate for much of the year. Cottonwood and Silver Creeks drained the area, providing a plentiful supply of fresh water year-round. So attractive was this particular section of Pleasant Valley that in 1878, Mormon apostle Erastus Snow and real estate magnate and Mormon land scout William Flake purchased the town site for the original Mormon colony named for them for $11,000.[2] In lieu of the $11,000 asking price, Stinson accepted an equivalent dollar amount in Mormon cattle. He then moved his cattle operation into the Tonto Basin (Pleasant Valley). He was in the cattle business in a very large way by then and needed some cowboys to help run the outfit. He hired the three eldest Tewksbury boys.

Back in Boone, Iowa, father and farmer Sam Graham was quite probably not too enthusiastic at losing three of his best hands, his sons Tom, John, and William, often called Billy. They all chose to leave Iowa in about 1885 and eventually found themselves in Globe as had the Tewksbury family just a few years before. The Tewksbury brothers and the Graham boys, along with the Grahams' cousin-in-tow, Louis Parker, became fast friends. The Tewksburys likely encouraged the Graham brothers to establish a ranch about ten miles upstream of the their own Cherry Creek operation. Soon the Grahams were working alongside their friends corralling, branding, and pushing Stinson cattle to market for him. However, there were also accusations that the team of Tewksbury and Graham were increasing their respective herds by a number of cattle curiously equal to those that went missing from Stinson's outfit, a coincidence not lost on ranch foreman John Gilliland.[3]

Soon, the parasitic partnership of the Graham-Tewksbury cattle-rustling empire began to come unhinged. John Graham rode to Prescott and registered the partnership's TE brand as his own. The TE had all along stood for the brand of Tom (Graham) and Edwin (Tewksbury). This undoubtedly infuriated the Tewksburys who, with a stroke of a pen, were summarily cut out of the very rustling operation they started with Stinson's stock and invited the Grahams to join. Worse yet for the Tewksbury clan, the Grahams had entered into a contract with Stinson whereby Stinson would pay the sum of one cow and a calf for providing information that would convict rustlers of his brand. Of course the Grahams did not have to look too far for the offenders. They pointed south about ten miles to the modest home and spread of John D. Tewksbury and sons.

Suddenly the Tewksburys found themselves in territorial court at Prescott answering to cattle-rustling charges. Along with brothers Edwin, James, and John Tewksbury, the indictment included George Blaine, William Richards, and W. H. Bishop.[4] Evidence was weak against the sextet and although all charges were soon dropped, the damage to the Tewksburys was done and any sense of honor among the thieves formerly employed by the Stinson Ranch was gone. The Tewksburys cried foul of course but were ignored and the stolen Stinson cattle became the sole property of the Grahams. The Grahams had managed to successfully take control of Tonto Basin's most profitable venture and with it control of much of the basin itself.

John Gilliland, the Stinson foreman, poured vinegar on the Tewksburys' wounded pride. Having summed up his boss's losses sometime in early 1884, he and ranch hand

Thomas H. Graham, May 1882, leader of the Graham faction in the Pleasant Valley War. *(Courtesy Arizona Historical Society, Tucson)*

Epitasio "Potash" Ruiz and others rode to the Tewksbury cabin to inquire about those losses and the probable Tewksbury involvement. Gilliland was met by Edwin Tewksbury. Tewksbury many years later recounted the incident:

> We was both a foot. Old John got sort of wringy an' was talking pretty strong about some folks stealin' some of Jim Stinson's cows. Nachelly I denied it. John he gits madder an' madder an' starts to draw his pistol. We both fired together. He missed me clean. I gits him through the leg. John he broke an' ran one way an' I sure hit the grit the other. Didn't want to hurt John nohow.[5]

Down but not out, the Tewksburys showed remarkable resilience. They concocted a scheme which they hoped would not only increase the family's coffers but quite possibly rid the country of the Grahams. Stinson had sold out any interest in his once vast cattle empire to a New York-based livestock conglomerate in 1885. The Aztec Land and Cattle Company set up a satellite office in Holbrook, from which it controlled more than 500,000 acres of grazing land on which ran incalculable herds. The Aztec named its local operation the Hash Knife and undertook an especially aggressive means of keeping sheep out of the area. Meanwhile, P. P. Daggs[6] and his brothers operated one of the largest sheep empires in all of the Southwest, which was headquartered at Flagstaff. The Daggs had been considering trailing a large herd of sheep to Pleasant Valley in the verdant Tonto Basin for some time. Still, they were not unfamiliar with the resentment such an undertaking would cause in the hearts and minds of the established cattlemen of the valley. The Tewksburys offered to trail the Daggs brothers' sheep right under the noses of the cattlemen. The Daggs men considered the Tewksbury offer a good option. They believed (correctly or otherwise) that few others would know how to deal with the perils of such an operation and that they would be prepared for any consequences.

The Tewksburys must have considered this opportunity to be a godsend and just the tool they needed to force cattle from the area with the overgrazing sheep operations usually entailed. The cattle would wander to greener pastures, none of which would be in Pleasant Valley. In addition to the "gotcha" quality of such an undertaking, the Tewksburys stood a better than average chance of making some real money without having to invest one single dollar by enlisting with the Daggs, who would let the brothers trail the sheep on consignment. That is, for every sheep they managed to keep alive and bring to market or whose wool they could sheer and sell, each brother would receive a share of the profits. These cowboys-turned-rustlers, derided and deprived by friend and foe alike, now relied on the much-maligned woolies to turn their luck and their fortunes around. The Tewksburys began sporting all manner of new weaponry, saddle horses, and tack, much more than might be expected from a failed gang of cattle rustlers. Daggs, it was rumored, was sponsoring the boys for their collective watchful eye over the company's sheep herds.

The Daggs brothers stood to gain quite a bit as well. They had been kept out of the Tonto Basin under implied or actual threats from the New York-based Aztec outfit. If the Tewksburys wanted in, then the Daggs Brothers Sheep Company would stake that game.

The Tewksburys, for whatever reason, early on chose not to take on the role of mountain shepherd themselves but instead hired a local man. That poor soul was either of Mexican, Basque, or Navajo descent.[7] The hired man likely had experience at sheep herding since the Mexicans had been running sheep in the territory for decades before the Anglos appeared in Arizona. Working for the Tewksburys in the capacity of a lone shepherd in Hash Knife cattle country would prove to be a really bad idea. No precise date can be given as to when the incident actually occurred, but the body of the Tewksbury sheepman was discovered sometime in February 1887 riddled by gunfire.[8] The sheep were scattered to the four winds. Any hope of a windfall for the Tewksbury family was shot to pieces somewhere along the Mogollon Rim or left to wander the mountain range unprotected and vulnerable to starvation, bludgeoning, stampeding, or wolf attack.

The tables had been turned on the scheming Tewksburys. Their plot to rid the country of cattle backfired with the death of the hired hand and the loss of most of the sheep. Seeing the likelihood of their own eventual ruin, John, James, and Edwin evidently decided to make a fight of it. John, Sr., along with his wife, Lydia, and the youngest children, Walter, Parker, and the daughter, were probably instructed to hunker down and wait things out.

Meanwhile a seldom-heard-of family entered the fray. Mart Blevins, usually referred to as Old Man Blevins, was not much older than fifty when his sons inserted themselves into the Graham-Tewksbury feud. Mart maintained a house in Holbrook but he and his older boys apparently hired on with the Hash Knife as enforcers of the outfit's deadline when they were not involved in stealing horses for their own take. The sons—John, Sam Houston, Charles, Hamp, and Andy Cooper Blevins—regularly aggravated the Tewksburys with repeated nighttime raids in which they routinely separated the Tewksburys from their livestock, especially their horses. The Old Man was said not only to know of his boys' depredations but to be the ramrod of their activities. The Blevins family came to Arizona through

Texas. And for reasons only guessed at, the Blevins clan had removed themselves from Texas rather hastily.

Once in Arizona, Andy Cooper Blevins denied his Blevins breeding, such as it was, and maintained that his true identity was simply Andy Cooper. This may have been an attempt at disguising his true identity for he was the same Andy Blevins who was wanted in Texas on a murder charge.[9] This family of thieves and murderers was just what the Hash Knife was looking for.

The Tewksbury bunch had had their fill of these men and their horse-stealing raids. It seemed like everyone in the Arizona Territory thought of the Tewksburys when they thought about who would be an easy mark. The trouble just kept coming and it had to stop or they would be the ones forced to leave Pleasant Valley. A new plan had to be concocted.

Joe T. McKinney was so thankful to get the job as under sheriff to the renowned Commodore Perry Owens, himself newly elected as Apache County sheriff, that at the inaugural dance in St. Johns in late 1886, McKinney accepted as his first order of business representing the sheriff's office. "I did the dancing for the sheriff's office," he said by way of explanation. "Commodore did not dance."[10]

A little later the next year, when both men officially took office, McKinney was out on the trail of two prisoners who had escaped from the jail at St. Johns under Owens' watch, according to McKinney. McKinney had been fast asleep in his hotel room at Sol Barth's when an excited Owens awakened him with shouts that the prisoners had escaped. Prisoners Bill and John Brown, McKinney reckoned, would head straight to their homes in Socorro, New Mexico.

After about a day's ride after the pair, McKinney learned that a bunch of cowboys shot and killed Bill after the brothers stole horses from a ranch near Datile, New Mexico. Joe knew he was on the right track. He continued his pursuit until he was intercepted by a New Mexico deputy who informed McKinney that John Brown had been captured. On his return trip to St. Johns, McKinney was again intercepted by a messenger. This one did not have very good news for the deputy: "Within about forty miles of St. Johns I met a Mexican who told me that I was no longer Under Sheriff, I had been fired."[11]

According to McKinney, Owens did not want to have his reputation as a hard man sullied with the knowledge that it was he who had allowed the prisoners to escape despite the warnings of his deputy. McKinney said the ride back to St. Johns was the longest two-day trip he ever made, attempting to reconcile in his own mind why he had lost his job. When he reached town a friend reported that Commodore was accusing him of allowing the prisoners to escape. McKinney went to his room, where he retrieved his .45 revolver. "I knew that I had done my duty," explained McKinney. "I had turned the keys over to him, and had given him every warning to be careful, that he had gone off to visit his lady-love and neglected his duty."[12] After McKinney confronted Owens in his office, the sheriff backed off his accusations and even apologized to the affronted but still former deputy, according to McKinney's side of the story. "We had an understanding . . . I walked out."

Today if a traveler intends to go from St. Johns to Winslow he or she would drive State Highway 180 out of St. Johns to Holbrook to the Interstate 40 junction. From there the traveler need just set the cruise control and enjoy the scenery for the next thirty-five miles until such time as Winslow comes into view. The whole trip is about a ninety-three-mile journey. When Joe McKinney lost his job working for Sheriff Owens and then accepted a position as constable at Winslow, the trip was a bit more demanding. He probably followed the Little Colorado River once leaving St. Johns. His first stop, a good day's ride later, may have been Woodruff, about seventeen miles south and east of Holbrook. The following day he likely sauntered into Holbrook, where he could have washed the dust off at a hotel while washing it down at a saloon. Then he would have pushed on for the next thirty-five miles or so, always riding at a comfortable pace along the banks of the Little Colorado, which, when trailing it north by northwest, would take him smack-dab into Winslow, his new home.

Winslow seemed a long way from the festering troubles back in Pleasant Valley, but for Constable McKinney it was his duties there which would place him in the middle of the Graham-Tewksbury feud. McKinney had not been on the job long when he was issued an arrest warrant for a horse thief. He and the suspect's employer, a man named Gorton, trailed the man for a day or so before learning the thief was camped at one of Gorton's cow camps. When Gorton gave up the chase McKinney pressed on alone. He was reassured of his progress by the fresh horse tracks he knew to be left by the suspect's mount. He was getting closer by the mile but still was not in sight of him. The constable forged ahead until, "I finally came to a sign board which had on it, 'Pleasant Valley 25 miles.'"[13] He was completely unaware of the torrid feelings festering there.

A few days ahead of McKinney's arrival in the valley in early August 1887, hard feelings between the Graham faction and the Tewksburys had exploded. Men from the Hash Knife had been riding the countryside to "encourage" nesters and others to leave the basin, and accounts that Andy Cooper had for some time been collecting signatures on an anti-Tewksbury petition did not go unnoticed. Meanwhile, Mart "Old Man" Blevins set out on a day in late July 1887 in search of some missing horses, most likely the result of an unauthorized Tewksbury visit. Within days the Blevins' patriarch was declared missing and presumed dead. Hamp Blevins, determined to find his father or his father's body, formed a scouting party—really a very well-armed posse—and started out for the all-too-familiar territory of the Tewksburys. As a kind of recruiting slogan, Blevins said that the purpose of the search was to take the Tewksburys "dead or alive."[14]

Blevins had enlisted an eager former Texan named John Paine, a cowboy working for the Aztec Land and Cattle Company's Hash Knife brand. Although his title was foreman, his real job was to "see that no sheep herds watered at the springs or grazed on the adjacent range [of the Hash Knife]." Paine kept a little place just southwest of Taylor in Navajo County called Four Mile Spring. Cattle rancher Will Barnes knew him and recalled that Paine "was pretty bad, drank excessively and was always ready to make 'six-shooter play.'"[15] The "scouting party" also included Bob Gillespie (often referred to as Glaspie in old-time memoirs), Tom Tucker, and one man with several identities, variously known as Thomas Covington, Carrington, or Edward Clark. However, Barnes, who was at the Hash Knife camp when the party started for the basin and wrote of the Pleasant Valley War in *The Arizona Historical Review*, denied that the multiple-christened man ever existed. "I certainly never saw him and I saw the party start off for the valley."[16]

Barnes stayed for a time at the camp visiting the camp's foreman, Ed Rogers. These two were unnerved by what they soon realized was not a search-and-rescue party but a witch hunt set on revenge. Rogers had just approached Barnes and told him that one of the party boasted they were going to Pleasant Valley to "start a little war of our own." On August 3, 1887, the Paine party left camp despite Rogers' and Barnes' best efforts to talk them out of going.

On the rain-chilled evening of August 9, Constable McKinney was no doubt gladdened by the amber glow of a cabin's window lamp as he neared Pleasant Valley. McKinney had ridden as far as the base of the Mogollon Rim. It was late, and he and his horse were fairly well spent. Rather than disturb anyone, he prepared to camp under a tree for the night. Unbeknownst to him he had ridden to within fifty yards of John Tewksbury's cabin. Two men were buried not too far from there at the place of Tewksbury friend George Newton. The dead men were members of a party who had ridden up to Newton's house just hours before.

Earlier that day Hamp Blevins, John Paine, and the other cowboys had reached the Newton place on Middleton Creek. George Newton, the owner of the ranch, was away conducting business for the Flying V outfit, a cattle enterprise he co-owned with J. J. Vosburg. J. F. Ketcherside, the operation's manager who made regular visits to Newton's ranch, was likewise away. The incoming riders announced that they were looking for Old Man Blevins. When the occupants said he was not there, the riders then asked for something to eat. Sensing the men were game for a fight, the occupants refused them food. As their request was denied, the horsemen turned their mounts to ride away, but much to the surprise of Paine and company, the people inside the Newton house were none other than the very men they were seeking. Bob Gillespie recounted the awful seconds that happened next: "When we turned to ride away the guns began firing and a general commotion ensued. John [Paine] and Hamp fell from their horses, Tom Tucker's horse fell, I got a bullet through my leg above the knee, the bullet went into my horse. I managed to get away on him but he quit on me and I had a time getting in with my wounded leg afoot."[17]

Constable Joe McKinney interviewed Ed Tewksbury sometime after that incident. Tewksbury, McKinney said, told a story identical to that of Gillespie's but added a bit of color to the tale. Ed Tewksbury expressed his amazement at the luck of Tom Tucker that day. "There never was as much lead missed one as missed Tom Tucker," he marveled.

Tewksbury said he and the six other men inside the cabin had been firing on the retreating Tucker when his horse was hit. The animal fell so as to land on Tucker's scabbard and trap its rifle beneath the horse, but Tucker managed to pull his rifle free and scamper into the bushes "while the seven of us were shooting at him with Winchesters."[18] With that the Pleasant Valley War was on. Tucker's wounds were serious and it took him days to crawl back to the Sigsby ranch and the chance to recuperate.

Sheriff William Mulvenon left Prescott with a small band of deputies to investigate the shootings at the Newton place. Along the way he recruited one Jim Roberts into his posse. Roberts had been with the Tewksburys on the day of the shooting. When the sheriff arrived at the scene in late August or early September there was not much left to provide any clues. The house and barn had been burned to the ground and a few days after the shootout the bodies had been buried. The man who took charge of interment was Charles E. Perkins, who owned a store in the valley and maintained as much neutrality in the festering Graham-Tewksbury feud as possible. So did the much-respected John Meadows, justice of the peace based at Payson.[19] Sheriff Mulvenon sensed he had just ridden into a very hostile situation with too few men, turned, and headed back to Prescott.

As Mulvenon and his party were leaving the valley, John and Ed Tewksbury and a third man busied themselves by shooting up two more interlopers who dared ride the trail near the Tewksbury ranch in broad daylight. Henry Middleton and Joseph Underwood were ambushed by the three men. Middleton has been identified as a Hash Knife cowboy who was continuously looking for trouble in the valley. He found it: Middleton was shot off his horse and killed.[20] Joe Underwood just had the bad luck to be a roaming cowboy who found himself in the middle of Arizona's

Pleasant Valley War. He first came to the attention of the Tewksburys, according to one source, when he offered aid to the mortally wounded William Graham after he was shot and killed on August 17, 1887, by Sheriff John Houck. Houck was actually laying in wait for Graham's brother, John, whom the sheriff was to serve a warrant. Billy panicked and drew a pistol when the sheriff stepped out from hiding, resulting in the sheriff shooting first in self-defense. Within earshot of another ambush, this time Underwood was one of its intended targets, next to Middleton when rifle fire brought him down. Underwood dismounted and sought the protection of a rather slim tree, leaving a leg exposed. A .45-caliber rifle slug promptly tore through that leg just below the knee. He later recuperated at the San Carlos Indian Agency under the care of one Dr. Davis.[21]

In an apparent act of retribution, the Grahams purportedly shot John Tewksbury and William Jacobs from their horses while they were returning from a hideout following the shooting at the Newton ranch. The *Flagstaff Champion* confirmed the incident and said that Sheriff Mulvenon was headed back into the valley in another attempt to quell the violence.[22] This time the sheriff had deputies George Bristow, E. M. Tackett, and S. J. Sullivan with him. This posse would later meet up with a Deputy Dan Francis and another named Odell. All of these men joined Sheriff Jim Houck and "a party from Apache [sic] county at Payson."[23] The Apache County party mentioned in the article was Joe T. McKinney.

The war was white-hot, as were the accounts, stories, and rumors stoking it. One in particular was especially horrendous. As stories go, the one relating the details of the John Tewksbury and William Jacobs murders and the undaunted courage of Tewksbury's wife, Mary Ann, is a white-knuckler. In this much romanticized treatise, once John and William are shot dead, the Grahams held off Mary

Anne (Marianne) and her father-in-law for up to four days
with hilltop sniping. The stories have it that feral hogs in
the area were allowed to root the corpses to entertain the
Grahams while intimidating those inside the cabin. So, too,
it is said that Mrs. Tewksbury finally reached her boiling
point, whereupon she marched from the cabin and strode
boldly to the two dead men. Once reaching the corpses, torn
asunder as they were by the rooting hogs, she went to work.
According to this tale, she knelt at her husband's mostly
consumed body and with nothing but bare hands dug John
a shallow grave. Once finished, she rolled the mangled body
into it and began to do the same for William Jacobs. Not a
sound broke as she braved the threat of gunfire to tend to
her downed men.[24] A very romantic story indeed, but not
altogether true.

The chronicler, Will C. Barnes, agreed this was quite a
compelling story but reported that it was hardly accurate.
Barnes said it was true that the Grahams did keep watch
over the cabin for several days after killing John and
William. He wrote that their motivation was a desire to
pick off additional Tewksburys who might happen along on
a trip home. He did not believe the act was engineered for
Graham pleasure or, for that matter, simply to torment Mrs.
Tewksbury and her father-in-law. Barnes also theorized
that the Grahams had suffered mightily at this point and
may have seen this as an opportunity to even the score. It
is understandable that they were probably still fighting mad
over the August 17 shooting death of young William "Billy"
Graham.

For as many as four days after that fatal September 3,
1887, ambush of Tewksbury and Jacobs the Grahams kept
watch from their hillside perch. When they received word
that Charlie Perkins and Justice of the Peace John Meadows
were coming, they folded up camp and left. Perkins and
Meadows, rather than Mrs. Tewksbury, finally buried the

John Tewksbury, killed with William Jacobs. Both bodies were left to the hogs before lawmen intervened. *(Courtesy Arizona Historical Society, Tucson)*

two dead men and told of the work the wild hogs had done on the corpses, according to Barnes.[25]

No matter who actually buried John Tewksbury and William Jacobs, the tale about the feral hogs feasting on the corpses is also open to question. Most notably, Joe McKinney claimed firsthand knowledge of the affair. He adamantly denied that the corpses were molested by wild hogs. There is the possibility, however, that McKinney may have simply been exercising gentility, for he was corresponding with a female acquaintance many years later about the incident.[26]

The very next day, Sunday, September 4, 1887, in the town of Holbrook, some ninety-plus miles northeast of Cherry Creek and the Tewksbury place, three men died and one man was seriously wounded when Yavapai County sheriff Commodore Perry Owens sought to serve a warrant on Andy Cooper Blevins for horse theft and other felonies. Sheriff Owens was convinced that Andy was inside the family cottage in the middle of town. John Blevins warned his brother that Owens was inside the Brown and Kinder livery stable talking with one of the owners. Andy did not want to face Owens so he instructed his brother to retrieve his horse and meet him at the house. John was successful at slipping out of the stable undetected with the horse. When one of Brown's hired men came into the office and handed his boss the money Andy owed for the animal's boarding, that meant one thing to Brown: Andy was preparing to hightail it back to the basin. Owens seemed rather casual and had even taken the time to dismantle his .45 revolver while in Brown's office, but when Brown told him of Andy's intent, "He put his pistol together, grabbed his rifle and stepped out into the street."[27]

The Blevins house had two front doors that were set back beneath a shaded porch. Owens saw Andy as he took quick refuge behind one of those doors—the one on the right side. The sheriff boldly stepped up onto the porch and announced that he had a warrant for Andy and was there to arrest him. There is little argument as to what happened next. Andy stalled the sheriff and went to slam the door but found it was blocked by the sheriff's boot. Owens threw up his rifle barrel and fired, with Blevins firing simultaneously. Owens' round splintered the door, slamming into the other's gut. He fell backward into the main room and into the arms of his mother, Mary Blevins. He would die the next day.[28]

Owens leaped from the front porch. Suddenly, Andy's brother John opened the door on the left and fired a pistol at the sheriff. Owens, still shooting from the hip, fired in John's direction, hitting him in the shoulder. The fight was not over yet. Owens heard a commotion to his right and observed the Blevins' brother-in-law, Mose Roberts, hurriedly clambering out a window. To Owens it must have had all the appearances of a sneak attack so he shot Roberts in the chest, killing him on the spot. The youngest Blevins brother, between the ages of fourteen and sixteen, grabbed Andy's pistol and ran onto the front porch screaming at the sheriff, cursing him wildly. As young Sam Houston Blevins cocked his dying brother's revolver, Sheriff Owens took aim from behind a wagon in the family's yard. The youngest of the Blevins boys hit the ground dead.[29]

At the time Owens' actions were considered those of a fearless hero, a man who, although outnumbered by a barricaded, armed foe, showed remarkable calm and courage while dispensing justice on the American frontier. His actions were seen as righteous retribution for what many read with horrified interest in headlines across the nation. "Sheriff Mulvenon was shot," screamed a headline in the *New York Times* dated September 3, 1887. The *Times* was repeating the story first published in the *Prescott Journal Miner* the day before. In that article it was reported that Mulvenon was killed and five of his deputies were wounded while as many as "eleven of the outlaws were killed."[30]

William J. "Bill" Mulvenon, 1887, sheriff of Yavapai County.
*(Courtesy Arizona Historical Society, Tucson)*

Later on the day of the Blevins gunfight, September 4, Sheriff Mulvenon and his entire posse rode nonchalantly into Prescott without a wound among them. The entire populace of the town was surprised; some were more than a little embarrassed.

But at the time Sheriff Owens was emptying his Winchester in the direction of any movement outside or inside the Blevins' home, neither he nor probably anyone else believed Mulvenon to be alive. It was quite likely that a majority of the citizenry blamed the Graham family and their adherents, which included most of the Blevins clan. So when Owens single-handedly exterminated most of the Grahams, the townsfolk were quite generous with praise. Practically before the smoke cleared, newspapers were lauding Owens' actions. With five shots Owens had secured his place with many aficionados of the legendary shootists of the Old West.

Yet not all agree that everything Owens did that day should be counted as heroic. Owens knew that there was at least one woman inside. He had seen Mary Blevins as she attempted to grapple with her son, Sam Houston, trying to thwart the boy's hysterical charge. One writer, Harry Sinclair Drago, said that after Owens killed his last victim, "Suddenly it was quiet." Then, inexplicably, the sheriff began pumping rounds from his Winchester blindly "through the thin walls of the cottage." The knowledge that Mary Blevins was still inside the house did not dissuade him from pumping lead through it. What he did not know was that there was a total of four females inside. Also cowering from incoming lead were Amanda Gladden and her nine-year-old daughter, Beatrice, and Mary's daughter-in-law, Eva Blevins.[31] Any one of them could have been riddled by his unexplained gunfire even though battle was ended. Drago wrote, "Afterwards, he [Owens] was vague about the purpose of that last fusillade."[32]

Although all the victims of the Holbrook shootout, save

young Sam Houston Blevins, had been active in the Graham-Tewksbury feud, Will C. Barnes argued that the event had nothing at all to do with the feuding going on at the time. Since he was present during much of the hostilities, he writes with some authority. In his memoirs published in 1932, Barnes wrote that he deliberately left out the Blevins fight and the triple lynching of August 12, 1888, of James Stott, Billy Wilson, and James Scott as merely coincidental occurrences that took place "while the valley troubles were at white heat. The hanging occurred almost a year after the last killing in Pleasant Valley, and like the Holbrook affair bore no earthly relation to it."[33] Barnes seems to stand alone in this position.

One compelling argument against Barnes' stance is that most of the lawmen of the region seemed to target the Grahams for arrest, even if their warrants were for offenses unrelated to the Tewksbury feud. Some might say that knowingly or unwittingly law enforcement of the times aided and abetted the Tewksburys in their fight against the Grahams since none of the Tewksburys were hunted with the same dogged determination as were their enemies in the feud. Graham partisan Al Rose admonished Winslow constable Joe McKinney that if McKinney was an officer, "you had better come and do something with the damn Tewksburys; if you don't then we are going to kill every damn one of them." McKinney, who until a few days before this encounter had worked as Owens' under sheriff and likely had good knowledge of the Tewksbury-Graham troubles, replied that he "could not take stock in any private scrap."[34] Likewise, Barnes considered the Holbrook shootout to have been nothing more than a lawman's attempting to exercise his duties, serving an arrest warrant. Of course Mart "Old Man" Blevins and his sons were no ordinary suspects.

Insults and injuries were the order of the day as skirmishes continued between the warring factions. Even after the events at Holbrook claimed the lives of a good number of the Graham adherents, each side took turns raiding or ambushing the other. Sheriff Mulvenon hit the trail a second time to bring in what was left of the Graham partisans. On September 9, 1887, the *Prescott Journal Miner* announced Mulvenon's intentions and intended tactics. The newspaper told its readers that the sheriff and three deputies, George Bristow, E. M. Tackett, and S. J. Sullivan, were planning to leave Prescott and ride to Payson, where they would be joined by Deputy Dan Francis and a posse he put together.[35] And of course Joe T. McKinney of Winslow joined a posse in search of Graham men. Altogether, Sheriff Mulvenon had gathered nearly three dozen men to ride with him into Pleasant Valley.

Several miles from the upstart town of Young, Arizona, Charles "Charlie" Perkins had built an adobe-walled general store seemingly in the middle of nowhere. Yet his location proved his business savvy, as the store provisioned cowboys and travelers, hunters and the hunted alike far away from the comforts and conveniences of any town. Charlie was prospering so well that near the end of September 1887, when Sheriff Mulvenon and his thirty-plus men rode up, he was in the process of adding a permanent residence to the existing building. The walls of the future home were then only about five or six feet in height.

Mulvenon commandeered Perkins' Store, as it came to be known, sending its proprietor and anyone else not connected to the work at hand out of the area. Mulvenon knew that his entrance into the valley was not hidden from those he hunted so he devised a plan to confuse the Graham contingent. Once he and his men gathered at the store, Mulvenon instructed at least half of them to ride on and to take all the horses with them. The men did as they were told and within one or two days a pair of riders could be seen in the distance. The riders would later be identified as John

Graham and Charles Blevins.[36] Mulvenon apparently fooled the duo into believing that the entire posse had left. After all, neither the posse nor their horses were in sight. Still, Graham and Blevins were cautious men so their approach was rather wary.

At the moment the two riders finally closed in on Perkins' Store and simultaneously leaned forward in their saddles to peer over the half-constructed walls, Mulvenon stepped out from behind them. With shotgun pointing from his hip Mulvenon calmly told both men to surrender. Both riders whirled their mounts on their hind legs while drawing their six-shooters. Mulvenon fired. The posse sprang from hiding and filled the valley with the echoes of a fatal fusillade. John Graham and Charles Blevins never got off a shot as lead ripped through their bodies. In the waning days of September the Graham and Blevins families lost two more fighters in the war against the Tewksburys. Later Mulvenon said he had not the heart to shoot "Johnny" but aimed at his horse instead, hoping to entice Graham to surrender.[37] It had not and John Graham became the second of his family to die in the feud.

By many contemporaries the shootout at Perkins' Store was considered the last major conflict in the Pleasant Valley War. As things stood following the killing of John Graham and Charles Blevins, Ed and James Tewksbury were all that remained of that family and only Tom Graham survived his brothers. In late 1888, James Tewksbury, already weakened by a long battle with consumption, contracted measles and died at his sister's home in Globe.[38] Ed Tewksbury and Tom Graham were all that were left. Pride stood in place of each family's fallen sons. The only two living combatants were unwilling to simply walk away from that which had cost them so dearly.

Tom nonetheless did move from the valley in 1889, perhaps after his wife became pregnant and he wanted the quieter, more sophisticated environment of city life. He moved to Tempe, leaving a man named S. W. Young in charge of his holdings. Young agreed to manage Tom's operation for a share of the take. Graham probably believed that time and now distance had quelled the fervor that once fueled the embers of the Pleasant Valley War. He would be proven wrong.

After his last arrest in 1888, Tom Graham stayed out of the limelight and jail. He spent his time running his cattle and buying and selling livestock while alternately farming on his new place at Tempe. Tom made the occasional trip back into Pleasant Valley to check on his holdings, but Graham was rarely alone on such trips and nearly always in the company of one Charles "Charlie" Douchet. During one trip Graham and Douchet encountered a few Tewksbury allies on the trail. John Rhodes was reportedly among them, as was one William Colcord. All riders reined their horses to a stop upon eyeing each other. Colcord broke from the Tewksbury bunch and rode up to Graham and Douchet with a plain question. "Well boy," Colcord began, "which is it, peace or war?" Graham is said to have preferred peace. Colcord took them off guard when he then shook Tom Graham's hand, nodded, and said, "Good morning," and then rode off.[39]

Three years after he moved with his family to the city, on August 2, 1892, Tom Graham was gunned down while driving a load of grain from his farm to market in Tempe. He lived long enough to tell those in attendance, including his horrified wife, Anne, that the shooters were two men: John Rhodes and Ed Tewksbury. Justice of the Peace W. O. Huson listened to eyewitness accounts and other evidence for three days before declaring, "I have listened carefully to all the testimony in this case and, although I was at first inclined to believe the defendant guilty of the murder, the defense has so conclusively proved their alibi that I must release the prisoner." That apparently was not what Anne Graham considered a fair and just ending. Having brought a .44-caliber pistol to the proceedings, Anne was ready to dispense a little justice of her own. As Huson finished his statement Anne ran up behind Rhodes, seated at the defense table, brought up the big, blue-steel revolver, and put it to the back of Rhodes' head. The unmistakable snap of the hammer falling on an empty cylinder followed. This allowed enough time for Porter Moffatt, a member of the galley, to attempt to restrain Anne from pulling the trigger a second time. As her father enveloped her in his arms and dragged her from the courtroom her baleful cry was heard, "Let me shoot him, for God's sake, let me shoot him!" On August 9, 1892, Rhodes walked from the courtroom a free man.[40] The courtroom assassination attempt of John Rhodes may have been the last desperate act of violence directly connected to the Pleasant Valley War.

# PART III

# Train Robbers and Man Hunters

## CHAPTER EIGHT

# Debacle at Nogales:
# The Fumbling Christian Boys

Most criminals today are not very bright, which is why so many of them end up in prison. The intellectual caliber of Western bad men was no higher, which not only earned lots of them a trip to jail, but lots more a one-way trip to Boot Hill. Along the way they committed some successful crimes; more often they got nothing but egg on their faces. So it was with the High Fives, the Christian brothers and their ever-changing entourage of hoodlums.

Numerous Arizona criminals were imports, usually men who left someplace else for their health. They were often in a hurry, with the law close behind them and their back trail liberally salted with corpses, hurt people, missing stock, and empty cash bags. The Christian boys were just such émigrés, products of Oklahoma Territory, refuse that drifted west when the territory got too hot for them.

The Christian boys, brothers Bill and Bob, traveled with their family from Texas into the wide-open land north of the Canadian River in 1891. In what was to become Pottawatomie County, Oklahoma Territory, this wild-and-woolly area was studded with saloon towns, dreary collections of booze-peddling shanties like Young's Crossing, Keokuk Falls, Violet Springs, and the Corner, a tiny patch of land on the South Canadian River whose collection of sleazy saloons attracted trash for miles in every direction. Even in the larger settlements like Shawnee, booze flowed in floods until all of Oklahoma went dry in 1907. At the turn of the century the Pottawatomie country boasted more than sixty saloons and two distilleries, and Shawnee town's daily booze intake in 1903 was said to be twenty-five gallons of whiskey and seven hundred gallons of beer.[1]

Entirely aside from the noxious rotgut they served, the down-at-heels bars were easy places in which to get killed. Keokuk Falls' booze parlors, for example, were quaintly known as the "seven deadly saloons." At the Corner lived a dedicated doctor named Mooney whose practice included a wide assortment of gunshots, knifings, and bloody batteries. The good doctor once managed an amputation on a saloon table while a drunken patron held a lamp to light the doctor's work and the usual revelry continued all around him. In Keokuk Falls somebody murdered a saloon keeper named Haning. The killer shot Haning in the head, left him on the floor of his bar, then came back "between daybreak and sunrise" to finish the process by the somewhat primitive means of driving a rusty nail into Haning's ear.[2] When trains of the Choctaw, Oklahoma and Gulf Railroad stopped in Shawnee, the conductor comfortingly announced: "Shawnee! Twenty minutes for lunch and to see a man killed!"

The Pottawatomie country was a natural shelter for both inept amateur robbers like Al Jennings and career outlaws like Bill Doolin, Zip Wyatt, and a pair of young hoodlums called the Casey boys, whom we will meet again. With Indian Territory on two sides, the country was a haven for the bootleggers who ran hooch into the Indian lands. It was here that the venerable term "bootlegger" may have had its genesis, describing those smugglers who rode into Indian country with pint bottles of John Barleycorn stuffed into the tops of their boots.

Oddly, the area was also known as a "fine country for the poor man," where crops grew well and game abounded.[3] Good people lived here too. One little town was named

Moral, and its founder decreed that no booze would be tolerated in his peaceful community. The Anti-Horsethief Association did what it could to curb widespread rustling, ordering that all horses must be branded with a "c" on the left jaw and have papers. Any man who rode a branded horse without carrying the proper papers was facing a vast amount of trouble.

The Christian family was considered respectable by most accounts although other tales characterize Old Man Christian as walking frequently on the wrong side of the law. Whatever the truth of that, by the time the brothers reached their twenties they had their own unenviable reputation as whiskey runners and horse thieves. Back then the Christian boys headquartered in a saloon in Violet Springs run by one Andy Morrison—he was eventually murdered while sleeping in his own back room—and in 1895 the brothers graduated from small-time crime to killing.

Their career in murder started in April, in a town called Burnett, but there is also a story that the whole sordid affair happened up in Guthrie, north of Oklahoma City. Wherever the dirty deed was done, it came to pass when the brothers and a drinking buddy, one John Mackey, walked out of a saloon and found the law waiting for them. Deputy Will Turner (or Turney) had warrants for the brothers' arrest, but he tried to make the arrest alone. Turner probably did not count on the brothers and Mackey all drawing on him at once. He died in the dusty street.

Tough Sheriff W. B. "Billy" Trousdale ran down Mackey, and the Christian boys surrendered, which turned out to be a bad idea. The court reporter on the case remembered that a "horde of people attended from the Four Corners District, and were about the hardest looking lot in my experience."[4] Disreputable audience or not, the brothers were convicted.

One story relates that county judge was the Honorable

J. D. F. Jennings, who is said to have been upset at the Christians because they had killed a friend of his famous son Al, one of the West's more celebrated—and inept— outlaws. Or maybe the judge just did not like criminals of any stripe. According to this story he gave the Christian boys life sentences and shipped them off to the Oklahoma City jail to await transport to prison.[5]

However, another story, probably the correct one, says the boys were tried and sentenced by Judge Henry Scott, and the court reporter remembered that Judge Scott gave the brothers twenty-five and twenty-two years for the killing. The *Oklahoma City Daily Oklahoman,* however, told its readers that the Christians had been sentenced to eight and ten years. In later days Jennie Cantelou, the court reporter, remembered the sentences as quite lenient, recalling, perhaps inaccurately, that the deputy had been "killed from ambush."[6]

After sentencing, the pair was transferred to the Oklahoma County Jail in Oklahoma City, then a two-story building outfitted with interior steel cages and thought to be a solid, secure lockup. Confined in the same cell as the Christian brothers was a nineteen-year-old loser called Casey, who with his brother had murdered Deputy Marshal Sam Ferris over in Canadian County in the latter part of May.[7] One Casey—either Jim or Vic depending on what account you read—had been shot up in the fight with the deputy and later died. But the surviving brother—the *Daily Oklahoman* said it was Vic—was going to stand trial for murder. He was due to be released on bond, but apparently he did not care to wait around for lawful delivery.

Since neither Casey nor the Christians wanted any part of prison, Bob Christian prevailed upon Jessie Finlay, his girlfriend, to smuggle in several guns, which he stashed in the stovepipe inside his cell. The outlaws chose Sunday, June 30, 1895, to make their break, for on Sundays the jailer, J. H. Garver, allowed his prisoners to move about in the corridor outside their cells. Garver was either unusually easygoing or just plain negligent, or maybe both. Only the day before the break, a Pottawatomie lawman had wired him, warning about a possible jailbreak. Garver did nothing.

At first the break went well. Casey and the Christians pistol-whipped the jailer and ran into an alley behind the jail. There one of the Christians—probably Will—stole a horse belonging to Police Chief Milt Jones and galloped out of town. The other brother and Casey fled on foot, stopped a couple in a buggy, and shoved their pistols into the driver's face. Carpenter Gus White, the driver, would not give up the reins and managed to pull the horses to a halt. Although the fugitives shot White in the leg and the stomach, he would survive.

Chief Jones was closing in on the two escapees, but as he got within eight or ten feet of the buggy, one of the outlaws turned and shot him down. Some observers thought Christian killed the lawman, but the coroner's jury decided Casey was the killer. After the fatal shot, the officer staggered onto the sidewalk and sank down against a building. He was dead in five minutes. A wild gun battle then broke out on Grand Avenue, the fugitives on one side and a couple of police officers and several armed citizens on the other. Bob Christian was hit yet managed to escape, and the lawmen drilled Casey through the neck and head, from which he expired in White's riddled buggy.

With Chief Jones lying dead in the street and both of the Christian brothers vanished, Oklahoma City reacted angrily, and a posse of "infuriated citizens" galloped after the outlaws. A daily paper opined that there was "little doubt" the fugitives would be captured. "Should they be caught," the paper editorialized, "a double lynching will surely follow."[8]

It was a fine idea and would have saved an enormous

amount of trouble later on. And it might well have come to pass, for the citizenry of Oklahoma City were indeed furious. One journalist accurately described the Christians as "noted thugs and desperadoes"[9] and another, having viewed Casey at the undertaker's emporium, somewhat spitefully wrote that Casey "looked much better in death than in life," which may well have been true.[10] But to do the justice everybody hungered for, the law first had to catch the Christians and that would prove very tough although posses searched high and low.

The authorities soon established that a number of people had been part of the planning for the break. Jessie, the loyal girlfriend, spent fourteen months in jail for her part. Jailer Garver discovered that he should have paid attention to the warning wire: his negligence got him ten years in prison, and he served two before he was pardoned. His incompetence should not have surprised anyone; ironically, the sheriff had planned to fire him the Monday after the break. Two other probable conspirators in the break, John Fessenden and Louis Miller, were riding with the brothers in the newly formed Christian gang. The most surprising conspirator was W. H. "Bill" Carr, an old-time U.S. deputy marshal whom authorities charged with supplying Bob's paramour with the very gun Carr had taken away from Bob when he arrested the outlaw. Carr got out on bond, but before his trial he "gave leg bail," as the saying went, left town abruptly and was seen no more. The *Daily Oklahoman* angrily commented that Carr had let down "everybody who trusted him or had anything to do with him."[11]

Not so the Christian brothers. They were on the run, but over the next couple of months they embarked on a string of penny-ante raids on country post offices and general stores. It was bush-league, nickel-and-dime thievery, but it kept the countryside in an uproar. They even managed to bungle a robbery of the Wewoka Trading Company, called the "richest institution in the Seminole nation." They got only a couple of hundred dollars in "provisions and equipment" because the only man who knew the safe combination had gone home for dinner.[12]

Other raids on local stores followed until on August 9 the gang ran into an ambush near the hamlet of Wilburton. A deputy marshal killed Fessenden, and gang member Foster Holbrook was captured. On the twenty-first, John Reeves, one of those who had furnished weaponry for the Oklahoma City jailbreak, was arrested near the town of Paoli. Later tried as a conspirator in Chief Jones' murder, he was sentenced to life. On the twenty-third the Christians shot their way past lawmen west of Purcell. Although Deputy Marshall W. E. Hocker was wounded in the fight, the posse believed Hocker had gotten a bullet into Bob Christian. In the small hours of September 30, Louis Miller, another of the jailbreak conspirators, was jumped by lawmen near Violet Springs. Miller decided to fight and came in second.

The gang reappeared in Oklahoma County in early September, breaking into the railroad agent's quarters in Edmond. And on the sixth of October, they tried a more ambitious task, holding up a St. Louis and San Francisco train east of Wilburton, but rode off with another measly haul. Their last hurrah came in December, when they robbed a mining company store in Coalgate, down in Choctaw country. This raid was another flop: a little over $200 in money, plus "goods to the value of some $200."

Oklahoma had just gotten too hot for the Christian boys, and they drifted west to quieter climes. A month or so later, they turned up in Seven Rivers, New Mexico, and soon ended up in Arizona's Sulphur Springs Valley. By this time, Bill was calling himself Ed Williams while brother Bob adopted the handle of Tom Anderson.[13] Bill went to work breaking horses for the 4-Bar Ranch and soon acquired the nicknames of "202"—maybe from his weight—and "Black

Jack," from his dark hair and mustache (not to be confused with another outlaw called Black Jack Ketchum, for whom Christian was and is sometimes mistaken). His partner, an honest cowboy named Ed Wilson, said of Christian, "A finer partner never lived. Big strong, fearless and good natured . . . ever ready to take his part, no matter what the game might be."[14]

Black Jack loved to whoop it up over in the mining town of Bisbee, along the border, and Wilson recounted that the big puncher "could spend more money than fifteen men could earn." Christian often said, according to Wilson, that "he had a good idea to get up [an] outfit and go train robbing." He repeatedly urged Wilson to join him, but that honest cowpoke refused. Considering what came later, it was a wise decision.

Others did not refuse, however, and Christian soon raised a new gang, including a Texan called Code (or maybe Cole) Young, whose real name was probably Harris. Then there was Bob Hayes, who was either a Texan or an Iowa hoodlum named Sam Hassels. Another notable gang member was George Musgrave, who also called himself Jeff Davis and Jesse Johnson. This able career criminal was yet another Texan. Then there was Jesse Williams, who may have been just another one of Musgrave's many aliases. Finally, add Tom Anderson, who was likely brother Bob Christian, and you have the gang known in the Southwest as the High Fives, named after a card game popular at the time.

The gang waxed and waned in the days to come as hoodlums came and went, were snaffled by the law or were killed by it. One Sid Moore rode with the High Fives, as did Van Musgrave, George's brother. Others drifted in and out, including a man with the peculiar handle of Alamo Hueco Dutch, and at least half a dozen others, one of whom was yet another Musgrave. Many of these people carried one or more aliases, so it was tough from time to time to know just who was part of the gang. Another complication arose from the fact that the gang did not all come together for every crime but sometimes operated in twos and threes.

All of these ne'er-do-wells, according to cowboy Wilson, were "crack shots" who removed the triggers from their pistols and simply thumbed back the hammer "when in a tight place" and fanned the pistol. "The speed," said Wilson, "with which they could shoot in this manner was simply amazing." No doubt, but could they hit anything farther than ten feet away?[15]

With his trusty henchmen, including another hard case called Three-Fingered Jack Dunlap—later extinguished by tough Jeff Milton—on August 6, 1896, Black Jack rode off to rob the bank at Nogales, right on the border with Mexico. Some of his band stayed outside with the horses; the others—probably Jesse Williams and Bob Hayes—went into the bank. They had excellent luck at first. Their mouths must have watered at the sight of a heap of hard money, maybe as much as thirty thousand dollars, counted out and waiting for a local rancher closing a stock purchase. Right after that, however, things quickly began to come unstuck. According to one tale, the bank's directors were meeting upstairs. Hearing a commotion beneath, they threw open windows and opened fire on the astonished robbers. Another attractive and improbable story says the rout of the bandits was begun by an act of God: a passing whirlwind slammed the bank's back door and scared the gang's inside men out of a year's growth, whereat they decamped in a great hurry. More probably, as other versions relate, the problem was a single tough bank employee, either bank president John Dessart or, more probably, cashier Frank Herrera. The most reliable tale of the bungled raid tells that Dessart ran for help while Herrera took on the outlaws. Whoever the staunch defender was, he was all wool and a yard wide. Alone in the bank, he snatched a pistol and began to blaze away. He did not hit anybody, but his heroics were enough to drive the bandits pell-mell out into the street, without their loot. To add to their woes, either just before or just after the bank's resident hero started shooting, a passerby also pulled his .41 Colt and opened fire on the confused robbers. This was customs collector Frank King.

Whatever the true sequence of things, what with the slamming of doors and folks shooting at them, these big tough men quickly concluded that Nogales was no place to hang around. The inside men tumbled out of the bank in a great swivet and the gang dropped their loot and fled, as cowboys said, at the high lope. The bank man was still firing behind them although all he hit was the bank ceiling and an unfortunate horse—or mule—parked across the street from the bank.

Frank King pursued, first on a buggy horse then on a pony requisitioned from a passing cowboy, turning back only when the outlaws began to shoot at him. Undaunted, King then raised a posse, but to no avail. Other posses took the field as well, among them Bisbee riders including Burt Alvord, soon to leave the side of the law to become a bandit in his own right. Sheriff Bob Leatherwood's party, with Alvord and Cochise County's pioneer photographer-turned-sheriff Camillus Fly along, got very near the outlaws. The fugitives littered their trail with abandoned food and cooking gear, even a loaded mule, in their haste to reach the Mexican border. But as the posse closed in, the gang turned on them. In the ensuing firefight, one of the posse members died.

The *Tucson Daily Citizen* reported that the lawmen, led by Sheriff Leatherwood, were ambushed in Skeleton Canyon, of evil repute. Deputy Frank Robson went down "at the first volley," with bullets through his forehead and his temple. The deputy's horse galloped off with him, dead or dying, and the waiting outlaws took not only the animal, but Robson's money, watch, and revolver.

Leatherwood jumped from his horse as the panicked animal bolted. Lawman Hildreth then killed Black Jack's mount, but the bandit caught the sheriff's horse and managed to switch saddles only to have the lawman's animal killed before Black Jack could mount. Hildreth's horse also went down, but the wounded Hildreth fought on even as the tree behind which he sheltered was filled with lead. Leatherwood, Fly, Alvord, and another posse member named Johnson also fought back as best they could, but they were shooting only at puffs of smoke.

After the firing died away, the battered posse found their quarry had vanished. The lawmen followed, reinforced by more posse men, including deadly man hunter Texas John Slaughter ("I say, I say, shoot first and shout 'throw up your hands' afterwards"). According to one version of the tale, Slaughter was not impressed with the posse's actions thus far and said so. "I say," he commented, "you're a fine bunch of officers. If there was any ambushing to be done, why in the heck didn't *you* do it?"[16]

Pursuit continued, but Leatherwood wrote from across the border in Sonora on August 18 that heavy rains had washed out the gang's trail. Southern Pacific detective and sometime Tombstone lawman Billy Breakenridge reported that the robbers were back in the United States, holed up at the San Simon Cattle Company's horse ranch.

The gang carried on its evil ways, hitting the San Simon railroad station and both the post office and Wickersham's Store at Bowie. In between, they "liberated" horses whenever they needed new mounts. In most cases they were careful to let the owners know where their stock was ultimately left as it paid to keep good relations with ordinary people when you were on the run. Things like paying for breakfast at the little Joe Schaefer Ranch with a couple of Bull Durham sacks of post office change were the sort of largesse that made people feel better disposed towards you, and after all, it is not hard to be generous with somebody else's money. They had a crude sense of humor—it is also not hard to be jovial when you have the gun. Cutting open the mail pouch during a stage holdup, they joked to the driver that if the government would only use baskets, the outlaws would not have to slice up government property. And sometimes they had the good sense not to take on a job more formidable than isolated stores. At one point they thought about robbing the paymaster's box bound for Fort Huachuca but gave that up rather than face the rifles of the U.S. Army's escort.

The frustrated officers kept up the pursuit, and the hunters now included Jeff Milton, the bulldog Wells Fargo man. Along the way Milton and a deputy stayed a night at Brandt's Store in San Simon. Brandt welcomed them with delight since he had already been held up once by the High Fives, and he feared the outlaws would visit him again. And while Milton was at the store, a cowboy came in bragging about how Christian was making fools of the officers and how he himself "could run the officers out of the country with a smoking corn cob."[17] Such boasting was never wise around Jeff Milton. "Go up there," he told the deputy, "and box his jaws. I'll be a-watchin' him, and if he beats you to the draw I'll kill him." "Sure," said the deputy, "it'll be a pleasure," and whopped the cowboy smartly under Milton's watchful eye. "I didn't see no smoking corn cobs," said Milton afterward.

But the High Fives had now determined to promote themselves to the criminal big time. And so, on a moonless night in October, the gang hit the eastbound A and P train at the Rio Puerco trestle over in New Mexico. The robbery should have been easy for the train obligingly stopped while the engineer inspected a faulty piston rod. The gang threw down on the train crew, shooting the brakeman in the hand when he came forward to see what the trouble was. But these were the High Fives, neither very bright nor very lucky. And so the fruits of bad luck and bad planning appeared again, in the form of a train passenger, Deputy United States Marshal Horace Loomis.

Loomis guessed something was wrong up front, and so he thoughtfully loaded his shotgun and stepped quietly out into the night. He saw the engineer uncoupling the express car as Code Young, who may have led the raid, shouted orders at him. Without ceremony, the officer dropped Young, who regained his feet and snapped off a couple of rounds from his pistol before the marshal gave him the second barrel. Exit Code Young.[18] The rest of the gang, uncertain what had happened to Young, at least realized that something was very wrong and galloped off into the night without their loot. Foiled again.

The gang returned to their small-time robberies, holding up a couple of stages and a series of isolated stores. As usual, their labors produced only pittances of money plus bits and pieces of clothing, liquor, and tobacco. There was a good deal of casual brutality connected with these robberies: Bob Hayes pistol-whipped one elderly country postmaster, for example, because he objected to giving up $5.50, all the money he had.

There was little profit in robbing isolated stores like the one in tiny Separ, between Deming and Lordsburg, New Mexico. After that strike, they ran into a posse at the Diamond A horse camp. The story goes that the gang had arranged with sympathetic cowboys to display a white cloth on the corral when it was safe to visit the ranch. They had not counted on the law moving in and detaining everybody at the camp, spoiling the signal system. When Black Jack and Bob Hayes rode into camp, all unsuspecting, the officers rose from their hiding place in a salt lick and blazed away. They blew Bob Hayes off his horse. He was probably killed by the rifle of Marshal Fred Higgins of Roswell although another story says Hayes was eliminated by a Santa Fe conductor somewhere around Kingman, Arizona. Black Jack got away from the Diamond A, even though his horse was killed by the lawmen. Supposedly Christian single-handedly heaved the dead animal up far enough to pull his Winchester clear then shot his way out of the ambush. A posse member named Dow shot five times at the outlaw leader at a range at which it seemed he could not miss, but Christian escaped unscathed, largely because of the bucking and twisting of his frantic horse.

One tally tells that by the end of 1896, in just six months, the High Fives had robbed a bank, a train, four stagecoaches, and a long list of little stores and post offices. On one occasion, they even robbed a traveler of his tobacco. Along the way, Black Jack had casually murdered one man and badly wounded his cook, and a couple of posse members had also died. On the plus side, career thugs Code Young and Bob Hayes were extinct.

Milton and the other hunters could not close with the gang. However, in February 1897, after a train robbery in New Mexico went sour, Black Jack's own paranoia moved him to kill one Red Sanders, whom, he thought, had talked to the law. It was after that unnecessary murder that Christian moved south, to hide out east of Clifton, Arizona, in a tangled, wild canyon to this day called Black Jack Canyon. And it was in that desolate place that the tireless law finally caught up with him. Christian had sent a gang member into Clifton to buy some two hundred rounds of ammunition of a most unusual caliber, probably .50-95 Winchester. Black Jack was known to carry a rifle of that caliber, and the law began to search.

As is common in the mythology of the West, there are a couple of different stories about the end of Black Jack Christian. After the failed attempt on the A and P train at Rio Puerco, the gang hid out at a "goat ranch" near Clifton.

There they planned another strike, but before they could do the job, the ammunition purchase alerted lawmen and/or an informer tipped off the law. Deputy Marshal Hall, the formidable Fred Higgins, and posse members Bill Hart, Crookneck Johnson, and Charlie Paxton set up an ambush in Cole Creek Canyon, down in Graham County.

Ironically, it was a lost hat that put paid to Black Jack's career. Disappointed, the lawmen had already folded up their trailside ambush and were riding toward the ranch to ask for breakfast when Fred Higgins turned back to look for his hat. It was at this moment that the posse saw three men on the trail behind them, already reaching for their weapons. The first shot came from Higgins, however, whom the outlaws had not seen. The three bandits broke for safety in the thick vegetation, but the posse saw one of them stagger before he reached cover. The officers, accurately assessing the area as very hostile and very dangerous, decided they had not lost anything in that heavy brush. They did not then try to search for whomever Higgins had likely hit but prudently withdrew to nearby Clifton.

Later that day, a cowboy named Bert Farmer passed down the same trail driving horses and stopped when the beasts shied at something. It was Bill Christian, mortally wounded. He was taken to a nearby ranch, but he did not last long. Dying, he murmured that it did not matter "who he was, or what his name might be." A Mormon freighter brought into Clifton all that remained of the bold bandit, tossed on top of a load of lumber. Self-appointed experts ran to identify the body, and some of them, inspired either by ignorance or by friendship for the deceased, identified the body as outlaw Black Jack Ketchum.

According to Tombstone lawman Billy Breakenridge— one of those who confused Christian with Ketchum—an ambush party led by Deputy Sheriff Ben Clark caught Christian's gang about daylight on April 27, 1897, killing both Black Jack and gang member George Musgrave. Another source differs and writes that only Christian went down, riddled with four slugs from the weapon of famous man hunter Jeff Milton. Both accounts are at least partially wrong. Musgrave seems to have survived the ambush in which Christian died. And Milton, the very tough Wells Fargo man, was not part of the ambush party that killed Christian. Afterward, however, he pursued other High Five members, and it was Milton's shotgun that finally did in Three-Fingered Jack Dunlap, veteran of the bungled Nogales raid and a journeyman villain in his own right. The bandits who got away were probably Musgrave, his brother, and Bob Christian. The Musgraves headed for Mexico, but Christian probably hid out in the mountains of southern Arizona. He surfaced there in the autumn of 1897, was arrested, and escaped, then dropped out of sight forever.

Musgrave deserves a few words of his own. He was a Texan, born in 1877, who by the time he was in his teens had embarked on a career in rustling. His first really serious trouble came when he was only seventeen. An experienced thief by then, he crossed ex-Texas Ranger George Parker. The difficulty seemed to stem from a disagreement over some stolen horses, and in the end Musgrave simply rode into a cow camp and murdered Parker. By this time, as young as he was, Musgrave had been indicted at least twice for stock theft. He did not tarry to answer the charges, being on his way farther west, where he would meet his friend Code Young, also a future member of the High Fives.

After the debacle in Cole Creek Canyon and his flight into Mexico, Musgrave returned to the United States and carried on in outlawry with his brother, Bob Christian, and one or two others. The gang robbed a train over near Grants, New Mexico, dynamiting the door of the express car—it took three tries—and then blew the safe, leaving the express car afire. The haul was a good one this time:

perhaps a hundred pounds of gold coins and a great deal of currency.

After that, the gang drifted apart, Musgrave's brothers apparently pursuing somewhat more peaceful ways as they added years to their ages. George himself worked as a cowboy and finally married in November 1908. But his past followed him. An old acquaintance spotted him in Grand Junction in the autumn of 1909 and he was arrested for the murder of Parker so long before. Handcuffed, Musgrave managed one last grand gesture, attacking a news photographer and trying to smash his camera. He failed, and the picture still survives.

Musgrave claimed self-defense and made the defense work. Acquitted, in due course he left for South America. Butch Cassidy and the Sundance Kid had tried the same thing but in November 1908 lost a gunfight with the Bolivian army. Musgrave tried Paraguay, sailing south late in 1911 or early the next year, and in time his wife joined him. He now called himself Robert Steward and is said to have lived on in South America, chiefly Paraguay and Brazil, as a businessman and rancher, maybe even taking sides in the area's endemic revolutions. He may have been also a rustler, holdup man, or murderer—or possibly all of these—depending on what tales you read. He never returned to the United States, dying probably in 1947.

One curious postscript remains. Black Jack Ketchum, a considerable villain in his own right, was mistaken for Black Jack Christian more than once. And Ketchum made an intriguing comment in April 1901, the day he was to be hung in Clayton, New Mexico. He knew Black Jack Christian, he said, and Christian was still alive. "Oh yes," said Ketchum, "I have an idea where he is but I won't tell."[19] And he did not. The secret, if there was one, went to the grave with Ketchum, both parts of him, for the shock of the drop parted him from his head, and he was buried in two pieces.

So passed the High Fives. Only George Musgrave achieved any sort of real success, and even he had to do it in exile from his own land. Considering the amount of time they spent living rough and running from the law and the nickel-and-dime scores most of their crimes produced, in the end they were a remarkably unsuccessful gang of outlaws with little to show for their efforts. Unless you consider the tally of the dead.

## CHAPTER NINE

# Shoot First: Texas John Slaughter Tames Cochise County

Tombstone in the 1880s was surely the toughest town on Earth. After all, at various times Tombstone boasted not only the Earps and the Clanton-McLaury gang, but Buckskin Frank Leslie, Luke Short, Doc Holliday, Zwing Hunt, Curly Bill Brocius, and dozens of other pugnacious gunmen of ability and reputation. If you wanted a fight, Tombstone was one of the easiest places to find one.

The raw, brawling town's Boot Hill grew steadily in population. There were a few fast guns buried up there, a lot of slow ones, some certified outlaws, and a few who were only suspected. The cemetery also held a substantial supporting cast, some of whom had names, some of whom did not, men who appealed to Judge Colt for justice and came out on the short end, men who got in the way of some hard case on the prod and departed this life abruptly as a consequence.

Some of Boot Hill's residents ended up in unmarked plots. Some of them did not, and the history of the town is writ large in their crude epitaphs. Some are short and specific:

KILLEN 1880. SHOT BY LESLIE

Others are more creative, like this much-photographed tribute, which blends history with a little art:

HERE LIES LESTER MOORE
FOUR SLUGS FROM A .44
NO LES NO MORE

Lester is said to have been a Wells Fargo agent in the border town of Naco. It seems a package arrived in his shop for one Dunstan. It showed up damaged, and Dunstan was much wroth. He apparently blamed Lester for the mishap, one thing led to another, and both men went for their guns. Lester, still behind his wicket, absorbed the four rounds commemorated on his wooden grave marker but got a fatal bullet into Dunstan. It is not recorded what happened to the package.

But there was one man the shootists would not challenge, one man who went quietly about his business on Tombstone's dusty streets without hindrance or trouble. His name was John Horton Slaughter, and he may have been the toughest man in the West, anyplace, ever. At least, that is what the hard-case gunfighters of southern Arizona thought for they left the stocky little man strictly alone.

It was not that Slaughter boasted or threatened or even raised his voice. He did not. In fact, he was a quiet man of quiet habits. Nevertheless, legends grew up around him. There was the time down in Douglas, Arizona, when Slaughter sat playing poker and steadily losing. At last he laid his pearl-handled revolver on the table. "I say, I say," said he, "there does seem to be an awful lot of aces in this deck." After that, there were far fewer aces, and Slaughter began to win his share of pots.

Slaughter was short, only about five feet, six inches, but he was built like a rock and heavily muscled. He did not talk tough—in fact he did not talk much at all—and he did not threaten. He was neither bully nor drunkard at a time when many of Tombstone's residents were both. There was something about John Slaughter, though, that made the town's toughest citizens want no part of him. There was something about his eyes.

Slaughter's eyes were jet black, obsidian black, and sometimes they seemed to bore right through a man. For all Slaughter's peaceful ways, men who considered challenging him could see death in those cold eyes and quickly found some pressing business elsewhere. A Tombstone man remembered those eyes:

> No one on whom Slaughter bestowed the most casual glance ever forgot his eyes. . . . When he looked at me, his eyes seemed to be burning a hole into my brain. I used to fancy he was taking an inventory of all my secrets. If someone had held a newspaper at the back of my head, it wouldn't have surprised me if Slaughter, looking straight through my skull, had read the want ads.[1]

John Slaughter was born in Sabine Parish, Louisiana, toward the end of 1841, but he grew up in wild West Texas, fighting Kiowa and Comanche raiders. He served a brief spell as a Confederate soldier then fought Indians and outlaws as a part-time Texas Ranger into the 1870s. For a while he ran cattle in Frio and Atascosa Counties, Texas, and drove his beef north to the booming Kansas railroad towns for shipment east. The price of beef had jumped from one to twenty dollars almost overnight, and Slaughter aimed to cash in on the boom. It was not easy. Along the line of the great trail drives lay all kinds of trouble and very little law. The route swarmed with raiders and rustlers, Indian and white. Only a strong man kept what was his: his herd, his outfit, or for that matter, his life. John Slaughter was tested early on.

One of those who was fool enough to try the taciturn Texan was a hoodlum called Bill or Barney Gallagher, an outlaw who rejoiced in the nickname of the "Man from Bitter Creek." Lots of punks invented themselves as hard cases in those days. Most of them did not survive long, but while they were kicking they gloried in their romantic names. There were a couple of Black Jacks and a bushel of Kids: Billy the Kid and Harry the Kid, the Sundance Kid and the Mormon Kid, the Narrow-Gauge Kid, the Mysterious Kid, and the Verdigris Kid. And that does not even count a rich assortment of other odd titles: Turkey Creek, Three-Fingered Jack, at least one other Bitter Creek, Peg-Leg, Cock-Eyed Charlie, Broken Nose, and Flat Nose. The list went on to include Dynamite Jack and Dynamite Dick, Black-Faced Charlie, Wyoming Frank, Texas Billy, Red Buck, Jack of Diamonds, and Tulsa Jack, plus a couple of miscreants who called themselves Shoot-'Em-Up whoever. The list abounded in Bills: Curly Bill, Wild Bill, Cherokee Bill, Old Bill, and the prize of the lot, Polka-Dot Bill. Some of these men were all talk and posturing, but Gallagher was the real thing. He had a deservedly evil reputation and was credited with killing thirteen men at least.

Gallagher ran into Slaughter around Devil's River in southwest Texas in 1876 as Slaughter was making up a trail herd. Gallagher cooked up a claim to several hundred of Slaughter's steer and pressed it with his usual bluster, but Slaughter was not impressed. "Hit the trail!" said Slaughter, and the outlaw went. But Gallagher was not through. He waited until Slaughter got his herd well on the trail toward Fort Sumner, up in the wild New Mexico Territory. He acquired a partner along the way, a man named Boyd, and they confronted Slaughter at last on John Chisum's South Spring Ranch. This time Gallagher meant business.

Gallagher charged Slaughter on horseback, and he came smokin', as the saying went. He drove in toward the little Texan at the gallop, brandishing a double-barreled shotgun, twin .45s slapping on his hips.[2] Slaughter did not wait for his attacker to close. Instead, he nailed Gallagher's horse at long range with his Winchester, and the outlaw pitched sprawling into the dust. Another version, more lurid and less plausible, has both men charging on horseback, with Slaughter killing his foe with a pistol as they galloped toward each other.[3] That does not sound like practical John Slaughter.

Gallagher may have been scum, but he did not lack courage. He staggered to his feet and advanced on Slaughter with a .45 in each hand, shooting as he came. He was still far out of effective handgun range, however, and the quiet Texan levered his Winchester and coolly shot Gallagher three times, breaking his arm and driving rounds through the outlaw's stomach and lungs. Gallagher collapsed in the dust and muttered his own epitaph as Slaughter walked up to him: "I needed killing twenty years ago anyway."[4] No doubt he was right. Boyd sensibly departed for parts unknown, and a sort of peace descended on that part of the Pecos country.

That was John Slaughter, unemotional, unaggressive, unafraid of man or beast, determined to assert what he believed were his rights—against anybody. For example, he never failed to cut cattle bearing his brand out of other people's herds, as was his right. He even relieved tough John Chisum of sixty steers although the legendary cattle baron protested strongly and showed Slaughter a bill of sale. Slaughter was unmoved and told Chisum, "You ought've known something was wrong with 'em, when they were that cheap. They're mine and I'm taking 'em."[5] And he did. John Chisum knew a fighting man when he saw one and did not press the point.

Others did. On one occasion Slaughter reclaimed over a hundred of his own steers from the herd of a man named Underwood. Flanked by two friends and armed to the teeth, Underwood approached Slaughter. As Underwood and his cohorts rode up, Slaughter thoughtfully unlimbered his Winchester and dismounted, putting his horse between his body and the three truculent men. "I bought and paid for them cattle!" shouted Underwood. Slaughter's answer got right to the point: "Try to take them!" And that was that. Underwood made the right choice and rode on home minus the steers but in one piece.

In 1878, Slaughter made the decision to move west. He had his eyes on Arizona, on the lush grass just above the Mexican border, the valleys of the San Simon, the San Pedro, and Sulphur Springs. He moved his herd alongside that of Amazon Howell, another tough and independent rancher. There was safety in numbers, but there was also something else. Slaughter, widowed years before, was taken with Howell's daughter, comely Viola. Slaughter was thirty-eight and Viola only nineteen, but the difference in ages meant nothing to either of them. In mid-April 1879, they were married during the drive, at Tularosa, and the match proved to be close and lasting.

Getting to Arizona at all was not easy. Besides Gallagher, Chisum, and Underwood there had been the flooded Rio Grande, the waterless gypsum of White Sands, Chief Victorio and his Apache band, howling winds and snowdrifts, and still more unpleasant people. Traditionally there was little law west of the Pecos, and just now rugged New Mexico swarmed with bandits of all kinds, unrest that would further delay Slaughter and his band. In 1878 the bloody Lincoln County War was raging, and Gov. Lew Wallace was determined to reestablish some kind of order. He was convinced that Slaughter's crew was a nest of outlaws. That was probably a bit of an overstatement, but it was certainly true that virtue was less important than ability to Slaughter when he hired his cowboys. There was also an allegation that Slaughter had stolen a couple of dozen steers and the unresolved question of Gallagher's death. There was not enough evidence to proceed against Slaughter, and he thankfully left Lincoln County, New Mexico, in his dust. In late summer of 1878 he reached the end of his long trail, the rich grass along the San Pedro River. His foreman, John Roberts, brought a second herd up from Texas a few months later, and Slaughter added still another during the next winter.

Slaughter contracted to supply beef to the San Carlos Reservation and to the ravenous railroad camp, then working up a huge appetite driving steel from Benson, Arizona, to Nogales, on the border. Slaughter's own herds would not fill the demand, and so he began to buy cattle in Old Mexico for hard cash and in large numbers. On one memorable occasion, Slaughter rode into Mexico on a cattle-buying trip carrying twelve thousand dollars in silver in his saddlebags to pay for the herd he would drive north. With him rode Roberts, his foreman; some vaqueros; and ex-slave teamster John Baptiste, called Old Bat. The pleasant jingle of all that hard silver money soon drew the intense attention of a band of more than forty heavily armed Mexicans. Slaughter turned to one of his vaqueros: *"Quienes son estos?"* he asked. *"Estos son bandidos,"* said the vaquero and promptly disappeared with all his fellows. Slaughter, Roberts, and Old Bat were alone and on their own.[6]

Abandoned by their vaqueros, Slaughter and his two hands were trapped in a tiny Mexican village by the expectant bandits. Considering the huge odds, Slaughter tried to avoid a fight, slipping out of the hamlet under cover of darkness and holing up with his men in a cluster of boulders. They were followed. Slaughter and his men were badly outnumbered, but Roberts and Old Bat were very nearly as formidable as their boss, and the night was dark. They turned to fight, springing a point-blank shotgun ambush that emptied several saddles and drove the rest of the bandits off in wild retreat.

Slaughter and his men were reported killed, however, and Viola drove south in wild alarm, hoping at least to recover her husband's body. Instead, she found Slaughter and his men hale and hearty, pushing a herd north out of Mexico. "It was," said Slaughter afterward, "the only time I remember ever having been murdered."[7]

After such a narrow escape, anyone else would have taken the trail back to the United States without a minute's delay. Not Slaughter. He had calmly gone on with his buying trip, found his herd, bought it, and driven it back north. He had come to Mexico for cattle after all, and no paltry gaggle of border thieves was going to stop him.

Neither were American thugs. Just north of Slaughter's ground lay the Clanton place, the lair of Old Man Clanton and his vicious, arrogant sons. The Clantons were hard men, famous for casting a sticky loop, as the saying went, and Slaughter soon noticed that some of his steers were missing. Knowing the Clanton reputation, Slaughter paid their ranch a call, cut out his steers, and confronted the Clanton clan. He spoke quietly and plainly to Old Man Clanton: "If ever I find you or any of your kin on my land again, I'll kill you."[8] That seemed simple enough, and if Slaughter's words sounded a little unfriendly, they were surely clear. Clanton, normally a man with a large and active mouth, looked into those terrible black eyes and was persuaded. After that it was hard to find a Clanton anyplace close to Slaughter's ground, and Slaughter's herds remained intact.

Old Man Clanton blustered a good deal about his one-sided conversation with Slaughter, but only once did he work up the nerve to go after the little Texan. He chose a moonlit night and followed John and Viola as they rode back to their ranch together. The evening was quiet and peaceful, but suddenly Slaughter's sixth sense called loudly to him. He turned to Viola. "You drive the team," he said. "I want my gun in my hand." Viola was startled. "What's the matter? I see nothing to cause alarm." Slaughter was insistent. "Neither do I. But do as I say." And then Viola noticed Clanton and nudged her husband. "That man has a gun in his hand," she said. "Why, so have I," said Slaughter, and Clanton disappeared into the night.

In another version of the same story, the threatening horseman is identified as Doc Holliday, another killer Slaughter neither liked nor trusted. Whichever version is the truth, the story starkly emphasizes both the constant danger that surrounded Slaughter and Texas John's preternatural awareness of danger.[9]

Honest, uncompromising Slaughter made other enemies as well. Once, as he and Viola left the rough, tough mill town of Charleston, Slaughter spotted a band of horsemen galloping to intercept him on the trail ahead. He calmly handed the reins of his team to Viola and picked up his shotgun. He spoke quietly to his wife: "Now we'll go on. If those fellows open up on us, you drive on out of danger. I'll fight from the ground."[10] The doughty Viola laid the leather to their team, and the couple outran the would-be bushwhackers. There was no pursuit. Nobody in his right mind wanted to chase John Slaughter and his deadly shotgun.

That episode was finished, but Slaughter was not. He had recognized two of the men, Ed Lyle and Cap Stilwell. He dealt with them in his own inimitable way. Lyle was first. Slaughter found him in a store and covered him with his Colt. "I'm not going to kill you," he said, but he continued, "Probably I ought to, but I'll give you this chance: this country isn't big enough any longer to hold the two of us. Twenty-four hours from now I'll be looking for you. I better not find you."[11] He didn't. Lyle might have been vicious, but he was bright enough to know that his continued health depended on living someplace other than Cochise County. He was not seen again. Slaughter found Stilwell in a saloon. The outlaw went for his six-shooter the instant he saw the cattleman, but Texas John beat him to the draw. And then, as Stilwell stared down the bore of Slaughter's Colt, Slaughter gave him the same choice he had given Lyle. And with the same result. Before the allotted twenty-four hours had expired, Stilwell was among those absent, and the Tombstone country knew him no more.

One more menace existed. It remained for Slaughter to come to terms with the Apache, whose roving bands periodically killed and burned all along the border country. Their tough warriors took the white man's beef when the spirit moved, even when they were not out for war. Slaughter dealt with the Apache raiders in his own way. He killed them. When a party strayed into his part of the territory, Slaughter tracked them expertly and remorselessly. Those he caught he shot, and even the fierce Apache soon accepted the inevitable. It was easier to travel trails that did not cross his land. Even the fearless Geronimo gave Slaughter and his cattle a wide berth. That formidable Apache warrior knew a kindred spirit when he saw one. A few beeves were not worth tangling with this deadly black-eyed man.

Again and again Slaughter heeded his inner voice, a psychic warning of danger. He paid close attention to his premonitions and repeatedly they alerted him to some menace on the trail ahead. He was convinced he was watched over by a sort of guardian angel, and time and again some power seemed to save his life. John Horton Slaughter's natural courage was reinforced by yet another mystic conviction, the profound certainty that he could not be killed. He himself put it, "No man can kill me. I wasn't born to be killed. I cannot explain it, but I know it. When my time comes, I'll die in bed."[12]

For all his belief in his destiny, Slaughter was a careful man. He was never seen without his revolver, even indoors at home, and in his later years it was always near to hand in his living room. He would allow no one behind him. Even his friend, lawman Jeff Milton, could not get behind the careful Slaughter although Milton jokingly tried many times.

Over the years Slaughter scouted for the army, serving under Generals Nelson Miles and George Crook as they harried the Apache war parties. Slaughter was present when Geronimo surrendered to Miles in Skeleton Canyon in 1886. In between he ran his cattle and helped chase down some of the lawless element who infested Tombstone and Cochise County. He did not waste time with such unredeemable riffraff. The *Tombstone Prospector* reported the result of one such law-enforcement expedition, the collection of a lowlife called John Horn, lately given to assaulting people and intimidating witnesses. After Slaughter caught up with him, Horn was, as the paper said tongue-in-cheek, "very badly used up, and is now lying at his room at the Way Up Lodging House."[13] No doubt he was, permanently so.

So were a lot of other men who thought they were tougher than the law. They were worthless in Slaughter's book, not people, and he did not hesitate to pull the trigger on them. Neither did his straight-shooting cowhands. In later years, Texas John's philosophy toward lawbreakers was put pretty graphically by John Swain, a tough black cowboy who had been with Slaughter ever since he had been "given" to his boss as a tiny child: "I helped kill a few triflin' 'Paches and no 'count thieves, but no, sir, ah didn't never kill a man."[14] This was of course John Slaughter's simple philosophy. There were good people and bad people. You cherished and protected the good. The rest of them, the trash, the world could easily do without, and Slaughter did his part to help with the cleansing.

In 1884, Slaughter and his Viola bought the ancient San Bernardino Grant, a monstrous seventy-thousand-acre tract straddling the border with Mexico. The Spanish land grant went back to 1822, but there had been a Spanish fort in the area as early as 1773 and a mission at about the same time. There was plenty of water and lush grass as far as the eye could see. It was cattle heaven, an empire to match the ability and drive of Texas John Slaughter. John and Viola built a large adobe house for themselves in 1890 and surrounded it with barns and sheds, a bunkhouse, and a forge. Slaughter built dams and canals, and in time a little settlement grew up around his house, with a store, a school, and a post office. Some thirty families settled there, and the land bloomed with grain, vegetables, and hay. "It was beautiful," Viola Slaughter said, "and it was ours."

In 1886, Slaughter took a partner, George Lang, who owned a spread next to the San Bernardino. Together they pushed cattle to California, hungry for beef, and even ran a slaughterhouse in far-off Los Angeles. Slaughter seemed to have achieved all that a man could want. But now a new duty called him, and Slaughter was not the man to turn away.

Tombstone and Cochise County still crawled with outlaws. The big names were gone, the famous shootists like the Earps and Clantons, but in their place the country was infested with thieves, rustlers, and murderers from all over the territory, plus a sizeable number of undesirable pilgrims from Texas and New Mexico. In Tombstone a back street called Whiskey Row was thick with criminals, and the good citizens of the county finally had had enough. There was little argument about who was the toughest honest man around. The citizenry appealed to Slaughter and he answered, winning election as sheriff of Cochise County in 1886. It was an ominous day for the outlaw element.

John Slaughter was not enchanted by the machinations of the legal system. He had his own somewhat original ideas about law enforcement and they did not extend to the niceties of due process. He did not clatter about the county with a posse as others had before him. Instead, he rode with only one or two deputies and often he traveled alone. He frequently went after horse and cattle thieves by himself, generally returning with the animals but without the rustlers. Knowing Texas John, the locals remained carefully incurious about the fate of the wanted men. As a San Pedro rancher put it, "Of course, I didn't ask John. That'd been a mistake. Nobody never asked Slaughter no questions. It never did no good to ask him none, and sometimes it was sorta dangerous."[15]

Tough lawman Jeff Milton understood his friend Slaughter well. Slaughter was noted for reading his warrants to the culprits after the shooting was over. Milton said, "[If] Slaughter believed a man needed killing, he thought no more of killing him than putting a hole through a can." Slaughter did not talk much about his law-enforcement activities. He did not talk much at all—he never had—but when he did, people usually listened. He had a habit of prefacing his remarks with, "I say, I say," and then saying it, as he did when he advised his deputies on their duties. "I say, I say, shoot first and yell 'throw up your hands' afterwards."[16] As one old Tombstone hand put it, "It was one of old John's ideas that the proper time to tell a man to halt was after you had fixed him so's he couldn't do anything else but halt."[17]

Taken altogether, he was not a good man to cross. It was not that Slaughter was a cruel man or even unkind; he was famous for his love of children and dogs. It was just that he had quite specific ideas about right and wrong and no use at all for people who broke the law. As a neighbor once described him, "Slaughter wasn't a bad man—but he was a very dangerous man—very quick with a pistol. He killed twelve men in the years he was sheriff and they all had it coming. And don't think they weren't damn tough!"[18] The count was twelve men unless you considered the missing horse thieves. His total may have been twenty—one estimate says it was—or it might have been a good deal higher, all without even adding Gallagher or Apaches or

Mexican bandits or what others he may have encountered on the long, dangerous cattle drives.

Slaughter did not notch his guns or boast or say much of anything about his work as sheriff. He wore fancy boots, dressed well and conservatively, sported a diamond ring, and carried a pearl-handled Colt. Generally puffing on one of his favorite Mexican cheroots, he was always courteous. He spoke formally to others—most men were "Mister"— and he expected to be treated with dignity himself. Folks who knew him hastened to oblige.

Deadly as he was, Slaughter still liked to avoid trouble before it happened. When he had decided that a local tough was dangerous and unreformable, Slaughter would call on the man. He would then reason with him briefly and specifically. He gave him a brief period to "buy a trunk," as Westerners were wont to say, pack up his possible, and leave the country. Otherwise, he would come looking for the incorrigible, who would then be forced to stay as a permanent resident.[19] It was hard to argue with logic like that, and when the gray dawn came on the appointed day, Cochise County was cleaner by one troublemaker.

That is how it worked with one Juan Soto, a career criminal arrested for a variety of crimes around Tombstone and nearby Charleston. Somehow a jury was not persuaded of Soto's guilt and turned him loose. Slaughter was unimpressed by the verdict and confronted Soto outside the courtroom. He had ten days to pack up, Slaughter told him quietly. After that, Soto would have to answer to the sheriff. The outlaw blustered a little, but from sunup on deadline day, Tombstone was rid of him. Soto did not go far, however, only to nearby Sulphur Springs. That turned out to be a mistake. The incidence of crime in that area increased immediately after Soto's arrival, and that was a mistake too. Suddenly Soto disappeared from Sulphur Springs, never to be seen again. John Slaughter did say he had had business over Sulphur Springs way about that time, but Slaughter went on solitary rides all the time, and nobody to speak of missed Soto.

Sometimes, though, gentle persuasion did not work. Then it came to shooting, and the men who crossed Slaughter invariably came in second. There was the Robles gang, six outlaws who held up a Northern Mexico and Arizona train and killed four crewmen at a station across the border. Four of the six bandits fled north into Cochise County. Slaughter and two deputies surprised three of them at dawn, still wrapped in their blankets. Refusing Slaughter's summons to surrender, the outlaws opened fire. Slaughter's first round killed Guadalupe Robles, brother of the gang leader. A second man snapped off a shot that nicked Slaughter's ear, then he went down dying from Texas John's return fire. Manuel Robles, the leader, ran for it. Slaughter nailed him twice as he ran, but the hardy outlaw vanished into the brush. Miraculously avoiding a revenge ambush—one of his deputies was killed instead—Slaughter relentlessly pursued Geronimo Miranda, the remaining member of the gang, seriously wounding him and driving him into Mexico with Robles, never to return.

At about this time a grateful citizenry asked Slaughter to run again for sheriff. Now, however, Viola put her foot down. His family and business needed him, she said, "and we don't feel that he would live through another term."[20] And that, even for tough John Slaughter, was that. The love of his life wanted him home, and he went back to his enormous spread and twenty-five thousand head of stock wearing his distinctive "Z" brand. But not to complete retirement, not Texas John Slaughter.

In 1894, legend has it, Slaughter again hit the back-trails, this time hunting for the notorious and extraordinarily dangerous Apache Kid. Slaughter, incensed by the Kid's killing of his friend, Bisbee sheriff John Williams, ran the renegade to earth in Guadalupe Canyon and put four bullets in him.[21]

Maybe so, maybe not, for it is only fair to say that no one is sure of the details of the Kid's demise. In fact, he was probably killed by a man called Yavapai Clark. Clark hit his man, the Kid or somebody else, but the blood trail petered out and Clark never found a body. Another story says the Apache Kid lived on in Mexico and died of natural causes, a tale espoused by none other than tough Col. Emilio Kosterlitzky.

Late in his career Slaughter also killed Peg-Leg Finney, a wanted thief about whom Slaughter was warned by telephone. This pioneering apparatus was the first in Slaughter's area. It traveled on iron poles of all things, but it worked, a great help to Slaughter and a bane to Peg-Leg, who made the grievous mistake of coming on to the San Bernardino and taking a nap under one of Slaughter's trees. When he awoke to find Slaughter and some other men staring down at him, he snatched his pistol and got a bullet from Slaughter's Winchester for his pains. By this time, John Slaughter was fifty-seven, a time when most men had begun to think of a little peace and quiet, but Texas John was not like anybody else, and he was not finished yet.

In 1900, a gambler-turned-thief called Little Bob Stevens stuck up a roulette game in Tombstone and fled on a stolen pony. Like the late unlamented Peg-Leg Finney, Stevens also made the mistake of seeking refuge on the San Bernardino and ran head-on into Slaughter. No expensive trial was necessary for Little Bob although there were some costs for a modest funeral.[22]

The next year, Slaughter joined a posse hunting a killer for hire who had murdered an entire family. When the posse finally ran him down, it is said, the murderer "resisted arrest"—maybe he really did—and Slaughter and the rest of the posse blew the man away. If Slaughter's hand was not quite as quick as it was in his salad days, his black eyes were just as steady and his philosophy towards criminals had not changed a whit with the years.

As the new century passed, Slaughter spent more and more time managing his thriving ranch and business interests, which now included a meat market in Charleston. In 1910 he acquired two more butcher shops in booming, copper-rich Bisbee. He was one of the founding members of the town of Douglas and its thriving bank and became a broker in mortgages on the side. Besides the San Bernardino and Viola, his lifelong love, Slaughter's consuming passion was poker, high-stakes games that often lasted from one day into the next. He and Viola entertained at San Bernardino cowboys, soldiers, and ranchers, men of every kind. Slaughter, who spoke fluent Spanish, often welcomed guests from Mexico, including Mexican presidents Madero and Huerta and the legendary Pancho Villa.

Slaughter's vital life stretched on into the 1920s, eventful almost to the end. In 1921, the year before his death, he suddenly looked up from his evening paper and reached for his Colt. The instinct was working again, and the old man was ready as ever to fight. Shots roared out just outside his house, and one of Slaughter's hands died in an aborted holdup attempt. The four assailants abandoned their plan to kill everybody at the ranch after Slaughter did not come out of the ranch house. Even though he was almost eighty, they dared not face that terrible little man, the man with death in his black eyes.

Towards the end of his life, Slaughter passed his days quietly in the sun at his beloved ranch, surrounded by a small pack of adoring dogs. He watched the children of his little empire playing in his yard, sat on the veranda with his memories and looking into Mexico, and brought Viola a rose from the garden each morning.

Old Bat, the fabulous black cowboy, passed away the year before Slaughter died, living his last years retired on the San Bernardino, well-supplied by his boss and old friend with his favorite treats, all the candy and soda he could ever want.

In his last days, Slaughter lived in the town of Douglas although he regularly visited his ranch and kept a hand in running it. He died in his sleep, as he had foreseen, in February 1922. Viola survived him by many years. So did his memory; it still does today.

## CHAPTER TEN

# Never Killed a Man Who Didn't Need It: Jeff Milton, Bob Paul, and Some Kindred Spirits

Fred Koch was not very bright, and he did not have much luck either. Fred was a bank robber, or at least he played the part. About noon on November 3, 1917, he stuck up a bank in Tombstone. That was bad enough, but worse was to come. In the process he mortally wounded banker T. R. Brandt when Brandt emerged from the vault with a shotgun instead of money. Where Fred wasn't very smart was in planning his big payday: he failed to assure himself a means of speedy retreat . . . and he failed to make sure that Jeff Milton was nowhere nearby.

As Koch fled Tombstone on foot, a stripped-down Model T rattled into the dusty town, driven by one of the deadliest men in the world. The quiet-voiced, hard-eyed driver was not far from sixty, but he carried the contempt for outlaws that had marked him all his days. Jeff Milton was cast in the same mold as Texas John Slaughter; he was not a good man to have on your trail. Milton stopped long enough to collect Guy Welch, the acting sheriff, then chugged off across the hills after Koch. It took a couple of miles, but Milton's hardy Ford gradually closed in on the panting robber. The lawmen got to within a hundred yards and the time came to reason with Koch. Neither Welch nor Milton had a rifle, but Milton piled out of the Model T with his handgun, yelling at Koch to halt. And when the fleeing man kept on running, Milton fired. The frontier Colt of previous years had given way to a .38 semiautomatic pistol, but Milton's eye was as keen as ever. The automatic banged, Koch went down with a slug in the arm, and Milton the man hunter had another scalp. Back in Tombstone, he stood between his trembling prisoner and an angry mob, preserving the simple-minded Koch for trial and an eventual one-way trip to an asylum. It had been just another day in the life for the fifty-six-year-old Milton, one of the deadliest—and least-known—man hunters in Western history.

Milton's long road had begun in 1861, near Marianna, Florida, and he came of fighting stock. His father, John, a planter and lawyer, was governor of Florida when Jeff first saw the light of day. The elder Milton, a passionate supporter of secession, named his new son for the president of the Confederacy. Jeff's great-grandfather had been a Revolutionary War captain, his grandfather was a colonel in the War of 1812, and Governor John had commanded an artillery unit in the Seminole War. Further back lay a long line of tough and civic-minded English Miltons, including the great blind poet who gave the world *Paradise Lost*.

After the Civil War, his father having committed suicide, young Jeff helped his mother fight to save what remained of the family lands. The lad was a devoted hunter and fisherman and an insatiable reader who even then loved tales of derring-do and gallantry. And in 1877, the restless young man moved west, out into a raw, new, dangerous land where only the strong survived, and the law was what a man carried on his hip. Out there a man made his own reputation, and where he came from did not matter. "The family had a coat of arms," said Jeff later. "I had it once, but I throwed it away. Didn't need it. Had my own coat and my own arms."[1] Young Jeff Milton, tall and tough, was on his way to Texas.

Milton worked in a store for a period then punched cows out on the Clear Fork of the Brazos. Out there this hardy young man learned the cowboy trade, and he also met a couple of men who would cross his path again in wild El Paso, for good or for evil. One was a young cowboy called George Scarborough, who in time would be one of the fabulous lawmen of West Texas and Milton's fast friend. The other was John Selman, gunman, rustler, and general no-good. But Jeff had a long trail to follow to West Texas.

In 1880, lying blandly that he was twenty-one, he was sworn into the Texas Rangers, and his long career as a lawman was launched. He spent three years as a Ranger, a liberal education in the ways of the scum of the Earth. In 1881, in Colorado City, Texas, as he tried to arrest a quarrelsome cowman with two other Rangers, the suspect drew and fired at one of Milton's companions, and Jeff cut the man down with a single .45 slug.

Law enforcement was the toughest business there was. A lawman had to be ready to fight at any time, and the quarry had to recognize that. The Rangers made the alternatives plain to the men they arrested, as in this exchange between Milton and one Dorsey. Dorsey began, "I won't go." Milton replied, "Let me tell you something, Dorsey. You either go or get killed, and I'll pull you in, just as you damned please." Dorsey said, "Well, if I've got to go . . ."

Milton and the other Rangers were constantly in the saddle—over a thousand miles on one manhunt alone—and were expected to keep the peace on short rations. Rangers lived mostly on beans, potatoes, rice, bacon, and coffee, and sometimes precious little of those. Even ammunition was rationed. Each ranger got twelve rifle cartridges each month and six for his pistol. They were expected to make each shot count or pay for the extras themselves.[2]

Three years of Ranger service were enough for restless Jeff, who drifted first to Fort Davis and then to Alpine (just plain Murphyville in those days). He ran a saloon for a while, thoughtfully attaching holstered revolvers to strategic points around the building. Those were tough days in a risky business, and it did not pay to be too far from a friend named Colt. Even a friendly game of pool had its hazards. Once, as Jeff played a self-proclaimed bad man and set himself for the winning shot, the hoodlum snarled, "Don't you knock that ball in!" Milton answered mildly, "Why, I don't see how I can help it." Threatened with "the damndest thrashing you ever got," Jeff calmly made his shot, reversed the cue, laid it across the bad man's head, "stomped him a little," and went on his way.[3]

And in time Jeff became a deputy sheriff in Murphyville, facing down the same wild, reckless cowboys he had chased when he wore a Ranger badge. With them he used the same direct, bluff approach as he did the day he confronted a saloon full of armed cowboys who had boasted they would run the law out of town. Jeff walked into the bar with a ten-gauge shotgun in his fists and made a little speech: "Boys, every damned one of you get your six-shooters off as fast as you can or I'll kill every damned one of you right here."[4] Coming from a hard-eyed professional like Milton, that was the kind of appealing logic cowboys understood. There was no more talk of running the law out of town.

In lots of ways, big Jeff Milton, for all his literacy and aristocratic background, was a simple, big-hearted man who could have been played by John Wayne in a movie. Like John Slaughter, he loved horses and dogs, all animals in fact, and would tolerate no cruelty to any of them. And to Jeff, as to Slaughter, all decent women were ladies, and real men treated them as such. Jeff would not tolerate gossip or backbiting about any nice girl. Nor, for that matter, about himself. Take the day a saddle maker told one Miss Levine that Jeff had made an indecent remark about her. Milton's reaction was predictable. Grabbing the saddler by the throat, Milton popped him with his pistol barrel and engaged him in polite conversation: "You're going up there and tell her you're a goddam [sic] lying son-of-a-b——, or

I'm going to kill you."[5] That seemed simple enough to the saddler, who acknowledged to Miss Levine—on his knees—that he was indeed a lying SOB. Milton oversaw the whole performance.

In later years, Jeff remembered the early days in Texas, and the chances he had had to invest in the new land and prosper with it: "It was a great country. And just to think what a man of my age could have done if he had had the sense of a louse. But I was a young buck who didn't give a damn whether school kept or not. I had a good time and I always kept one hundred dollars to bury myself if I should die."[6]

In 1884, Jeff moved on into New Mexico and soon became a deputy sheriff in Socorro County. New Mexico was as wild and woolly as places got in those days, as Jeff soon found out. When he and another man were ambushed by Mexican bandits down on the Gila River, Milton went down with a dead horse and a hole in his leg. Still, he got his Winchester clear, and when the smoke blew away three bandits were dead. Milton matter-of-factly dumped a liberal dose of turpentine into his wound, straddled his pack horse, and rode on to safety.

Around the same time, Milton had a close encounter with an even more dangerous enemy. This one was a grizzly bear, angry at Milton and intent on opening him up with those fearsome claws. Before the beast could do any major damage, Milton crammed the muzzle of his Colt into the bear's mouth and got off a round.

Not content with the dangers of law enforcement, Milton added hazardous sidelines. He became a stock detective, tracking the rustlers who plagued cattlemen, and he joined the volunteer force called Russell's Army, which tracked and fought the Apache raiders who still haunted Arizona. In 1887, Milton moved on to the border service, becoming one of twenty-five mounted officers responsible for almost a thousand miles of wild, unfenced, lawless border. Two years later, still restless, he drifted on to other things: operating a little horse ranch, service as a fireman, and a job as a conductor with the Southern Pacific. And then came El Paso.

In 1894 this dusty town on the Rio Grande needed law badly, and so it hired as sheriff the toughest man it could find, Jeff Milton. El Paso crawled with gunmen, outlaws, whores, con men, and criminals of every stripe. The town constable was gunfighter John Selman, who "protected" the local fancy houses for a fee. Selman did not like the looks of this tough young sheriff and quickly started boasting about where he would stick this young upstart's gun. Milton, in his own direct way, dealt with the problem by confronting Selman in an El Paso saloon. "How about the six-shooter?" said Milton. "I've got it on. Think you wanta use it on me?" And Selman, the famous man killer, backed down.

Milton had to confront Selman and his deputy one more time. This time he arrested the deputy for levying protection money from a couple of the town "Nymphs," and he explained to Selman and his man in his clear, simple way, "If you try it again, I'll put you both in jail. And if either of you ever starts any-thing with me again, I'm going to kill you, certain."[7]

Next Milton confronted the blustering bully who worked as enforcer for some of the worst saloons in town. This man he grabbed by the ear and kicked sprawling into the street. When the man started to get up, he was looking into the muzzle of Jeff's Colt. After forcing the man to crawl ignominiously into a saloon and deposit his pistol behind the bar, Milton gave him some of his usual wholesome instructions: "Next time you speak to me, come up and take your hat off. And don't pass me on the street without taking your hat off—at no time!"[8]

And that was that, at least until Milton had to face down John Wesley Hardin when that famous shootist came to El Paso to practice law. Jeff met Hardin armed in a saloon and told him he would have to check his pistols at the bar. Hardin looked at him quietly. "Do you know who you are talking to?" Jeff nodded. "I evidently do, sir . . . and I think if I were you . . . I'd take 'em off right now, before anything starts." Hardin studied the big quiet man with the level black eyes. "All right, Chief, we'll abide by the law."

In El Paso, Jeff renewed acquaintances with George Scarborough, who had been sheriff down in Jones County, Texas, and in the 1890s was a deputy U.S. marshal in El Paso. Dee Harkey, a very tough *hombre* himself, knew both men well. "There were some shooting sheriffs, good and bad. George Scarborough and Jeff Milton were . . . both good officers; they used to say, 'Kill the outlaws and get rid of them,'" he described.[9]

Milton and Scarborough shared the same feelings about outlaws, and now they were about to go through the fire together.

Jeff Milton (left) and fellow lawman George Scarborough, ca. 1895, El Paso, Texas. (*Courtesy Arizona Historical Society, Tucson*)

On a June night in 1895, Scarborough crossed the railroad bridge in Juarez on the Mexican side of the Rio Grande to meet and return with one Martin Morose (or M'Rose or Morocz). Although Morose was wanted for a variety of delicts in Texas, his heart was in El Paso, where lived his voluptuous wife and his money, the lady increasingly courted by John Wesley Hardin. As Morose and Scarborough approached the American side, Milton and a Texas Ranger ordered Morose to surrender. Instead, the man went for his gun, and a slug from Milton's .45 knocked him down. As he started to rise, shooting, Scarborough shot him again, and this time Morose did not get up. One tale quotes Morose as saying, "Boys, you've killed me," which led Scarborough to reply, "Stop trying to get up, then, and we'll quit."[10]

The shooting caused a tremendous uproar in El Paso, as men took sides with or against Milton or Morose. Both Scarborough and Milton were accused of murder, a charge which hung on in the courts for years before it was finally dismissed. And the affair brought Milton head to head with an increasingly alcoholic Hardin, who boasted he had hired Milton to kill Morose. Milton dealt with Hardin's lie directly, in front of a city saloon and a crowd of witnesses. "You're not only a goddamed [sic] liar; you're a goddamed [sic] lying son-of-a-b——, and you are now going to tell these gentlemen you are."[11] Hardin, the icy killer of a least fifteen men, abjectly told the witnesses exactly that.

Although no one ever established that either Milton or Scarborough did anything wrong in connection with the Morose affair, the dispute and accusation after Morose's death drove both men out of El Paso. However, Wells Fargo knew a good man when it saw one and hired Milton as a special agent out in Arizona. In short order both he and Scarborough were in action again, surviving a wild shootout with a gang headed by killer and holdup man Bronco Bill Walters.

In July 1898, they came upon Bronco Bill and two of his men in the wild country of eastern Arizona, near the settlement of Solomonville. Walters instantly jerked his pistol and opened up on Milton, but the lawman's return fire ripped through the outlaw's lungs and knocked him from his saddle. Scarborough and Milton killed a second hoodlum's horse then turned their fire on a third wanted man, one Bill Johnson, who was working his rifle overtime from behind a juniper. Johnson left a bit of one hip exposed, however, and went down with a bullet from Milton that travled all the way up into his abdomen before it stopped. He died that night. Milton dispatched a rider to the Solomonville sheriff. His courier, who rejoiced in the peculiar handle of Climax Jim, carried a message that was pure, vintage Milton: "Send a coffin and a doctor."[12]

On another occasion, according to one legend, Milton and a posse laid a successful ambush for the High Five gang along the Arizona-New Mexico border. This tale tells that Milton shouted an order to surrender, but the outlaws dug for their weapons. Milton put four slugs into a bravo called Bill "Black Jack" Christian, who hit the ground mortally wounded. In return, Milton was nicked by a bullet from the gun of Three-Fingered Jack Dunlap, who escaped in the confusion. It is an appealing story, but it probably did not happen that way. Black Jack Christian was indeed exterminated by the law near Clifton, Arizona, but the exterminators were headed by Deputy Marshal Fred Higgins. No doubt Milton would have loved to be part of that action for he had hunted the High Fives in the past.

In time, Milton became a Wells Fargo express messenger, another ultra-hazardous occupation in those days of regular train robberies. And in February 1900, Milton went up against five outlaws from ex-lawman Burt Alvord's gang. One of them, says the abiding myth, was the same Dunlap who held a longstanding grudge against Milton, dating back to the killing of Black Jack Christian. Grudge or no grudge, as Milton's train pulled into the station at tiny Fairbank— a wide spot in the road not far from Tombstone—Three-Fingered Jack and the others were waiting. The gang fired on Milton, smashing his left arm, cutting its artery, and knocking him to the floor of the express car. The terrible wound would have finished anybody but Milton. Instead, Jeff fired both barrels of his shotgun one-handed, dropping Three-Fingered Jack with eleven shots in his worthless body. As Dunlap went down, gang member Bravo Juan Yoas yelped with a buckshot in the behind, and the other three bandits ducked. Milton managed to slam the car door, lock the safe, and throw away the keys. He had passed out by the time the remaining gang members broke into the car, which probably saved his life.

The bandits got nothing, thanks to Milton's courage, but he would never recover full use of his shattered arm. Though he successfully resisted his doctor's advice to amputate, even Jeff realized he would have to find a somewhat quieter line of work. In 1904, with the help of friends, Milton was appointed the Chinese agent along the Arizona border, trying to stem the hordes of illegal oriental immigrants being spirited from Mexico. Milton stayed on with the agency, which became the Immigration Service as of 1913, as it became bigger and more formal. Then, in 1919, lifelong bachelor Milton met and married a maiden New York schoolteacher. He was fifty-eight and Mildred Tait was forty, but the match was made in heaven, as people said in those simple days. Jeff labored happily on for the United States, begrudging only the time away from his beloved Mildred.

Neither then nor afterward did Milton talk much about his decades of law enforcement. He was quick enough to tell stories of the wild country, of tough rides and long manhunts, but he seldom got to the details of the ends of those expeditions. Once, when his wife saw a bullet scar on his jaw and asked who had shot him, Milton replied tersely, "A man who is not alive," and said no more. And when a doctor friend asked what happened to the subject of still another manhunt up in the Mogollons, Milton said simply, "He's still there."

Milton retired in 1933 at age seventy-two and died quietly in Tucson in the spring of 1947. As he wanted, Mildred had his ashes scattered in the desert southwest of the city. In 1936 the Immigration Service named a patrol boat for him, a pleasant monument to a life of uncompromising courage and enforcement of the law.

Jeff Milton was not a man for speeches, certainly not speeches about the profound meaning of life. His philosophy was as simple as you can get, and this is the way he put it: "I never killed a man who didn't need killing; I never shot an animal except for meat." Which isn't a bad epitaph for anybody.

Milton was one of a tough, dedicated breed of men who regularly took long chances for meager wages, enforcing what law there was in the raw new West. Arizona had its share of these lawmen, hard men like Commodore Perry Owens, the Earps, and Bob Paul. There were others less well known today but just as tenacious. Take for example Dan Tucker, a quiet man who did not know fear. Like so many of his compatriots, he came from someplace else. Born in Canada, he spent some time up in Colorado before he arrived in New Mexico, where for a time he ran a stage station along the Jornada del Muerte. As a deputy in Deming, New Mexico, he walked the streets carrying a shotgun and is said to have killed three bad men in three days. In September 1881, he blew away one Jake Bond, a rustler from Arizona's San Simon Valley. Bond had more sand than sense and grabbed for his rifle when Tucker told him he was under arrest. "Without further parleying," a newspaper reported, "the officer fired, landing nine buckshot in Bond's body." Bond "instantly fell to the ground, a corpse."[13]

Jeff Kidder was of the same breed, a handsome young man who came out of Vermillion, South Dakota, and ended in wild and wooly Arizona. All his teenage and adult life, Kidder practiced endlessly with his pistols, and by the time he came south in 1903 to join the recently established Arizona Rangers he was an accomplished shootist. Ordinarily, Kidder was courteous and well-behaved, but when he had been drinking, he turned into a different man. He did not lose his temper during the Rangers' successful opposition to a strike by hundreds of angry Bisbee miners, but in 1904, outside the Turf Saloon in Bisbee, he clubbed down—"buffaloed"—three men. Whatever the cause of the fracas, Kidder was vilified in the press and charged with assault. Convicted on one count only, he paid a fine and went on his quarrelsome way. He even locked horns with formidable Jeff Milton in Cazobon's Restaurant in Nogales one day. The result depends on whose account you read. Milton said he backed Kidder down; a witness said Kidder insulted Milton even though Milton had a gun leveled at him; still another related that the two shot at each other, fortunately without result.

When he was sober, though, they did not come any tougher than Kidder. The captain of the Rangers said the young man was the best he had, and when Kidder received an inheritance from his father, he spent much of it—perhaps thousands—on more ammunition for his endless practice. In the end, he was almost miraculously fast and accurate. And deadly. Another Ranger said Kidder "in a pinch would shoot first and ask the questions later on, if there was anybody left to answer them." Shades of John Slaughter.

He operated, as did other Arizona lawmen, on both sides of the Mexican border, for in those days the Sonora Rurales, the Mexican Rural Guard, were commanded by the legendary Col. Emelio Kosterlitzky, who was perfectly willing to ignore little things like borders and jurisdictional niceties. And back in Arizona, there remained endless work for lawmen. Kidder killed a man who resisted arrest in Douglas, buffaloed another in Benson, and in Flagstaff flattened a bully in an epic fistfight. Promoted to sergeant, he did much to bring relative peace to Nogales. He was both feared and respected, a useful combination for any lawman.

In the end, it may have been too much drink that brought Jeff Kidder down. Just across the border in Naco, Mexico—a dismal place then and afterward—he spent some time with a lady of the evening called Chia. When he left, he accused her of stealing money from him, whereat she yelled for the police. Two of them appeared, and one immediately shot Kidder in the belly. Sitting on the floor, Kidder downed both men. What happened afterward was brutal in the extreme. Kidder tried to reach the border fence, fighting all the way and wounding still a third policeman. Out of ammunition, he surrendered and was dragged to jail, repeatedly clubbed with pistols. Not until the next day could two American doctors reach him, and by then they could do little for his battered body.

Kidder was dying and he knew it. Game to the end, he told a friend, "They got me, but if my ammunition had not run out, I might have served them the same way." After Kidder died, a full day elapsed before the local authorities gave permission to take his remains back to the American side. It was a good thing they did, said Captain Wheeler of the Rangers, for if they had not, "a thousand men were coming to take it."

One postscript remains. Billy Old, Kidder's close friend, is said to have remembered his friend's murder and decided it was up to him to do something about it. After the Rangers disbanded in 1909, he vanished into Mexico. Some who knew both men thought he spent the next two years running down and killing those responsible for Kidder's death.

George Scarborough also gets a few paragraphs here although he really deserves a chapter all to himself. A one-time Texas cowboy, Scarborough is now chiefly remembered for killing veteran gunman John Selman in El Paso's Wigwam Saloon in April 1895. But Scarborough was much more than a shootist. Over a considerable career as a lawman, he rode with Jeff Milton and others in pursuit of some of the worst hoodlums Arizona ever saw.

Scarborough spent his life taking chances, and at last the odds caught up with him. Tracking rustlers said to be part of the Wild Bunch, the Doolin-Daltin gang, near San Simon in April 1900, he and another man came up with their quarry and chased them into a box canyon. In the fight that followed, Wild Bunch alumnus Harvey Logan got a bullet into Scarborough's leg. A doctor in Deming, New Mexico, tried to save him by amputating the leg, but the radical surgery did not work, and the lawman died the next day. Just a little more than four years later, Logan, badly wounded by a posse near Glenwood Springs, Colorado, put a bullet into his own head rather than be captured alive.

Finally, there was Bob Paul, whom some say was the best and toughest lawman ever to keep the peace in Arizona. Paul was a quiet man, reluctant to kill, but as formidable an officer as ever walked. Born in Massachusetts, he went to sea on whalers for at least three long voyages of storms and dreary months at sea and survived a broken leg inflicted by an angry whale. In 1849 he had had enough of the sea and came ashore to stay in booming San Francisco. He headed for the Sierra gold country and did well in a series of mining camps. He then became a deputy sheriff in Calaveras County—home of Mark Twain's jumping frog—and ran to earth the notorious Bell gang, plague of honest miners across the mountains. He and his posse killed one and captured the rest, saving them for prison and Bell himself for the gallows.

His popularity sky-high with law-abiding people, he was elected sheriff and served two terms. But then the lure of placer mining called him back in 1865; he was stone broke by 1874. Paul began to ride shotgun for Wells Fargo, and by 1877 the company made him a detective and sent him to Arizona. Tombstone, by 1880 in the throes of the Earp-cowboy struggle, ran Paul for sheriff against Charlie Shibell. Shibell won the election narrowly, largely on the returns from lawless Galeyville, where he beat Paul 103 to 1. Considering the dubious margin and the fact that more votes were cast than there were registered voters, Paul contested the election and the courts agreed with him.

There are all kinds of fanciful stories about the Galeyville election. One of them—the best one—says that Wyatt Earp, a friend of Paul's, told Curly Bill Brocius he would swear Brocius had been guilty of murder in the death of respected marshal Fred White on the street in Tombstone. The price of his silence, said Wyatt, was information about the stuffing of the ballot boxes in Galeyville. Maybe, but the essence of the fraud at Galeyville is caught by a different story more likely to be true. In the San Simon precinct, where Galeyville lay, those charged with seeing the democratic process safely followed were the election inspector—Ike Clanton of all people—and two election judges, none other than John Ringo and one H. A. Thompson. The election results were certified by a man called Henry Johnson, and he turned out to be James K. Johnson, a follower of Curly Bill and present when Brocius killed Marshal White in Tombstone. The *Weekly Star* paraphrased the Bard, commenting that there was "something very rotten in Denmark."

While he awaited the outcome of the litigation, Paul again rode shotgun for Wells Fargo. And so it was that on March 15, 1881, he rode the Benson stage with driver Eli

"Bud" Philpot, beginning the tale of murder and pursuit that resulted in the Earp-cowboy shootout. Paul was a staunch ally of the Earps, so much so that he refused to join Behan and a posse of Clantons, John Ringo, and the like, fearing the Earps would be murdered once disarmed and in Tombstone. Thereafter he traveled to Colorado, where Holliday and the Earps then were. Still apprehensive for their safety if they were returned to Arizona, he and the Arizona governor appealed to the governor of Colorado to deny extradition. It was denied.

Paul went on serving as sheriff, arresting a rich variety of murderers and thieves. Some of his quarry included the Red Jack Almer gang, murderers of a Wells Fargo messenger on the stage between Glove and Florence. Three of the gang were quickly captured; two of them were lynched (see "Pearl Hart and Other Losers") and the third died before trial of something somewhat vaguely called "nervous prostration." Paul ran down the rest, following so closely that the outlaws lost their supplies, including Red Jack's hat, a copy of the reward notice stuffed inside.[14] In the Rincon Mountains, Paul's posse blew away Red Jack and badly wounded Charlie Hensley, said to have been the actual killer of the Wells Fargo messenger. Hensley fled, but the posse soon caught up. He fired on the posse and managed to kill Paul's horse, but the return fire tore a hole in his head.

In 1884, Paul ran for sheriff again, again lost, and again asserted some of the votes were false. A judge ordered him to vacate the office, but he hung on for more than a year, until he peacefully yielded the office to his opponent. Paul tried mining again, without notable success, then hired on with the Southern Pacific Railroad in January 1888 as a "special officer." He went right to work, chasing three bandits who had held up a train at Stein's Pass, pursuing them all the way into Mexico. With the help of a Mexican army detachment, he and his posse ran down the robbers, who took refuge in a house. Paul solved that problem by setting fire to the house and simply blew the outlaws away when they ran out shooting.

Bob Paul was appointed United States marshal of Arizona Territory in 1888, to the rejoicing of Arizonans. One newspaper put it this way: "Paul is known throughout the Southwest as a fearless man, who has frequently taken his life in his own hands in the pursuit of criminals." When the administration changed, he was replaced as marshal. He was feeling his years by that time, and ill health caught up with him in March 1901. He left behind his wife and five children, a towering reputation, and an admiring public. The *Arizona Daily Citizen* wrote a warm obituary and perfectly caught the essence of the man: "He was a brave man, and did his duty."

CHAPTER ELEVEN

# Pearl Hart and Other Losers

Early Arizona was as tough a land as ever men saw in the United States. A Bostonian lecturer told his audience what a wonderful place Arizona was. Why, he said, "all they lacked was plenty of water and good society." To which a member of the audience replied, "That's all they lack in hell."[1] They were both right. The member of the audience might have added that this promising land was also overstocked with dangerous, lawless people. These undesirables were much given to stealing anything of even marginal value, but they were especially fond of the stagecoach.

Hoodlums have been robbing stages ever since the days of England's dashing Dick Turpin. The same crime was a staple of the American West, providing lawless men with a sort of rolling repository of money, gold watches, bullion, and other highly desirable goods. Once trains arrived and started carrying things of value, especially gold and silver in the express car, the criminal fraternity turned to robbing them as well. Nobody knows for sure who the first American train robbers really were. Generally, the dubious honor of being first is awarded to the Reno brothers, a set of Midwestern criminals. The price tag for the Reno gang's brief notoriety quickly proved a trifle steep: the brothers and seven of their confederates were summarily lynched. That did not stop imitators, however, including the Dalton boys; two of them ended up dead on the streets of Coffeyville, Kansas, and another in prison. No wiser, a batch of imitators carried on.

Some of them briefly infested Arizona although no one

had much lasting success. They seemed to suffer from a raging case of criminal's disease, known nonclinically as "terminally dumb." Take the case of Grant Wheeler and Joe George. In January 1895, these two stuck up a Southern Pacific train near Willcox, dynamiting the through safe. The through safe was an innovation of the express business. It went from origin to destination without keys; it could only be opened at its destination, an expedient which often discouraged or disappointed the covetous. Wheeler and George discovered the safe held more than a thousand dollars in paper money, but what they did not figure on was several thousand dollars in pesos carried in sacks. The sacks did seem handy to stack on their dynamite, and when they touched off the explosive a shower of pesos screamed off in all directions, a silver shrapnel that whined through the air and slammed into trees, telegraph poles, and the wood of the express car itself. The robbers survived the storm of pesos, however, and galloped off with what was left of their loot.

The next month they came back to the well, this time at Stein's Pass, and this time what passed for their plans came quickly unglued. The density of the robbers led them to cleverly detach the car. Trouble was, they cut loose the mail car instead of the express car. No safe; no money. Sheriff Billy Breakenridge and a posse chased Wheeler all the way into Colorado and surrounded him near a place called Mancos. Wheeler fired a few shots at the posse and the last one into himself. A high price for a handful of bills and some battered silver pesos.[2] Joe Boot did not fare any better, unless a piece of transitory notoriety was worth a sentence of thirty years in Yuma prison. Joe escaped after a couple of years, but the dubious fame would cloud his life.

Joe had a cohort in crime, a diminutive female called Pearl Hart, shrouded to this day in a swirling mist of mythology. She was grandiloquently called the "bandit queen" in some accounts, more elegantly the "lady bandit" in others. The truth was far more prosaic. In fact, Pearl was a mining camp cook, possibly a prostitute, or maybe a singer, depending on which story you read. One newspaper somewhat vaguely said she "wrestled with the world in a catch-as-catch-can style,"[3] which could mean about anything.

She was Canadian by birth, said to have run off at about sixteen with a ne'er-do-well named Hart, who didn't work very well and didn't do it much. He was worthless by all accounts, brutal, lazy, and unpleasant, and that was on his good days. Pearl had a child by Hart (she would later have a second, rumored to have been fathered by another man), but in time she got tired of his sloth and brutality. She left him repeatedly and took him back almost as often. At last even Pearl had enough, took her child back to her mother in Canada, and returned to Arizona, the land of her dreams.

The mythology gets thick here. Some tales of Pearl cast her as a sort of early-day feminist, inspired by watching Annie Oakley at the Chicago Columbian Exposition in 1893 and listening to suffragette speeches there while Hart carried on with his fumbling career as barker. In any case, the story goes, Pearl settled in Arizona, cooking, performing, and turning tricks until she heard that her mother was grievously ill and in need of money. She turned to crime purely to raise money for her mother, or that was what Pearl would later tell a jury.

Pearl drifted from town to town, ending in Phoenix. "I was good-looking, desperate, discouraged, and ready for anything that might come . . . I do not care to dwell on this period of my life." Or so she (or someone claiming to be her) wrote in *Cosmopolitan* in 1899.[4] In Phoenix she reunited with her husband. This time the honeymoon continued for some three years and another child, until he started raising lumps on her again. That was the end of the affair, and Hart went off to join the war in Cuba.

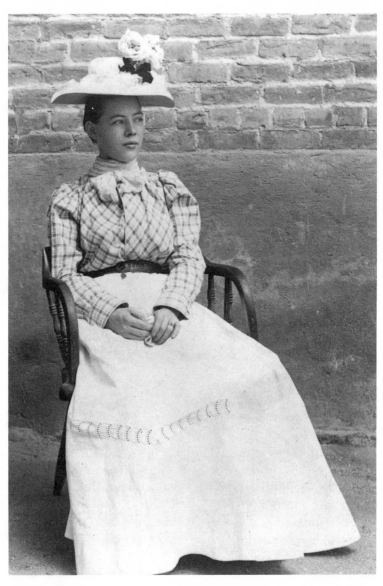

Pearl Hart, the last stage robber in American history—male or female. (*Courtesy Arizona Historical Society, Tucson*)

By now Pearl was deeply depressed and tried suicide, but friends intervened. She found work as a camp cook at Mammoth, living in a tent, her health declining. Then she met Joe Boot, variously described as a miner, farmer, cowboy, or musician. Joe wanted to go to Globe. She went with him and found work as a cook in a miner's boarding house, until the mine or mill shut down and she was again unemployed.

Re-enter the egregious, omnipresent Hart. This time Pearl refused to support the lazy slob, and he left, never to be seen again. About this time someone wrote her that her mother was seriously ill and she must return home quickly. "That letter drove me crazy," she wrote. According to Pearl her brother had already hit her up for what little money she had, so she had no money for train fare back to Canada. As she searched for an answer to her financial dilemma, Joe Boot told her he had a fine claim where they would hit pay dirt. They set out and Pearl swung a pick and shovel just as he did: lots of dirt, no pay.

Some sources say Pearl was the moving force in inspiring Joe to forsake the path of righteousness for the fast lane. In a piece in *Cosmopolitan* magazine in 1899, she said he was the villain of the play, as far as robbing a stage. Joe convinced her robbery was the only way to raise money, and she relented: "Joe, I said, if you promise me that no one will be hurt, I will go with you."[5]

One version of her legend says that before they went stage robbing, the two robbed passersby interested in a roll in the hay with Pearl, something of a looker, at least by frontier standards. Once in her room, however, the avid stranger would be whopped by Joe, who took his money. That ploy either proved to be too dangerous or it did not pay enough—maybe it never happened at all—but it may have been the basis for still another tale that has them running a brothel.

The claim being a bust, Joe proposed they rob the Globe stage, according to the *Cosmopolitan* article. Pearl, however, later boasted that she was the leader, demanding at gunpoint that Joe accompany her. Joe, in this version, went along for love of her. Besides, she is supposed to have said that if he did not go along with her plan "I would have killed him and he knew it, too."[6] No matter who proposed the crime, Pearl finally decided it was her ticket to Canada. They posted themselves at a curve where they knew the stage would have to slow down. When the stage got close, they walked their horses down the road, and when they met it, hauled out their handguns. It all worked as they had planned, and Pearl ordered the passengers out into the road.

There are stories about the passengers falling all over themselves as they tried to exit the stage and Pearl giving them orders. But the driver, one tale tells, recognized both Pearl and Joe. Pearl searched not only the passengers, but the coach, finding a couple of pistols stashed down in the passengers' seats and taking them, a casual act that would in time generate a vast amount of trouble for her. "I can't see why men carry revolvers, because they almost invariably give them up at the very time they were made to be used."[7] A fair comment, for the three passengers offered no resistance. Two of the passengers did not have much money, but one was carrying almost four hundred dollars, which would buy a lot of railroad tickets. Pearl, sorrowing, or maybe posturing as the big-time road agent, returned to each of the victims a whole buck to eat on. She called it a "charitable contribution." There was no violence, and the two robbers rode off toward Benson, where they intended to catch a train and disappear.

One version of Pearl's storied exploit tells that she was identified in the newspapers, called by one the "daring lady bandit." The same story called Boot "a miner well known in Florence." Whether they were immediately identified or not, their lack of prior planning made the pursuit a lot easier than it should have been. They had apparently not thought about an escape plan or even looked over the countryside through which they would have to flee. Pearl described part of their ride as "awful . . . over perilous trails and the precipitous cañons." They camped on the east bank of the Gila but instead of moving on quickly stayed a full twenty-four hours, riding on the next night. The next camping spot was close to road traffic, so they sought out a cave, shooting a wild boar who was there first. The next night they again set out. Joe went into Mammoth for some supplies, and they kept moving. Rain was pouring down and their horses were bone weary, so they camped for another full day, moving on at night. According to one account, by now they were hopelessly lost and found themselves back on the stage road only a little way from the site of the holdup.

Along the way, says one version of their odyssey, they tried to jump a creek on their worn-out horses. Pearl, "a good rider" (of course) cleared the creek, but Joe did not. He "went down twice" before Pearl hauled him out and spent "the next hour fishing muddy ditch water from the lungs of her outlaw lover."[8] Pearl told the tale a little differently: "Joe's horse fell in, and for a while I thought they would both be drowned. . . . I sat in my saddle perfectly helpless."[9]

After Joe was "rescued" from the creek, the two spent a miserable night in the rain, eating cold beans. If the night was bad, the morning was worse, for they were unpleasantly awakened by the baleful stare of the bores of a couple of rifles. The owners turned out to be members of a sheriff's posse, and Joe and Pearl were out of the crime business.

Joe took up residence in the jail at Florence, county seat of Pima County, where the holdup had taken place. Pearl tried suicide again—or pretended to. One story says she gobbled talcum powder, which fooled no one, and she was moved to Tucson, where there were better accommodations for women. She apparently traveled in ladylike garb, prompting the *Phoenix Republican* to comment somewhat spitefully that she "proved not as good looking a girl as she had been as a boy." For her part, Pearl said afterward, "I did hate to leave Joe, who had been so considerate of me during all the ups and downs of the wild chase."

Pearl was not through playing tough bandit. After supper one night she used a knife from the jail silverware to dig out enough bricks in her cell to make a hole large enough to slither through. She may have gotten help from one Ed Hogan (or maybe Ed Sherwood), said to be, of all things, a well-known bicycle thief. The two escaped together, planning to form an outlaw gang, reported one paper, of which she was to be the "bandit queen."[10]

Caught with a male companion—presumably Hogan— by lawman George Scarborough, Pearl was "in a state of undress" and told Scarborough she could not possibly go with him, all her clothing being in the Chinese laundry. Scarborough was not sympathetic. He told her to dress in her boyfriend's clothing, and back she went to jail. She was, said Scarborough, one of the most foul-mouthed people he had ever heard.

Pearl found herself a celebrity. After all, female bandits did not come along every day. There are a couple of tales that she trumpeted a good deal of claptrap about refusing to be tried by a law for which as a woman she could not vote. One tale quotes the *Arizona Star* as editorializing, "Why should a woman be indicted, put on trial, convicted and sentenced under a law she or her sex had no part in making."[11]

At trial, Pearl turned on the tears for the jurors, claiming she would never have participated in such crimes except for the need for money and out of devotion to her mother. And it worked. Acquitted in spite of the evidence, Pearl rejoiced.

The judge did not. Quickly re-arrested, Pearl was tried for larceny relating to one of the pistols she had purloined during the holdup. This time a new jury saw the evidence in a different light and convicted her. The sentence was five years, not excessive in view of Joe's thirty.

Joe cut himself some impromptu amnesty, escaping after a couple of years to disappear from history. After serving something like half her sentence, Pearl was pardoned. One wonderfully lurid legend tells that she was pregnant—or claimed she was—when she got out. That made the situation somewhat delicate, or so the story goes, since the only men who had been alone with her in her cell were a minister, a trusty, and the territorial governor.[12] Nevertheless, there is no record of her giving birth to anything thereafter except more tales of her short, unsuccessful career as an outlaw. What is certain is that she continued to play the celebrity while in jail, the center of attention of various writers who cranked out fanciful stories and had her photographed carrying an assortment of firearms, presumably unloaded. Since the jailers had access to her too, the story about impregnation by clergy or state officials is a little thin, but the tale is too good to leave out.

What happened to Pearl after that is unclear. There is a tale that she journeyed north, intending to capitalize on her notoriety as the famous lady bandit. Maybe she was to sing or act in a play about herself written by her sister, a Mrs. Frizell, a drama somewhat prosaically entitled "The Arizona Bandit." Whatever she did, it does not seem to have been a smashing success. Other tales have her running a Kansas City cigar store, getting arrested as part of a gang of pickpockets, and working for Buffalo Bill's Wild West show. In fact, Pearl probably came back to Arizona, her first love, and lived for many years peacefully in Dripping Springs as wife of a rancher. Far from robbing stages, she ended her days "gardening and writing in a diary." It is worth noting that her mother was alive when Pearl got out of prison.

Fast forward about twenty-five years for the best part of Pearl's legend. The story goes that an "elderly lady" walked into the Pima County jail and asked to look the prison over. When asked why, she said that she was Pearl Hart and wanted to see her old cell. She was accommodated by the jail staff, thanked them, and walked away into history.[13]

Pearl remained unrepentant, it is said, telling and retelling the tale of her undistinguished criminal career. Would she do it again? You bet, said Pearl. She would have enjoyed a latter-day fable that told of her planning a robbery with none other than Jesse James, helping Jesse escape the law and riding melodramatically off into the sunrise with him to her hideout. Never mind that Jesse had been dead since 1882, in which year Pearl would have been about eleven.

Pearl commemorated herself in poetry, not very good but apparently florid enough for the times. It went in part like this:

> My partner speaking lightly said the stage would be here
> soon;
> We saw it coming round the bend and called to them to
> halt.
> Then to their pockets we did attend;
> If they got hurt 'twas their own fault.[14]

As with Pearl and Joe, determined pursuit by the law had a lot to do with the generally poor return on train and stage robbery. In March 1889, for example, four men held up an A and P train at the station in Canyon Diablo and made off with loot from the express car money box. The crooks' major error was committing their crime in Yavapai County, where Sheriff Billy O'Neill held sway. O'Neill and three deputies promptly gave chase and hung on the criminals' trail all the way up into southeastern Utah. When the long pursuit ended, a wild and ineffective gun battle followed, some fifty shots producing only a wound to one of the robbers' horses.

But the lawmen did succeed in routing their quarry, who fled into the surrounding hills without their all-important mounts. The lawmen followed on horseback and in short order rounded up John Smith, Bill Sitrin, D. M. Haverick, and a man who rejoiced in the name of Long John Halford. After all the agony and danger, the bandits were carrying only about a thousand dollars in booty.

Their brief, fruitless career was typical of most of Arizona's amateur outlaws, whose cupidity always outdid their ability. Old Man Clanton's son Peter is a good example of these losers. He became a student of horse thievery and joined up with a likeminded gang in rustlers' heaven around the village of St. Johns. In due course the good citizens had enough and in 1877 a "citizens' committee" rode out to abate the nuisance. A wild fight followed in which two of the committee were killed. Peter forted up in somebody's house, but the committee pulled away part of the roof and blazed away inside, killing Peter. Two of his compatriots surrendered, but on their way into town in the care of a single lawman, they were taken from the officer by a band of citizens and summarily hanged.

If sheer determination were the sole criterion for success in the stealing business, Frank Armer should have been a worldbeater. It did not work out that way. Frank was a cowboy out of the Tonto Basin who partnered up with a buddy named Rogers to get rich on train robbery. Frank, only twenty at the time, clambered across the coal of a tender to stop a train near Maricopa, where Rogers joined him. They did not get much for their pains, but they got away—for a while. The two had obviously thought long and hard about their maiden voyage into crime, for they rode around in circles through the surrounding desert, presumably to leave tracks to confuse any pursuit. They did not reckon with the expertise of Indian trackers, who cut across the circles of tracks and sorted out the bandits' escape in short order. The bandits had split up, but all that meant was that they were swept up individually, Rogers down on the Gila River and Armer in Phoenix. Armer tried to shoot it out with the law but ended up wounded and on his way to Yuma, sentenced to thirty long years.

Here begins the saga of Armer's grim determination. First he tried to tunnel out of prison, and his tunnel was not discovered until he was almost clear of the walls. Undaunted, Armer later ran for his freedom while working outside the prison. This attempt ended with him ignominiously clutching the earth, sheltering from the fire of a Gatling gun mounted on the prison walls. Again permitted to work outside, Armer ran for it a third time, but his brief freedom ended on the Gila River when Indian trackers ran him down. That was almost literally the end for Armer. He did breathe free air again, but only briefly and not very much and only when he was released in the last stages of tuberculosis. He died very soon afterward at his mother's home.

In September 1899, a westbound Southern Pacific train was held up when it stopped at a small station at Cochise. The bandits struck at midnight, and there was no resistance from the train crew, which included express messenger Charles Adair, who only the previous year had killed a would-be train robber on the same run. The haul was unusual, much better than most train or stage holdups brought in, some ten thousand dollars in gold and paper, and the four bandits got away into the wild ridges and draws of the Chiricahuas. Although the law pursued, led by, among others, the formidable George Scarborough, the bandits were not caught—until the next February, that is, when the Nogales-Benson train was robbed at Fairbank. Only this time the express messenger was Jeff Milton, lawman and man hunter.

A couple of versions of the fight that followed have the gang making certain Milton was not the messenger on this train, but somebody went down sick and Milton stepped in to take his place. Summoned to surrender, Milton held his fire: the railroad platform was crowded with people, the bandits mixed in among them. He knew that if he fired on the outlaws, he would almost surely hit one or more innocents. Knowing no such civilized scruples, the bandits shot Milton several times. As Milton fell back into the car and the bandits starting climbing in, with the civilians now out of his line of fire, Milton replied with his shotgun, ushering career criminal Three-Fingered Jack Dunlap into the hereafter by the slow route. He also got at least one buckshot into the fanny of fleeing felon Bravo Juan Yoas, who forthwith lost all interest in larceny. Milton lost consciousness but before he did, he managed to throw away the keys to the safe. The holdup men fled, along the way abandoning the dying Dunlap at a place called Buckshot Springs.

Dunlap was not pleased with being left behind. When the law collected him, at first he remained stoically silent, but as he sank away he named names before he passed to his reward. The officers ran down two of the robbers, and Yoas was captured later in Mexico. More information followed, there being no honor among these thieves. Some servants of the law were involved in the planning of the crime, they said: Burt Alvord, Billy Stiles, and Bill Downing. All three ended up in the calabozo.

Alvord and Stiles had a history of law enforcement, Alvord in particular having few scruples about using his gun. A man called Six Shooter Jim, real name unknown, became a resident of Tombstone's Boot Hill courtesy of Alvord. Downing is a more enigmatic character, a two-time jailbird improbably said by some to be Frank Jackson, survivor of the Sam Bass gang's 1878 shootout with local lawmen in Round Rock, Texas.[15] Alvord and Stiles eventually escaped. Alvord is said to have spread a rumor that he and Stiles had been killed, and even ordered a couple of coffins. The

ruse did not work, and Alvord spent a couple of years in
Yuma before he was released and vanished from the United
States. According to legend, Stiles ended up in China, of
all places, eventually returning to the United States and
getting himself killed in Nevada while working as a lawman
under an alias. One tale has Stiles and Alvord cutting a deal
with Arizona Rangers captain Burt Mossman to help lure
Augustine Chacón out of Mexico and back to captivity and
death in the United States.

Then there was vastly overrated Tom Ketchum, known
to outlaw history as Black Jack, chiefly famous for his
spectacular exit from this life. He was a Texan by birth,
big, strong, and, like most of his fellow outlaws, not awfully
bright. He was and is often confused with Will "Black Jack"
Christian. He led a small gang of likeminded thugs who
managed a couple of successful crimes until they made the
error of trying a train holdup at Stein's Pass, just across
the New Mexico line. The express car was not the traveling
bonanza they looked forward to: it was full of Wells Fargo men
who promptly opened fire. In the ensuing battle, outlaw Ed
Cullen absorbed a load of buckshot and announced, "Boys,
I'm dead." Sure enough, he was. That was the end of the
gang, who had lost confidence in Black Jack's leadership.
His followers, including his brother, departed. Brother Sam
joined longtime robbers Elzy (or Elza) Lay and Will Carver,
but both he and Lay were soon captured. Shot in the arm,
Sam went off to jail, where he died of blood poisoning from
an officer's bullet.

Black Jack became the chief suspect in a pointless
murder of two men in Yavapai, Arizona, and thereafter
tried a singlehanded and unsuccessful train holdup in
Folsom, New Mexico. All he got was a mangled arm from the
conductor's shotgun. The arm was amputated, and to add
insult to injury, train robbery being then a capital offense,
Ketchum was sentenced to hang. His departure from this

life was spectacular. Somebody miscalculated the length of the drop in relation to Black Jack's weight, and he left the world in two pieces, parting with his head in the process.

Newt Harold was an import from Missouri who moved to Arizona to further his criminal career. On the evening of November 23, 1892, he stuck up a little grocery store-cum-bank in San Marcial, New Mexico. Masking himself with a handkerchief, he removed his mask and used the handkerchief to wrap up and carry away his loot. Harold fled into Arizona, ending up in little Snowflake, where he killed one lawman and was shot down by a second officer.

On August 10, 1883, two men masked with gunny sacks of all things stopped the Florence-Globe stage near Riverside Station on the Gila. The Wells Fargo messenger was callously murdered, and the bandits got away with about four thousand dollars, a substantial haul for the time. The law made inquiries and learned that one Jack Almer had spent some time around the Florence stage office, had ridden the stage partway along the line, and had appeared upset when at one station he asked vainly whether two men had left a horse for him. The law perked up its ears.

Almer had a couple of aliases but was generally called Red Jack or Red Jacket. It turned out that he was part of a fairly extensive conspiracy that involved among others a shadowy figure called Prospector Bob, a ranch owner suspected of harboring outlaws, and a former justice of the peace. The justice of the peace rolled over on the rest, and lawmen learned that the Wells Fargo man had been murdered by one Charles Hensley. Arrests followed. So did a legal tug of war between two courts over who had priority to try the case. In the end, a citizens' committee solved the niceties of the jurisdictional dispute by simply invading the jail and hanging two of the conspirators, including the justice of the peace.

Direct extralegal action was not unusual in the Arizona

of the day, nor for that matter anyplace in the West. As one newspaper commented with some truth, men lynched by the citizenry "were cured of killing others, and others were deterred from the commission of crimes." Thus with killer John Heath, convicted of second-degree murder in a cluster of killings committed during a robbery. The good citizens of Tombstone deemed the sentence a clear miscarriage of justice; they set out to make up for the shortsightedness of the court and lynched Heath in February 1894. According to a coroner's jury verdict authored by county coroner Dr. John Goodfellow: "We the jury of inquest . . . find . . . that he came to his death from emphysema of the lungs—a disease common to high altitudes—which might have been and probably was, caused by strangulation, self-inflicted or otherwise."[16] The next month, five other outlaws were hung—legally this time—for the same crime.

Heath's departure was extralegal of course, but the West was prone to a sort of rough justice largely unknown in other parts of the country, both in dealing with malefactors like Heath outside the courts and in excusing others who personally rid the world of the undesirable. A memorable example is a madam who rejoiced in the title of Pussycat Nell. She operated her parlor from above a saloon in Beer City, just across the Kansas line in the Oklahoma panhandle. Nell had a disagreement with the town's lawman and dispatched him with her shotgun. Nobody seemed to care very much, for the dead man was known to do some rustling on the side. Like so many similar cases across the burgeoning West, the townsfolk applied the age-old twin maxims: "He had it coming" and "Who cares?"

So it was with Red Jack's two coconspirators. As for the rest, a posse led by the formidable Bob Paul caught up with Red and Hensley, killing Red and putting several holes in Hensley. The latter escaped briefly, but the posse caught up to him the next day. He decided to fight, and somebody drilled him through the head, adding another hole to those he was carrying from the skirmish the day before, thus ending the ring involved with what is today called the Riverside stage robbery.

Red Jack was not the only small-time troublemaker given to fancy names. Around the towns of St. Johns and Springerville in the late 1880s, rustling was endemic, with horses and mules stolen in southern Arizona and Mexico traded in for horses and mules from farther north and then herded one way or the other for sale. Among the more virulent rustlers was one Billy Evans, known also as Ace or Jack of Diamonds, maybe from the song of the same name. For a while he ran with another punk also called Jack of Diamonds. They are not to be confused with still another loser, one Jack Brenen, or Brennan, called the Jack of Clubs for reasons now forgotten.[17]

The two Diamonds rustled here and there and then made the mistake of stealing stock from rancher Charles Thomas. They and a third man even stayed overnight with Thomas, eating his food before disappearing before daybreak with three of Thomas's horses and the mounts of two friends also staying the night. The angry rancher and his friends gave chase. In time they came up with the Ace and the Jack and another thief, who may have been either one Kid Swingle or one Lee Renfro. The pursuers went right to work, killing both Ace and Jack. The third man fled. Thomas and his friends left the remains where they fell. If the third robber was Renfro, he did not last long either, falling to a lawman's bullets only a few days later.[18]

The newspapers of the day gloried in the sensational, even more than they do today. One of them rhapsodized over the gunslinging ability of lawman Christopher Columbus Perry, known for a fondness for killing folks he considered bad men. Talented Perry truly was, but the reporter did it one better: "[Perry] carries his revolver in front of his belt instead of behind, so that by a quick muscular movement of the stomach he can toss the pistol into his hand before his adversary has time to draw on him."[19] Why, sure, although it is a little tough to visualize how he carried a gun "in front of his belt" without a holster of some kind.

And then there was Barney Riggs. Barney may have been one of the two or three meanest men ever to carry a gun in the West, which is saying a great deal. He was a Texan who left the Lone Star State in his twenties when the local sheriff came to his home and invited him to the office to answer a question or two. Barney, not desirous of such a talk, according to legend dressed in his sister's clothing and walked out the house right past the sheriff. It makes you wonder just how alert the lawman was or how ugly Barney's sister might have been.[20] A more probable tale has Barney leaving Texas after he "accidentally" shot a friend with "an empty gun," which, one newspaper commented, did about as much damage as "non-explosive coal oil lamps."

Barney then turned up in Cochise County, Arizona, where two uncles were already in business. According to legend, Barney shot a good many people, including a relative whom Barney thought was overinterested in Mrs. Riggs. The unfortunate relative was Richmond Hudson, called a "step-cousin," killed from ambush. Barney took it on the heel and toe after the shooting but was captured and tried for murder.

On trial for the murder of Hudson, Barney listened with mounting anger while the district attorney compared him to an "Apache renegade," until Barney could stand it no longer. His outburst was a reflection of the man. "Yes, you son of a b——," he shouted, "and I'll murder you."[21] But veteran lawman Fred Dodge pounced on Riggs and murder or mayhem was averted. "Thank you, Fred," said the DA calmly and went on with his summation.

Barney was convicted of murder one, and away he went to Yuma. He won his freedom when he intervened in a violent escape attempt in which several prisoners were killed. Barney fended off death or injury to prison officials, including the superintendent, who later joined in signing a petition for clemency. Barney served only a year and later joked that he had killed one man to get into Yuma and another one to get out. Encouraged by the law to depart Arizona without delay, he returned to Texas.

For a while he served as a lawman in Reeves County, where he was noted for his propensity for violence. Even with a badge, Barney never changed. In fact, while serving the law, he became more and more aggressive and pugnacious as time went by. In late 1893 or early 1894, he was accused of shooting four men. His trial ended in a dismissal of the charges, and Barney continued his lawless ways. He married again—maybe without a divorce from wife number one—and sided with his wife's family, the Frazers, in a feud with a family called Sosa. After casualties on both sides, one tale tells that the surviving Sosa was tracked to Presidio, Texas, by an avenger still unidentified who killed him, cut him up, fed the pieces to some hogs, and returned with a purse made of the man's scrotum.[22] It could have been Barney; it sure sounds like him.

Then came the murder of relative Bud Frazer, shot down by Deacon Jim Miller, a career professional assassin who boasted that he had killed fifty-one men, until the day the good citizens of Ada, Oklahoma, hanged Jim unceremoniously from a stable roof beam. Barney, ever loyal, even moved his family to hunt down Miller. Miller was afraid of him, the story goes, so he sent a couple of henchmen to do in Barney. Barney, warned by others, was also told of the rumor that the two men—like Miller—wore some sort of iron body armor. Barney laughed. That was not a problem, he said; "I'll just shoot them in the head." Sure enough, meeting the men in a saloon, Barney dropped them both, each with a single shot apiece to the head. There is one tale that he took the precaution of wearing a steel vest of his own; he did not need it.

Barney's foul personality did not change either. After a quarrel with his second wife, he began to break up the household furniture. When his wife tried to stop him, he knocked her down and "attempted to pour coal oil on her and set her afire."[23] But when his wife left him amid violence and recrimination, Barney blamed her son-in-law, one Buck Chadborn, who was the designated trustee for Riggs' child-support payments. Riggs seems to have attacked Chadborn more than once with his cane, until the day came when Chadborn had enough and put a bullet in Barney's chest. Barney died a day later. It just goes to show you, never bring a cane to a gunfight.

Another ne'er-do-well who came to a violent end early in life was Pony Deal (or Diehl), not to be confused with Pony Neal. Deal started life as Charles Ray, but it was as Pony Deal that he graduated to stage robbery. He is believed to have been part of a couple of stage robberies in 1881, along with perpetual nuisances Frank Stilwell, Curly Bill Brocius, Pete Spencer, and maybe Sherman McMasters, depending on whose opinion you read. He was arrested in a saloon in the autumn of that year by a local peace officer who walked up behind him, yanked Pony's pistol from its holster, and covered both Pony and a companion.

Whatever happened to him after that arrest, according to Wyatt Earp, Pony was part of another pair of stage holdups on successive days in January 1882. There is no record of him being tried, and according to Earp, Pony was present with other cowboys during the fight at Iron Springs in 1882, the day Curly Bill Brocius passed to his reward, urged on by Wyatt's shotgun.

Deal was twice reported killed in gunfights—probably wishful thinking—but in fact was apparently arrested for rustling in New Mexico and sentenced to the state penitentiary. He had gone to work shipping stolen cattle for a gang of wholesale rustlers, and when the gang went down, Deal went with them. He tried once unsuccessfully to escape and in the end was pardoned in 1891 and disappeared. With luck, somebody shot him, somewhere, but his end remains a mystery.

Southern Arizona was the stomping ground of a whole covey of lesser lights, wannabe criminals, and groupies, and a few of these deserve a passing mention, if only for comic relief. A small-timer who called himself Shoot-'Em-Up Dick and another second-rate hoodlum stole a valuable horse and were promptly run down by a small posse. Dick made bail but failed to appear for his court date. Afterward, he apparently attempted to traded on his dubious reputation, trying one night to walk away without paying his dinner bill at Jim Sam's Chinese restaurant. Sam remonstrated and Dick brandished his reputation. "No, you damned heathen," he is quoted as saying, "I'm Shoot-'Em-Up Dick." Undaunted, the restaurant owner produced a pistol and announced, "You Shoot-'Em-Up Dick. Me shoot-em-down Sam. You pay pretty dam [*sic*] quick." And Dick did. He went on to steal a pair of mules belonging to rancher Maj. William Downing, already suffering from widespread rustling. Downing, a decisive sort, followed Dick and found him asleep under a tree. The story goes that Downing woke him up and then killed him. Nobody much cared, for rustlers were not highly thought of and Downing was not charged.[24]

Two-bit criminals could be as savage as their more famous criminal brethren. Curtis Hawley and Lafayette Grimes stopped a stage near Globe at a spot appropriately called Six-Shooter Canyon. As they escaped from the scene, they fell in with a respected Globe druggist, Dr. Vail, whom they wantonly shot three times and left for dead. After that they met the coach's express messenger, who apparently did not recognize them. Nevertheless suspicious, the killers put eight rounds into him. By this time a posse was on the track. Following the description given to them by the dying Vail, the law arrested Curtis Hawley and the two Grimes brothers, the second of whom, Cicero, had been in on planning the robbery. They were brought into the Globe jail without trouble, but then the angry citizens decided to save the state the expense of trial and avoid inconveniences like hung juries, judges, and lengthy appeals. Accordingly, they hanged two of the killers in front of the St. Elmo Saloon. The ad hoc sentence was carried out to the accompaniment of the tolling of the bell on the Methodist Episcopal Church, lending a vaguely civilized touch to the proceedings. They exercised some clemency too, sparing Cicero Grimes after much speechifying by others on his behalf.[25]

Cicero went off to Yuma, and with him went an outlaw with the quaint handle of Billy the Kid Number Two. Billy would not give his real name and went to prison under his unconvincing nickname. He was a pain in the neck in prison, nearly digging his way out at one point, briefly escaping at another. He seems to have been in perpetual disciplinary trouble but was at length discharged and disappears from history, leaving no footprints.

Which brings us to El Peludo. In the dubious pantheon of Arizona bad men, Augustine Chacón probably deserves the top spot, which is saying a great deal. He was unforgettable in lots of ways, even when he was not riding about killing people. For one thing, he was a huge man for his day, over six feet, his tall figure crowned by a mass of black hair and a large, droopy, Pancho Villa-like mustache. He looked like a fur-bearing animal elsewhere as well, the mat of black hair all over his body earning him the title of El Peludo, the Hairy One.[26]

As is the case with many Western hoodlums, a good deal of mythology surrounds the history of El Peludo. The story

Chavez (left), killed by Sheriff Wakefield in the Santa Rita Mountains. Augustin Chacón (right), hanged November 23, 1902. *(Courtesy Arizona Historical Society, Tucson)*

goes that he had been a vaquero south of the border before he rode up into Arizona about 1888. He may have worked as a farmhand as well and later claimed to have spent some time serving with Mexican police along the border. He hired on as a cowboy in Arizona, but the lure of easy money robbing people beat the prospect of long miserable days on horseback in blazing sun or driving rain, pushing animals who did not want to go where the cowboys did. And so, perhaps as early as 1889, Chacón embarked on a new career.

On a night in December 1895, he and two confederates, Morales and Franco, set their hearts on the merchandise and the till of Mrs. McCormack's store in Morenci. The clerk, Paul Becker, closed up that evening long enough to walk down the street to a saloon to get some dinner. While he was gone, Chacón and company climbed through a transom and fell to looting the store. Becker, full of dinner, walked in on them. Open the safe, they told him, or get shot. Becker, a tough man in his own right, took on all three, knocking a gun from one bandit and grabbing for the knife another one held. The blade sliced open his hand and the robbers went on threatening, but still Becker refused to open his boss's safe. Chacón rammed a knife into Becker's side, leaving him on the store floor, believing him dead. But Becker was not, and when the robbers left he managed to get on his feet and stagger back to the saloon, where a town constable jerked the knife from his side. Becker would survive, and now the law was after Chacón and his pals. And the law was not going to stop looking.

Chacón and an assortment of his friends had been a perpetual nuisance in the Morenci area for long time. Chacón had gone to work punching cattle for rancher Ben Ollney, and at first the relationship went well. Then the two men fell out over the size of Chacón's paycheck, and Ollney died with his employee's bullet in him. When other cowhands ran to help their boss, Chacón killed five of them as well. A posse pursued, and when they came within shooting distance Chacón killed four of them. That made ten murders in short order if the tales are true. The outlaw was well on his way to the estimated fifty dead he would leave along his trail.

Chacón stayed on the run for months after that, but at last someone recognized him near Fort Apache, and a band of local citizens tossed him in jail. There was talk of a hanging the next day, but when the sun came up Chacón was nowhere to be found. All that remained of his presence was a pile of dull hacksaw blades. No one ever discovered who got the saws into Chacón's cell although one highly unlikely fable has Ollney's daughter smuggling them in because she "never believed Chacón murdered her father."[27] That myth aside, the killer was back on the loose.

Chacón worked both sides of the border, rustling impartially in both Mexico and the Unites States and selling his booty where he could. By 1894 he was around Morenci again, and his next victims were a pair of young men who were encamped to hunt and fish for a few days. They were murdered for their guns and ammunition by Chacón and several other hoodlums.

The Hairy One later appeared in Tombstone, and that proved to be a great mistake because sheriff of Cochise County was Texas John Slaughter, a very tough lawman given to shooting first and worrying about due process of law afterward. Hearing Chacón was nearby, Slaughter gave chase, aided by his deputy—and future outlaw—Burt Alvord. They found Chacón all right, but the outlaw was infernally lucky. Slaughter and his deputy, both carrying shotguns, separated to approach the tent where Chacón was shooting the breeze with some friends. Alvord moved toward the front of the tent and Slaughter closed in from behind. The plan, a sound notion, was that Alvord would shout to Chacón to come out and surrender. Almost surely, Slaughter reasoned, the murderer would run from the rear of the tent, where Slaughter's shotgun would be waiting.

John Slaughter was a dead shot, and he pulled down on Chacón as the outlaw ran from the back of the tent as expected. Slaughter was sure he had hit the man. According to one version of the tale, Slaughter commented, "I say, I say, I gave him both barrels. He pitched off into the gulch. He must be lying down there." He and Alvord, carrying lanterns, looked for their quarry in the ravine behind the tent, for Slaughter had seen a tent rope broken on the side next to the ravine and guessed his man had torn it as he fell. But there was no corpse in the ravine, and the lawmen concluded that Chacón had tripped over the rope just as Slaughter fired. Chacón's clumsiness saved his life for Slaughter did not miss with a shotgun at close range. The outlaw must have had a horse nearby as he was long gone.

Then came the invasion at McCormack's Store, and this time the law had some luck. A posse was quickly gathered, led by Constable Alex Davis, and Chacón, Morales, and Franco were run to earth in a cabin. A full-fledged war ensued. After a good deal of shooting, Morales and Franco got to their horses and ran for it, but they did not get far. Some of the posse followed, and both outlaws ended up dead. That left Chacón. He fought on from a spot behind boulders near the cabin until at last a very brave posse member volunteered to talk him into surrender. The posseman was one Pablo Salcido, who had punched cattle with Chacón and thought that friendship might prevail on the fugitive to give himself up. He called out to Chacón, and the outlaw told him to come in and talk. Salcido started toward the outlaw's position and got a bullet through the head for his courageous attempt to make peace. The vicious act was vintage Chacón.[28]

The response from the furious posse was a hailstorm of bullets, and when a period of silence suggested Chacón might have been hit, the possemen cautiously approached. A round had punched a hole in their quarry's shoulder and another left a red gash across his chest. He was dazed and quickly captured, bound for jail again, this time in Solomonville, charged with the murder of Salcido. The lockup there was not famous for its strength, and sure enough, when he had recovered a little Chacón wandered off, hiding out in a ditch to await the coming of night. That proved to be a poor idea too. A member of a posse searching for him fell into the same ditch and landed on top of the fugitive, who found himself back in jail.

To the charge of murder, Chacón pleaded not guilty, not surprisingly, but the jury disagreed and the sentence was predictably death by hanging. He appealed, of course—so did a group of people opposed to the death penalty—but the Arizona Supreme Court affirmed the verdict. Before justice could be done, Chacón got out of his shackles on his return trip from Tucson to Solomonville, but again he was recaptured.

Chacón was still not through. Just a little over a week before his execution date, he again escaped, this time cutting through the adobe walls of the jail and hacking through beams, then running through the sheriff's office while other prisoners sang songs and played guitars to cover the sound of his labors. Again, nobody knew who ran tools in to him, but he was allowed visitors and he apparently still had some friends willing to stick their necks out to bring him the means of escape.

And so honest citizens worried and watched their backs for the next four years. As he had before, Chacón worked both sides of the border, and at least two more murders were attributed to him. This time it was two men killed in their home in the Black River country. There had been more than one in the group that murdered them, and one description fit the distinctive appearance of hairy Augustine Chacón.

Mostly, though, he stayed in Mexico, only venturing north to peddle rustled stock.

Now the newly minted Arizona Rangers were looking for him, and their leader was Burt Mossman. Mossman had been a range boss for the Hash Knife outfit over near Holbrook, and they did not come any tougher. He was not going to give up until Chacón was hanged. Mossman's term as captain of the Rangers ran out in 1902, when a new governor came on board. Tom Rynning was appointed to Mossman's position, but Mossman became a United States deputy marshal and remained in the law enforcement business. He had been chasing Chacón for years, and he was determined to run him down.

Mossman had also been pursuing Burt Alvord, sometime lawman and professional train robber. Alvord was at large, as was Billy Stiles, also an ex-lawman and one of the coconspirators with Alvord in the botched stage robbery at Cochise Junction in the autumn of 1899. The Cochise Junction plan had been simple. Alvord would stay in a saloon in Willcox, being suitably obvious so he would have an alibi. He could then provide alibis for the rest of the robbers, including Stiles. When news of the robbery arrived in Willcox, Alvord gathered a posse and galloped about the countryside, of course catching nobody. Meanwhile, according to legend, the loot was stored in Alvord's chicken coop.

The loot from Cochise Junction had been substantial, and so Alvord and Stiles decided on another train holdup, this time at Fairbank, again to be committed by other hoodlums while Alvord and Stiles established alibis elsewhere. But this job ran head-on into Jeff Milton, riding as agent in the express car. Badly wounded himself, Milton mortally wounded one of Alvord's followers, Three-Fingered Jack Dunlap, and got a shot into the backside of still another, Bravo Juan Yoas. Dunlap, dying, implicated some of his companions, who in turn squealed on Alvord and Stiles.

Arrested, both men made a break for it in April 1902. Stiles had been granted immunity in return for testimony against the other bandits, but he used his status to break Alvord out of jail. Alvord and Stiles were at large, probably in Mexico, when Alvord, at least, tired of living on the run. And so Mossman made a little deal with the devil. While Stiles and Alvord were still fugitives themselves, Mossman managed to make contact with them. The idea was to use them to lure Chacón back into Arizona, thus avoiding irritating details like jurisdiction and extradition papers. Mossman did not even tell Mexican border police commander Emilio Kosterlitzky, who had also been known to turn a blind eye to little things like national frontiers. Mossman was going to do this one alone.

What exactly Mossman promised Stiles and Alvord is not entirely clear, but it was enough to gain their assistance. It may have included an offer to share the reward still outstanding for the apprehension of Chacón. Mossman also carried a letter from Judge William Barnes in Tucson, advising Alvord that he might win leniency by helping the law and telling Alvord that his wife was in financial difficulty. Mossman also contacted Stiles' brother and in time got together with the outlaws. They agreed to help.

One account tells that new Ranger captain Rynning was aware of the plan and concurred. The two men met in Bisbee, and Mossman told him what was afoot. Rynning turned out to be a kindred spirit. "This conversation never took place," said Rynning, winked, and went his way.

Mossman's part to play in his little farce was to act the greedy horse thief, eager to set up the larceny of some valuable horses on the ranch of Col. Bill Greene, near the border. Once the stock was rustled, it would be sold off in Mexico. Chacón was loath to cross the border these days, but Mossman hoped the lure of a quick, easy haul close to the safety of the border might tempt his quarry.

It did. Some four months later Chacón took the bait, and Mossman received telegrams or letters from both Alvord and Stiles. Chacón, still cautious, arranged for a meeting at a spot some twenty-five miles inside Mexico, reasoning that the American law could not get at him there. Technically it could not, of course, but he did not know Burt Mossman.

The four men met on a bad night, huddled against a drizzle around a sputtering fire. Chacón was not inclined to be either welcoming or trusting, and according to one version of the story Mossman spent the whole night with his hand on the butt of his handgun underneath his slicker. When daybreak came, Mossman lit himself a cigarette, touching it off with a twig from the fire. About this time Alvord, never overly public spirited, announced that he would go and get some fresh water and rode off into the morning. He would not return, and Mossman probably guessed he would not. Deputy Marshal Mossman dropped the twig he had used to light his cigarette, and in one motion jerked his revolver from beneath his slicker. Even the suspicious Chacón was caught off guard, and Mossman kept him at pistol-point until Stiles could get him handcuffed.

And so the three rode back toward the border, Mossman and Stiles alert for any sign of Rurales or Federales or anybody else who might object to what amounted to kidnapping, carting a prisoner illegally back to America. They were lucky, made the frontier, cut a fence along it, and crossed into the United States near Naco. Mossman flagged down a train bound for Benson, and there he was reinforced by Sheriff Jim Parks of Graham County. Parks brought along another set of handcuffs and some leg irons; nobody wanted to take chances with the most elusive and murderous man in the Southwest.

Coincidentally, a reporter shared the three men's train ride to Solomonville, and in his story commented on Chacón's appearance, his "bent form" and graying hair.

Chacón was despondent. "I want them to kill me this time," he said. "I prefer death to a term in the penitentiary." If that was really his wish, it was surely going to come true. The newsman also asked Mossman where the arrest occurred. He replied blandly that it had happened "on a pasture located about seven miles this side of the Mexican line."[29] Sheriff Parks did not contradict him, and so a world of legal hassling was temporarily avoided.

Back in Solomonville, extra guards reinforced the jail, stronger now than the puny affair it had been when Chacón had last departed unbidden. Behind fourteen-foot adobe walls, the gallows loomed. Three ropes on this gibbet, no waiting—the sort of forethought that had gone into the construction of the six-rope gallows at Fort Smith in years gone by. Entrance to the hanging itself was to be by admission only and some fifty people showed up, not counting those perched in nearby trees high enough to see over the walls. Hangings were a favorite form of public entertainment in those days, and Chacón was as infamous as a man could be.

Newspaper accounts called Chacón "nervy" as he drank coffee and smoked cigarettes on the scaffold, talking to people in the crowd. He made a sort of speech complaining that he was accused of more crimes than he actually had committed—although through the years he had admitted to dozens of killings. He especially denied killing Salcido, his one-time saddle companion. "I have a clean conscience," he said, a notably nonsensical notion.

His many escapes seem to have turned him into a sort of folk hero, presumably because of his unusual talent for breaking out of a series of dilapidated jails. It certainly could not have been the tally of the dead, several of them law officers. By one count he had killed some seventeen Anglos and something like thirty-seven Mexicans as he carried on his murdering, rustling, and looting. At least that's how the story went, and nobody denied that there was a great deal of truth to the claim.

The braggadocio of frontier punks like Chacón was frequently an attempt to lend themselves superstar status, a little like the minute Wizard of Oz shouting down his huge megaphone to terrify the citizenry. Men with swashbuckling names like Bitter Creek, Shoot-'Em-Up Bill, the Verdigris Kid, and the Narrowgage Kid lasted quick, as the saying went in those days; so did fumblers like Elmer McCurdy and much-overrated Al Jennings. But Chacón was the real thing by all accounts: strong, tough, fearless, and apparently empty inside, as befitted an outlaw without scruples or compassion. When the gallows trap dropped on November 21, 1902, Arizona Territory was at last rid of as despicable a man as ever robbed and killed in the West.

Very few of the hoodlums in this chapter lasted very long. Most of them died violently, and none of them accomplished much while they were around besides hurting other people. If they had a collective epitaph, it would have read something like this: Good riddance.

# PART IV

# Closing the Arizona Frontier

## CHAPTER TWELVE

# Rustlers in Twilight: The Long Arm of the Arizona Rangers

The eradication of the Tewksburys and the near extinction of the Grahams did not produce a like effect on the Arizona cattle rustlers. Ranked sixth in the country by land area with its 113,635 square miles, Arizona had a contrastingly small population in 1900, some 123,000, yet it was one of the country's leading spots for outlaws. This was a prime place to conduct robberies, holdups, and rustling with more than enough space for gangs of criminals to hide out with little fear of encountering their various pursuers.

The trend toward lawlessness continued even as the march of modernity made its way to Arizona and into the lives of the people living there. Ringing telephones began replacing the clattering telegraph as residents delighted in their first-ever ice cream cones, pretzels, and even Coca-Cola. So vast was the landscape that even with the introduction of toothpaste in a tube, other inhabitants continued living in primitive conditions ranging from dugouts and log shacks to adobe-walled cliff dwellings. The trek to the twentieth century was just as fraught with dangerous men and their depredations as bandits continued to attack railroads, stagecoaches, banks, and cattlemen with impunity throughout the territory.

Politicians and business leaders grew more concerned with the report of each new criminal act as outlaws routinely fended off their pursuers or managed a successful escape once in custody. Of the movers and shakers expressing grave concern over the outlaw plague was Arizona's governor, Nathan Oakes Murphy. With one hand in public affairs and the other hand in business matters, he rose to become the territorial governor in 1892. When his first term ended, Murphy, a Republican, was replaced when Pres. Grover Cleveland, a Democrat, appointed a likeminded soul.[1] This did not slow down the ever-active Murphy. He was elected to the U.S. Congress representing Arizona from 1895-1897 and was reappointed as Arizona's governor in 1898. From that time on, Governor Murphy increasingly heard from fellow civic and business leaders crying out for action against the outlaws who seemingly operated at will within the territory.

Eventually, Governor Murphy looked east to Texas for inspiration and the Arizona Rangers were established. About six months later, he appointed the organization's first captain. Burton C. "Burt" Mossman was born in Illinois in 1867. His family moved to Missouri and then to New Mexico in 1882. He spoke fluent Spanish and for a time worked for a survey crew under constant threat of attack from Apaches in the Sacramento Mountains. In 1884, he took up work as a cowboy and was good at it, but his quick-triggered temper cost him several jobs. However, as dependable, hard-working, and knowledgeable cowboys were hard to come by, Mossman had little trouble finding work. Despite his quick temper, Burt collected friends easily. Most were very much like himself: imposing, hard, honest men who knew little if no fear.

By 1901, Mossman was working as foreman of the Aztec Land and Cattle Company's Hash Knife outfit, a two-million-acre spread located eighty miles west of Holbrook.[2] Under his management, the massive operation turned a fourteen-year run of red ink into a profitable enterprise. He set into motion this reversal of fortune by promptly arresting those of the outfit's employees he suspected of being moonlight rustlers of their employer's beef. Mossman did this without the consent or knowledge of law enforcement. He also fired fifty-three of the Hash Knife's eighty-four cowboys. Mossman so impressed the local sheriff, Frank Wattron, that he was pressed into service as his deputy. Mossman wore the star with ease and caught the attention of one Bucky O'Neill, who offered him a commission with the Rough Riders. Mossman declined, saying he preferred to keep his job as deputy sheriff.

Mossman was also working with the Aztec Land and Cattle Company in 1900 when it sold off its Western ranching interests and discharged its employees. He then went into the retail end of the business, buying out a slaughterhouse in Bisbee and opening up a second one in Douglas. He eventually sold all of his mercantile interests and "retired" to Phoenix in 1901. The money earned from his earlier business dealings allowed him to spend much of his time playing poker with influential friends at his new residence in the Adams Hotel.

Word had been out for some time that Governor Murphy intended to establish a new Ranger force and that he was actively soliciting candidates to head the outfit. "What we need is a hard riding, sure shooting outfit something like the Texas Rangers or the Mexican Rurales,"[3] and a man to lead them, the governor told a group of influential businessmen and Mossman acquaintances. All thoughts turned to Burt.

The governor convened an impromptu panel whose word, he believed, would convince Mossman to accept the job as captain of the Arizona Rangers. The group consisted of Governor Murphy; Graham County councilman Charley Shannon; the head of Southern Pacific Railroad operations in the Southwest, Col. Epes Randolph; and J. C. Adams, the owner of the hotel which Mossman called home. Mossman was summoned to the governor's mansion, where to his surprise this group of movers and shakers and card-playing buddies were awaiting him. He did not refuse the men he liked and respected, and on August 30, 1901, nearly six months after the bill calling for the creation of a Ranger force was signed into law, Burt Mossman became its first captain.[4]

Within the week Mossman had established Ranger headquarters at Bisbee. By Friday two new recruits had signed up to become Arizona Rangers. On the last day of the week, September 6, 1901, Tom Holland and Bert Grover were the first to pin the badge to their shirts. They were followed by Texans Leonard Page and George Edgar "Ed" Scarborough, the former Texas Ranger and the son of lawman George W. Scarborough. Including Mossman, that made five of the mandated force of fourteen. Then came Carlos Tafolla, who signed his enlistment papers at St. Johns. Seven days later, on Friday the thirteenth, three more men added their names to the roll. They were Fred Barefoot, James Warren, and another Texan named Don Johnson. The following week Mossman saw his company of Rangers increase to eleven as Richard Stanton—previously a waiter from New York who said he saw combat with Teddy Roosevelt's Rough Riders in Cuba at San Juan Hill—and Pittsburgh, Pennsylvania, native John Campbell joined the ranks. On September 20, Duane Hamblin joined the group. Two men were all that Captain Mossman needed to realize his full complement of Rangers. In October the remaining two positions were filled by Frank Richardson and forty-seven-year-old Henry Gray, the oldest of the enlisted men. Other than Mossman, only Ed Scarborough, Tafolla, and Johnson had any previous law-enforcement experience. Regardless of that lack of experience, Burt believed the men he had chosen were each qualified to represent the Arizona Territory as her Rangers.

One man, however, proved him wrong, and on December 3, 1901, after serving less than two months the waiter from New York, Richard Stanton, was asked to leave the force. Stanton and Grover had taken a disliking to each other. Stanton did not help himself by shooting Grover in the leg;

it led to his dismissal.[5] The remaining twelve men under Mossman's command were all privates. A sergeant was mandated in the service's original charter but it would be some time before Private Campbell would amass enough experience to rise to that rank.

The call of adventure was more important to these men than the prospect of riches. Each private was paid $55 dollars per month for his service and was allotted a per diem of $1 a day for food for himself and 50¢ a day for grain for his horse. The individual Ranger had to provide everything else, including the horse. The men were required to furnish their own camping equipment such as bedrolls, tents, coffee pots, and cups and cooking utensils. Only the captain received what at the time would be considered a livable wage of $120 per month. The sergeant's pay was set at $75.

Out of their meager salaries, the recruits were also expected to pay for the weapons they were provided. Mossman made sure they were equipped with the same weapons he used a few years earlier when he was trailing rustlers. His men had to furnish their own six-shooters and Mossman chose the Colt .45 single-action revolver as the company's official handgun. Mossman himself carried a Model 1895 .30-.40 Winchester. Governor Murphy mandated that the territory provide the Rangers' ammunition.

In early October, before trigger-happy Richard Stanton was culled from the Rangers, Mossman dispersed his crew along the trail of fugitive outlaw gangs. Mossman and Governor Murphy wanted these men to make a good showing: the public had recently seen their property taxes increase by five cents for every one hundred dollars' worth of taxable property in order to pay for this outfit. One significant target was the Bill Smith gang. He and his siblings and their mother all lived in Graham County in southeast Arizona, located in or very near what today is known as the

Apache-Sitgreaves National Forest. The family home was situated along the Blue River, which parallels the border with New Mexico; it functioned as the gang's headquarters as well.

Bill Smith was arguably Arizona's most infamous cattle rustler. Smith's first encounter with the law in Arizona came with an arrest in 1898. He escaped and three years later he and his brothers were up to their old ways, robbing trains, stealing cattle and horses, and generally making nuisances of themselves. One victim, Henry Barrett, was a former friend of the Smiths, but that relationship dissolved quickly when Barrett realized his supposed friends were stealing horses from his ranch. Barrett caught wind of Smith's presence in St. Johns, where one gang member stopped to buy supplies. They were, Barrett learned, herding a bunch of stolen horses south to Springerville and likely would eventually continue on southward, where they would corral the horses at the family headquarters on the Blue River.

Barrett gathered three men to form a posse. Elijah Holgate, Hank Sharp, and Pete Peterson accompanied Barrett to Greer. There they met with Rangers Tafolla and Hamblin, who agreed to ride with the Barrett posse in search of the Smith gang. The posse recruited three more men: Lorenzo Crosby and brothers Arch and Bill Maxwell.[6] They continued south, skirting Big Lake before camping for the night on the ranch of Pete Slaughter, where the trail showed signs that the outlaws, too, had camped. The following morning Barrett, his posse, and the Rangers broke camp and continued their slow-paced, dogged hunt.

Just before sunset, the outlaws settled in at their makeshift camp in a steep-walled canyon protected on each side by the Ord and Baldy Mountains. Some in the gang were field dressing a bear they had shot earlier and making small talk when their dog let out a howl. Nervous and suspicious, Bill Smith clambered up to the snow-covered ridge and poked his nose over just far enough to see nine riders closing in. It was a posse, he knew. The shots that felled the bear had also alerted the posse as to the presence of others in the area. While the Barrett posse could not have known for sure that it was Bill Smith and his gang, they sensed it. Smith hurriedly scampered down from the rim's edge and ordered his men to hide the horses and ready themselves for battle. Long shadows began to fill the gorge as the outlaws prepared and waited.

The sunset behind the mountain's rim contrasted sharply with the darkness hovering above the canyon floor upon which was nestled the bandits' camp. These contrasts made it all the more difficult for the posse to pinpoint their targets below. They would have to wait until nightfall. After six of their number positioned themselves along the rim, three men brazenly walked straight toward the outlaw camp. Rangers Hamblin and Tafolla led the way and Bill Maxwell followed. The trio emerged from the cover of darkness the tree-lined canyon provided and stepped out into an open expanse just yards short of the outlaw campsite. Their comrades on the rim saw the dark figures of Maxwell and the Rangers against the snow, which made the men as starkly visible as three raisins floating in a bowl of milk.

Bartlett shouted from above for the men to take cover. Hamblin did but Maxwell and Tafolla ignored Bartlett's hollering and strode toward the campsite undaunted. Maxwell called out for the gang to surrender. Bill Smith agreed and started toward the possemen. The two Rangers could not see that Smith was dragging his Savage .303 rifle behind him.[7] When Smith was within forty feet of the lawmen he swung the rifle up and began pumping lead. His first shot hit Tafolla in the midsection. Another round struck the forehead of Bill Maxwell. He was probably dead before he crumpled to the ground. From above, Arch, Bill's brother, and the others opened fire, sending the bandits scurrying in search of cover.

In the meantime the mortally wounded Tafolla kept his Winchester pumping hot lead in the direction of the bandit camp. Henry Barrett inflicted the most damage on the outlaws as rounds from his Spanish Mauser ripped through the trunks of the smaller trees used by the gang to take cover. He wounded two desperadoes—one in the foot and the other in the leg. One of the steel-jacketed rounds also killed that old baying dog who had sounded the alarm.

While the battle was still white-hot, Ranger Hamblin managed to creep around to where the outlaws had hidden their mounts and a pack mule. Hamblin released the animals and drove them off. The notorious rustlers were now on foot and that is how they made their escape.

The rest of the posse members converged on the clearing where Tafolla and Maxwell lay. Tafolla had been shot a second time, again through his torso. He was mumbling and groaning for water. Maxwell was dead. His hat lay nearby with three bullet holes in its crown. The posse located all of the gang's horses as well as the pack gear, tack, and supplies hastily left behind. While the others stayed with the wounded Tafolla, Arch Maxwell and Hank Sharp rode in the direction of the Maxwell homestead near Nutrioso to find help for Tafolla. Probably before the men ever reached their destination, Ranger Tafolla died at midnight in the company of fellow Ranger Duane Hamblin and the rancher Henry Barrett, who had once been a friend of Tafolla's killers.[8]

The deaths of their friends caused the Ranger company to delay the pursuit and capture of Arizona's other active bands of thugs and miscreants. Worse yet, however doggedly they trailed the Smith gang into New Mexico and Mexico, the Rangers could not find them. Citizen naysayers, politicians, and local law-enforcement groups scrutinized their every move and viewed the Rangers as a waste of money, while local sheriffs viewed them as infringing on their own ability to collect rewards. Governor Murphy even received criticism that the outfit was too Republican and that he and Mossman ought to have some Democrats on the rolls. Murphy weighed the remarks as potentially damaging to his future in politics, but Mossman dismissed them, making light of the situation. Even though Mossman was a staunch Republican himself, he said he never once chose a man to serve by asking him first what his political persuasions were.

The Rangers did manage an arrest or two in early October, but the arrests of suspected murderers Hete O'Conner and Andrew Griffin did not help much. Their record of apprehensions increased the following month, but only by two. With the arrests of James Head and William Williams on November 11, 1901, the total number of persons arrested by the Rangers rose to a mere four. By year's end the neophyte company of Rangers improved that record somewhat when, in separate incidents, they apprehended six more desperadoes, four of whom were suspected murderers. By February 1902, it appeared as though these Rangers were on their mark. The loss of the newly appointed sergeant of the company, Dayton Graham—who resigned twice to accept positions in local law enforcement—and others who resigned before their tenure of one year was fulfilled, kept the Rangers constantly shorthanded. Nonetheless their apprehension record gradually improved.

As Captain Mossman and his men scoured the vast expanses of the Arizona Territory, cattle rustlers, murderers, thieves, and bandits of all kinds were put on notice that Arizona was no longer a safe haven. Until the Rangers felt competent in their new skin as a territorial police force, many a New Mexico and Texas outlaw had found refuge in the mountains of eastern Arizona, where they routinely relieved ranchers of livestock and anything else not nailed down. County sheriffs were too few and spread too thin to be much of a deterrent. But things were a-changin' in that neck of the woods and many of the Blue River's part-time inhabitants began to move elsewhere.

When notorious outlaw leaders George and Canely Musgrave[9] slipped across the New Mexico-Arizona border with their gang, they probably envisioned the kind of temporary respite outlaws of the pre-Rangers era had experienced. But within two months of arriving at a female friend's house north of Clifton, the gang was severely downsized. New Mexico authorities alerted Mossman that members of the Musgrave gang had held up a post office in Fort Sumner, killing the proprietor, and were most likely headed to the girl friend's place on the Blue River. Mossman in turn told his men stationed in Clifton to be on the lookout.

When Graham County deputy sheriff Jim Parks was informed of a group of heavily armed men riding in the area of the woman's house, he formed a posse. The posse, numbering twelve horsemen, included several special officers and citizens as well as Rangers Pollard Pearson, Fred Barefoot, and Henry Gray. The posse arrived at the suspected hideout late at night on March 9, 1902. They hid themselves from view after surrounding the place. It was a long wait, but at daylight they sprang to action, taking Musgrave associate Witt Neill by surprise as he slept on a cot on the front porch. Neill offered no resistance as he slowly stirred from sleep. When the covers were thrown back a virtual weapons storehouse was exposed.

Three of the officers escorted Neill back to Clifton. Two more of the gang were caught when the posse divided and captured Joe Roberts and George Cook while the pair was herding stolen horses through the mountains. An unidentified accomplice was later arrested by authorities in New Mexico. Two others the posse was trailing managed to escape the law but not, perhaps, the terrain. Years later in 1936, the skeletal remains of a man and a horse were discovered north of Glendale in the Hedgepet Mountains. Those remains are thought to have been of one of the fleeing rustlers and his horse.

With the arrests of four of the Musgrave men and the likely death of a wandering fifth, the Musgrave gang was rendered nonexistent in Arizona Territory. A great coup had occurred in the Rangers' fight for legitimacy. With the political winds at their backs, the Rangers pressed forward with grit and determination. By April 1902, the Rangers had brought in eighteen law breakers and that number would continually increase.

During the next three months even more outlaws succumbed to Ranger tactics. Arrests were effectively conducted in counties and communities throughout the eastern portions of the territory, with criminals summarily thrown into local hoosegows to await their various fates. In the months of May, June, and July the Rangers rounded up seventeen suspected rustlers, robbers, murderers, rapists, and anybody else whose noncompliance with territorial law made them fair game. The Rangers were riding high on the reputation of their most recent arrest record, but with the prevailing winds of favorable public sentiment whisking the Rangers into a state of high confidence, a dust storm arose in the form of a card game.

By August things in the eastern part of the territory had calmed down enough to allow Captain Mossman and a couple of his men to enjoy a little rest and relaxation at their headquarters town of Bisbee. On Saturday, August 16, Mossman entered the Orient Saloon, a dive in the town's Brewery Gulch section. Here the inhabitants and their frequent guests caroused with impunity. And apparently, as long as everyone behaved according to local law and custom, Brewery Gulch and its various sordid enterprises were allowed to flourish.

Mossman's particular downtime activity was card playing. On August 16, Mossman was so engaged at a table that included a professional gambler from an establishment called the Fish Pond. The gambler had just laid claim to a four-hundred-dollar pot when another player, Ranger Bert Grover, accused the self-proclaimed winner a cheat. Things only deteriorated from that point. A rowdy brawl ensued that headed out into the street with Grover, Mossman, the Fish Pond gambler, and two town policemen all tugging and yelling and wrestling one another in front of the Orient. The spectacle was observed by several townspeople, all marveling at how the supposed peacekeepers were acting against the peace and dignity of the territorial laws. The ruckus was only broken up when Bisbee policemen managed to restrain Grover, and Mossman rescued the gambler from the continued pummeling of Ranger Leonard Page. Grover was taken to jail but was quickly sprung when Page snuck inside and freed the Ranger, who hightailed it to high country until things settled down.

The public outcry was swift. The incident was seen as a most tasteless display by the once-heralded territorial law-men and was widely derided as "to say the least, disgrace-ful."[10] Citizens, including the sporting element of Brewery Gulch, expressed outrage at the Rangers' participation in the brawl and demanded Mossman's removal.

But down in Mexico in a mountain base camp near Sonora, one particularly villainous outlaw paid little attention to the shenanigans going on in Bisbee. If anything, the apparent disarray of the territory's police force worked well in his favor. Augustine Chacón was a cold, cruel man who took pleasure in killing those he robbed. As we have seen in Chapter Eleven, Burt Mossman eventually captured Chacón, who was executed in November 1902, and restored his credibility among Arizona's law-abiding citizens.

Mossman left the Ranger service a hero. He cited as the

reason for his stepping down the need to tend to his private interests in Bisbee. But the real reason likely was that his longtime friend, Governor Murphy, the man who gave birth to the idea of an Arizona Ranger service, fell out of favor with Pres. Theodore Roosevelt's administration. Murphy had refused to support a federally sponsored bill that would have created numerous projects for the territory at federal expense. Having been appointed governor by the president meant that he served only by the will of the president, who now wanted him replaced. That hastened Mossman's decision to quit the service, and President Roosevelt wasted no time in filling the gubernatorial vacancy with a man he knew from his days leading the famous Rough Riders. Alexander O. Brodie took the reins and found himself in need of filling the vacancy created by Mossman's resignation. Brodie tapped Thomas H. Rynning to lead the Rangers and he accepted.[11]

One of the first actions Captain Rynning took was to move Rangers headquarters out of Bisbee. Bisbee was by then well enough established that Rynning determined local law enforcement could handle the town's problems, but a settlement west of there was crying for law-enforcement protection. The town of Douglas was founded in 1900 and named for James S. Douglas, the son of the president of the Phelps Dodge company, the mining operation that laid claim to the area. Douglas was not much at that time. It had one bathtub to serve anyone with the occasional need and only one well to supply the entire town with water. About the only real convenience was the telephone Rynning had installed at headquarters.[12]

Douglas was established to benefit the workers of the smelter the company planned to build; the Copper Queen smelter would process ore mined in Mexico. This was a wild place with many of the "trappings" of a frontier mining town, and the Rangers would have their work cut out for them.

Not only were there homegrown incorrigibles, but Mexican outlaws would regularly cross the border into Douglas to escape the Rurales pursuing them. The Rangers would get a double dose of miscreants to deal with in Douglas.

On October 1, 1902, the Rangers occupied a small adobe building as their headquarters. Furnishings were sparse, with the front room set up as the office. The only other room, in the rear of the building, housed the men's clothing, bedrolls, tack, and sundry other equipment and supplies. The men erected a corral adjacent to the rear of the building and laid a broad board floor to alleviate the dust associated with gusty winds, grassless turf, and livestock. One horse per day stood with its saddle and bridle on in the event a Ranger was called to immediate action away from town.

Rynning's force was akin to a temporary employment service for a while, but within weeks he was appointing men of his own choosing to fill vacancies created by Mossman men. From the time of Rynning's appointment in September 1902 through December of that year, the Rangers made an impressive number of arrests, exceeding twenty. They had managed to greatly reduce the number of livestock thieves and other offenders in many of the former trouble spots in southeastern Arizona.

In October, the Rangers were pressed into service as strikebreakers in Globe when employees of the Old Dominion Copper Company threatened the destruction of one of the company's mines and the death of a mine boss. Not a shot was fired by the Rangers. Apparently their presence alone convinced the striking miners to seek other avenues to settle their grievances.

The Ranger successes had not gone unnoticed, and on March 19, 1903, the service was rewarded, so to speak, when the Twenty-Second Legislative Assembly, acting in Phoenix, passed an act authorizing the doubling of the Ranger force. In addition, the Rangers would be provided pack animals at public expense and for the first time since its creation, and the men serving would be issued badges identifying them as Arizona Rangers.[13]

The increase in the number of Arizona Rangers would prove most valuable conducting an assignment the Rangers liked least: strikebreaking. They had had a taste of it in Globe and did not care much for it, even though that incident was a relatively minor affair. The situation in and around Clifton, Metcalf, and Morenci would be quite different.

When a law meant to limit the number of hours miners toiled beneath the terrain for the rich mine owners went into effect, it was meant to ease the burden under which these men strained. While it may have done that by mandating an eight-hour workday rather than the more common ten- or even fourteen-hour workdays, it also had an effect unforeseen by the benevolent lawmakers. The mine owners believed that if the men working the mines were going to be doing less work—in terms of hours spent below ground— then they would receive less pay. This led to grumbling and threats of walkouts at first, but when Chicago-based labor agitator W. H. Lastaunau arrived, things escalated rapidly.[14]

The handful of county law officers and the few citizen-deputies Sheriff Jim Parks recruited for riot duty were no match for the nearly three thousand riled-up miners. And so the Rangers were called to the convergence of the San Francisco, Eagle, and Gila Rivers, near the border of New Mexico and the towns of Morenci, Clifton, and the now defunct Metcalf. Rynning was in command but as was his usual custom he commanded from an established headquarters while delegating field operations to Lt. John Foster. Rynning set up his headquarters at a Morenci hotel, where he coordinated with Sheriff Parks on tactics. One Ranger, Bud Bassett, once stated that he actually saw Rynning in the field on one occasion but the captain was merely out making a round of Ranger camp inspections.

The Rangers arrived in Morenci via train on Sunday, June 7. They made sure everyone both in and out of town knew they were there. Now wearing their polished silver Ranger badges prominently, they also sported Winchesters and handguns as they passed through town to set up camp and corral their horses. The company had managed to deploy only half its force but word reached the other Rangers who had been scouting in assigned districts and the men were soon reinforced.

On their first full day in the region, the Rangers spent much of their time observing the miners. That Monday the schedule consisted mainly of boisterous or grumbling men tramping back and forth from Morenci to a lime pit outside of town. Much of their time was spent shouting among themselves and getting drunk well into the night. On Tuesday, June 9, about two hundred miners from Metcalf began marching toward Morenci, even as Lastaunau was whipping the men back at the lime pit to a fever pitch of hostility. The Rangers and the few deputies and citizens who came to their aid would soon be facing a riot of armed and angry men headed toward town. They held their lines and waited. The anticipated clash and its likely firestorm of hot lead did not transpire that day. Instead, a deluge sent the approaching combatants running for cover as hail and rain fell relentlessly.

The San Francisco River could not hold all the accumulated water within its banks, and within minutes of the start of the raging storm, the town of Clifton braced for the worst. An eight-foot wall of water took the city, many of its buildings and animals, and at least twenty residents to the rushing river, where all was lost. The flood took the fight out of the striking miners, who redirected their efforts toward rescuing their neighbors and cleaning up the town.

On Wednesday, June 10, the Rangers arrested the agitator from Chicago, quelling lesser hostilities committed by some still-angry miners. With Lastaunau in custody many of his minions readily gave up when confronted by the Rangers. After the arrival of some 230 Arizona National Guardsmen joined by 280 horse soldiers from Forts Huachuca and Grant, and with an additional cadre of soldiers on their way from Texas, the miners elected to vote in favor of the lowered wage for the fewer hours worked. The Rangers could now go back to chasing cattle and horse rustlers and other incorrigibles, as they were meant to do.[15]

But the incident left a bad taste in the mouths of several Rangers, who were unhappy with nearly having to kill citizens and foreign workers over something as meaningless, to them, as wages. And by September, five Rangers resigned while two others were dismissed. Two of the Rangers who resigned did so within one month of the strikebreaking duty in the Metcalf-Morenci district. Fred Barefoot and John Campbell, who had been charter members of the force, dating back to Captain Mossman's leadership days, were among those who left the company. Down but not out on account of the turnover in personnel, Rynning continued to recruit men and tour Ranger stations from his headquarters at Douglas.

A capable and proud administrator and a decorated former Rough Rider, Captain Rynning could also prove himself in the field. On one of his regularly conducted station inspection tours, this one in Aravaipa Valley, he arrested Ike Clancie, a Texas fugitive wanted there for two murders. Tom Bell, a Stafford, Texas, rancher who sought the refuge of the Arizona mountains after murdering a man in his home state, became Rynning's second arrest that year. Rynning noted with particular pride and enthusiasm that cattle rustling, in fact rustling of all kinds of livestock, had sharply declined on his watch. Governor Brodie had also noticed this and issued a public statement proclaiming that "cattle stealing has been practically wiped out in Arizona."[16] That was late in 1903.

On December 20, former Ranger Billy Stiles and compatriot Burt Alvord escaped from the Yuma Territorial Prison, closely followed by seventeen others. The escape of Stiles and Alvord provided a welcome distraction from the distasteful memory of the Rangers' strikebreaking duties. Three Rangers were assigned to hunt down the outlaw duo while little notice was paid to the nearly two dozen other escapees. After some rather unconventional interrogation tactics, which included shooting the horse of one suspected sympathizer out from under him and confiscating one of his steers, the Rangers did manage to get a bead on their prey. The assigned Rangers sent word to Rynning that the outlaws Alvord and Stiles were soon to be snared. The lieutenant responded by personally taking the lead in the hunt. His information came too late, however, and he missed capturing the pair. Days later on Friday, February 19, 1904, Sgt. Johnny Brooks of the Rangers, one of the men who allegedly shot the outlaw sympathizer's horse out from under him, locked in the location of Stiles and Alvord.

Brooks enlisted Sheriff Del Lewis of Cochise County to join forces. Lewis in turn gathered three deputies and the small posse dipped into Mexico. They crossed at Naco, Arizona, and rode around Naco, Sonora to the Young Ranch. It was evening when the riders approached the ranch house, but in the gray light they spotted Alvord and Stiles and another man on the porch having a late supper. Brooks and Sheriff Lewis were silhouetted at the top of a hill. Thinking the pair were acquaintances, the men yelled a greeting from the porch. When one of the outlaws hollered up the ridge inquiring whether one of the riders was a man named Skeeter, his inquiry was met with silence. Sensing trouble, the trio on the porch drew their guns. Brooks and Lewis got off the first shots, however, and Alvord was wounded in the ankle. Although not serious, the injury

Constable Burt Alvord with an arm around Deputy Constable Billy Stiles. *(Courtesy Arizona Historical Society, Tucson)*

hobbled him. His dinner partners turned and ran, crossing a stream before disappearing into the wooded darkness, leaving Alvord to face the posse alone. Incensed that his friends had callously abandoned him, Alvord ignored the lawmen and instead turned and opened fire on the fleeing tablemates. He missed, and Alvord again found himself in the Yuma Territorial Prison. This time he would not escape the two-year stretch that lay before him. Stiles, however, was still on the loose with a five-thousand-dollar reward hanging over his head. Sergeant Brooks was promoted to lieutenant for his success in capturing Alvord.[17]

Skirmishes with the few remaining cattle rustlers continued in various parts of the territory, but evidence abounds that those incidents had been dramatically reduced by the Rangers. Their success may have been their eventual downfall for there had been a spate of calls for the Ranger force to be reduced in size if not completely abolished. Most of the detractors cited the growing expense of maintaining such a company of lawmen, the cost of which was estimated at more than three thousand dollars a month (seventy-one thousand dollars today). A few county lawmen supported efforts to suppress the Rangers, but as before, their main concern was the reward money lost to them whenever the Rangers scoured an area and arrested bad men the county officers had hoped to capture.

Still, the Rangers had a powerful ally in the Arizona Cattlemen's Association. On November 15, 1906, Rynning extolled the successes of his force to an assembly of association members and emphasized the necessity of keeping it intact. He reminded the ranchers that the Rangers' average arrest rate stood at 1,000 incorrigibles per year and of those arrested no fewer than 80 percent were convicted. The enthusiastic crowd adopted a resolution calling for the legislature "not to reduce the Ranger force at this time." Another powerful associate in the Rangers' corner was Joseph H. Kibbey, who became governor by appointment on March 7, 1905, after Brodie accepted a presidential appointment to the War Department.[18]

Despite their powerful associates, Rynning and his Rangers found themselves on shaky ground when they decided to cross the line without orders and enter Mexico to rescue Americans faced with riotous miners. On June 1, 1906, as many as five thousand angry Mexicans marched through Cananea demanding an eight-hour workday and a raise in pay. "Colonel" William C. Greene, who operated the mine, attempted to quell the uprising as the surly crowd reached the office building housing his Cananea Consolidated Copper Company. While standing in a convertible, Greene appealed to the men gathered in the street. The protestors were unsympathetic and marched to a lumber yard, where they killed two Americans, a father and son, employed there. Greene and his security chief, former Texas Ranger William D. "Dave" Allison, gathered what Americans they could and made a stand at Greene's thirty-four-room mansion.

As rioters attacked the estate repeatedly throughout the night, women and children were secretly loaded onto train cars whose seats had been removed to accommodate the more than one thousand seeking refuge in Arizona. As they arrived, anxious citizens there clamored to hear of the horrendous actions taking place south of the border. Men began gathering, armed and angry, with the threat of mounting a movement to reinforce the beleaguered Greene party. A friend of Greene's back in Douglas was manning the telegraph when he received this message from his beleaguered friend: "FOR GOD'S SAKE SEND US SOME ARMED HELP."[19]

Rynning was moved by the desperation he had heard in the voices and seen in the faces of the returning Americans. He knew he had to do something but Governor Kibbey had just telegraphed Rynning with orders not to cross into Mexico. Nevertheless, Rynning gathered up a force of former soldiers, Rangers, and a couple of currently serving Rangers to act as a volunteer rescue group. By the time they reached Naco, Arizona, just yards north of its sister city Naco, Sonora, the volunteer group numbered more than two hundred fifty men.

Rynning and his contingent did not know that Gov. Rafael Yzabel and Gen. Lui Torrez were headed to Cananea. In addition, Col. Emilio Kosterlitzky, formidable leader of the Mexican Rurales, had broken off a fight with Yaqui Indians and was also headed to Cananea to quell the violence. Rynning's volunteers were the first to arrive. They were instrumental in suppressing the gunplay around the Greene estate but sporadic incidents continued with sniper fire and men tossing dynamite at suspected American strongholds. At the arrival of Colonel Kosterlitzky and his Rurales much of the violence subsided. All became quiet when it was discovered that fifteen hundred Mexican soldiers were marching toward Cananea. Also known was the fact that American troops had assembled along the border, awaiting orders to cross. The miners weighed the odds and returned to work on Monday, June 4, 1906, just three days after their rampage began.[20]

When Rynning and his men returned to Arizona they were hailed as heroes, but Rynning was immediately called to Governor Kibbey's office in Phoenix. The governor expected Rynning to render a full accounting for the unauthorized deployment into Mexico. In the end, the governor was appeased by the support of Arizonans back home as well as Rynning's own eloquent explanation and let the matter drop. Rynning kept his Ranger's commission and his captaincy.

The year 1907 brought very visible changes to the Arizona Rangers. The first and most notable was the resignation of its longtime leader, Captain Rynning, who had held the reins of control for the better part of its five-year existence. On March 20, 1907, he resigned his Ranger commission to become the superintendent of the Yuma Territorial Prison. He began his new assignment, a promotion, just ten days later. Hardly anyone was surprised when Rynning's right-hand man and field commandant, Lieutenant Wheeler, became the Ranger's third captain.[21]

A second change in Ranger operations was the relocation of its headquarters. Douglas had become quite tame with the help of the Phelps Dodge Mining Company's investments and influence. Douglas was so tame, in fact, that despite its rip-roaring past, it became known as "the City of Churches." Now that Douglas seemed to have been relieved of its criminal element, newly appointed captain Harry Wheeler looked south to Naco, Arizona.

Wheeler also changed the direction of the Ranger service itself. Instead of running up large arrest numbers by collaring inebriated citizens and other misdemeanor offenders, Wheeler turned to real crime prevention in outlying areas. He directed his Rangers to pair off and ride the range to dissuade rustling. But Wheeler's new strategy was nearly the end of the Rangers. Fewer arrests were recorded, while the mileage for which the Rangers sought recompense increased. The critics of the force once again demanded the demise of the organization. The detractors relied on Captain Wheeler's own records. For the month of August 1907, there were only twenty-seven arrests made, whereas the mileage the captain submitted for payment reached a whopping nine thousand dollars.

By this time, the Rangers had faced two political challenges. One called for a reduction in their force of twenty-four by half. Another more severe measure before the legislature called for the complete abolition of the force. Neither measure was signed into law, but Governor

Kibbey realized something needed to be done in order to quell the mounting resentment toward what some saw as an unnecessary tax burden. Kibbey decided to reduce the number of Rangers through attrition. When men left the force the governor simply refused to fill their vacancies. This act seemed to temporarily satisfy some who were calling for the collapse of the service.

The following year was both valiant and tragic for the Rangers. Their efforts in southern Arizona, where they nearly eradicated livestock rustling, were already legend. Most offenders foolish enough to rustle in southern Arizona did so within jumping distance of the Mexican border. Many rustlers, gamblers, and assorted criminals falsely believed that crossing the border to Mexico would make them immune to United States' laws. But a pact existed between the Rangers and Mexican Rurales to cooperate on a prisoner exchange when either group apprehended one of the other's fugitives. This arrangement worked rather well, except in a few isolated cases where local police and government officials were in cahoots with the bad guys. This occurred on both sides of the border, especially in Naco, Arizona, and Naco, Sonora. However, many of southern Arizona's cattle and sheep ranchers now only had each other to worry about.

In fact, the Rangers were so effective that even Captain Wheeler complained of the lack of action and the stale morale his troops suffered because of it. His August report to Governor Kibbey noted, "The whole country seems remarkably quiet and scarcely any crimes are being committed anywhere." Later, Wheeler wrote to Kibbey, "There has been absolutely no trouble of any kind and I am getting tired of so much goodness as are all the men."[22] That is not a complaint one is likely to hear from any law-enforcement officer today, but in the late nineteenth and early twentieth centuries these men joined such services for one thing—the thrill of the chase. Without it they became bored. The rank and file probably did not consider the outcome of their own proficiency, but Wheeler perhaps knew that with eradication of the professional outlaw from much of the territory's wildest ranges and the constant political pressure to disband the organization, the Rangers were unwittingly working themselves out of a job. The shooting death of William F. Downing, "the last of the professional bad men in this section," which should have been a celebratory event, may have been the last nail in the Rangers' coffin. The Rangers were a tremendous law-enforcement success, but that success hastened the outfit's demise.

Tragedy came earlier in April when longtime Ranger Jefferson Parish "Jeff" Kidder wound up in a gun battle with Naco, Sonora, police in the middle of the night. Saloon-hopping, Kidder walked across the border from Naco, Arizona, where he arrived on Friday, April 3. He was supposed to meet Wheeler at Rangers headquarters to sign his reenlistment papers as his commission had expired two days earlier on April 1.[23] Wheeler was out on one of his many scouts for outlaws, however, so Kidder decided to spend time with a senorita on the Mexican side of the border. None of the Rangers were allowed to venture alone to the town, near the site of the Greene mining company labor dispute in 1906, because hard feelings still existed among many of the Mexican miners. Rangers could cross the border in pursuit of a fugitive but generally only after notifying local officials and receiving permission.

Kidder crossed into Sonora late on the evening of April 3 and stuck his badge in a pocket. He removed his gun belt but stuck his pearl-handled .45 in his trousers' belt covered by his coat. He left behind a Winchester rifle, for he did not want anyone in the Mexican town to view his presence as a threat. He found his woman friend, named Chia, but all hell broke loose after a presumably amicable rendezvous. Upon leaving the back room of the saloon where he and Chia had spent time together, Kidder discovered that a silver dollar was missing from his pocket. It was the last dollar he had on him and he accused Chia of swiping it. Chia was enraged by the accusation, threw open the door, and started yelling for the *policia*.

Their first shot went straight through Kidder's midsection and exited his back. Thrown from his feet, Kidder managed to return fire and struck both of the two policemen in their legs. The officers were incapacitated and the severely wounded Kidder staggered to the street. He made it as far as the border fence when Mexican police began sending bullets his way. He hadn't the strength to crawl either through or over the barbed wire, and he sank to the ground. Sitting, he reloaded his pistol and fended off his attackers until he emptied his gun, grazing the police chief, Victoriano Amadore, only slightly. At the sound of the "click" of the hammer, Kidder called out that he had no more fight. The police and others rushed him, dragged him back into the Mexican town, and gave him such a ferocious beating that even the undertaker could not disguise its effects.[24]

Kidder died on Sunday morning, April 5, 1908. The incident rallied more than one thousand citizens in Naco, Arizona, who, when informed the Mexicans would not return the body, armed themselves to go in and get it. Later, cooler heads prevailed; Kidder's body was returned to the United States and shipped to his mother in California for burial.[25]

The New Year brought the Rangers more troubles. This time the challenge was not from gangs or rogue outlaws, but from the Democrats. Long regarded as a Republican force, the Rangers had been criticized at nearly every turn by Democratic opponents. For years the Rangers were little more to the opposing parties than a political Ping-Pong ball.

By 1909, with the Democrats having regained a majority in both houses of the territorial legislature, any attempt to bring down Governor Kibbey, a Republican, had to include the tactic of bringing down the Arizona Rangers.

Even though Captain Wheeler was able to muster a show of support from several county sheriffs and district attorneys, sentiment for and against keeping the Ranger company tilted in favor of those wanting to abolish it. Early in 1909, county councilman Thomas Weedin, a member of one house of Arizona's legislature, passed a bill calling for the abolition of the Rangers.[26] On Saturday, January 30, a joint caucus was held with members of both houses, and the Democratic majority voted to abolish the Arizona Rangers. Their demise would take fifteen days, a few false claims by the author of the bill, and a few pen strokes. On February 15, 1909, the necessary votes to abolish the Rangers were in and the Arizona Rangers were out of business.[27]

# Afterword

Sixty-four-year-old William J. Mulvenon, who served as Yavapai County sheriff from 1885 until 1888, was one of the more distinguished participants in the Pleasant Valley War. He died of Bright's disease on May 26, 1915, while still active in Prescott's emerging business and political community. Mulvenon served in the territorial legislature until 1896 and found time to establish the Crystal Ice Works and the Arizona Brewing Company, both located in Prescott. Since he had an abundant supply of ice and beer on hand, it was only natural that Mulvenon next opened a saloon after the completion of his Mulvenon Building in August 1901.

As the saloon was located just outside the city limits at Gurley and Granite Streets, authorities had little say about the daily operations of Mulvenon's latest enterprise. And there was plenty of speculation as to the goings-on inside the two-story brick building. Mulvenon openly operated the saloon on the first floor. After Prohibition began, he claimed to serve harmless "sodas," but the second floor with its six rented rooms coincidently occupied by six young ladies raised more than a few eyebrows from time to time. Today the saloon lives on as the Gurley Street Grill near the former red-light district.[1]

Commodore Perry Owens shared a name with both his father, Oliver H. Perry Owens, and the famed naval commander Oliver Hazard Perry. Owens' mother christened the boy Commodore at his birth on July 29, 1852. His gunfight in Holbrook in September 1887, in which Owens killed Andy Blevins (Cooper) along with his teenaged brother, Sam Houston Blevins, and Mose Roberts made the sheriff famous throughout the Arizona Territory. This wide-ranging popularity was short lived, however, and Owens was voted out of office at the next election. He was replaced by a former deputy, St. George Creaghe. Owens left Holbrook and Yavapai County to take positions as a deputy U. S. marshal and in 1895 became the first sheriff of the newly formed Navajo County. He eventually retired to Seligman, where he dealt in real estate and opened a store and saloon. In 1902, he married Elizabeth Barrett and by 1910 the couple was living in San Diego, California. The Owens returned to Seligman and saw Arizona become the forty-eighth state on February 14, 1912. Commodore Perry Owens died of Bright's disease on May 10, 1919, at the age of sixty-six. He is buried in the Citizen's Cemetery in Flagstaff.[2]

Pleasant Valley War observer William C. Barnes was born in San Francisco in 1858. He received his education in Minneapolis, Minnesota, and La Porte, Indiana. He joined the military and in 1880 was sent to Arizona Territory, where he served as a telegrapher while stationed at Fort Apache. During an Indian raid on the fort, Barnes distinguished himself by slipping through hostile enemy lines only to return with reinforcements, thus liberating the besieged fort. He was given the Congressional Medal of Honor in 1881. The next year Barnes left the military and dove head and hoof into the cattle business. He eventually became the principal owner of the Esperanza Cattle Company, one of the largest operations in Apache County at the time. By 1890, Barnes was appointed to the Apache County Board of Supervisors. The next year, he was elected to the territorial legislature. In 1893, he was named to the Arizona Commission to the Chicago World's Fair. Barnes next agreed to serve as chairman of the Arizona Live Stock

Board in 1897, serving three years. Also that year he found time to court and marry Edith Talbot in Phoenix.

Barnes moved to New Mexico in 1901 and was immediately pressed into public service there when he was elected to its territorial legislature the same year. Not surprisingly, he also accepted an appointed position on New Mexico's Live Stock Board, as he had in Arizona, serving from 1902 until 1907. His resignation from that board only meant that the ever-moving-forward Barnes now had time to serve another government agency. This time he went to work for the Forest Service. Barnes retired after twenty-one years but again found time to fulfill his desire to be the consummate public servant by becoming the secretary of the U.S. Geographic Board in Washington, D.C. When he retired in 1930, he returned to his beloved Arizona and immediately set out on his next project. After working five years he published *Arizona Place Names*. Barnes laid down his ambitions entirely, however, when on December 17, 1936, he died.[3]

Many of the Arizona Rangers alumni fared as well as the survivors of the Pleasant Valley War. Burton C. Mossman, the first captain of the Arizona Rangers, resigned but lived well for a while thanks to the generosity of mining magnate Col. W. C. Greene. Mossman ran a huge ranching outfit in South Dakota called the Diamond A. In 1905, while stopping in Kansas City on the way to New York City, Mossman met and then married a woman named Grace. She died nine days after giving birth to the couple's second child, a girl.

Mossman moved to Roswell, New Mexico, in 1916, and from there managed the Diamond A Ranch. In 1925, Mossman met and married thirty-three-year-old Ruth Shrader; Mossman was fifty-eight. Tragedy again struck the Mossman clan when his son, Maj. Burton C. "Billy" Mossman, Jr., died in a plane crash in 1943. Mossman Sr. retired from ranching in 1944 and died in 1956.[4]

Harry Cornwall Wheeler was the Arizona Rangers' third and final captain. And despite the passage of Act No. 64 by the Twenty-Fifth Legislative Assembly of Arizona Territory on February 15, 1909, immediately abolishing the Arizona Rangers, Wheeler remained in law enforcement. He served as a deputy sheriff of Cochise County before being elected sheriff in 1911. He would serve two more terms with reelections in 1914 and 1916. His experience putting down labor disputes as a Ranger came in handy in 1917, as workers with the Copper Queen Mining Company in Bisbee halted production with a massive strike. Sheriff Wheeler hired an impressive number of "special deputies"—275— to help quell the problem. In a somewhat shocking tactic, Wheeler and his deputies force-marched 1,187 strikers and their supporters to waiting boxcars on the outskirts of Bisbee. From there the miners were railed out into the desert and unloaded at a small community near the border of New Mexico.[5] The army later provided rudimentary provisions such as tents, food, and water. Wheeler's questionable method was railed against in the local press, who called the forced march and railroading the "Bisbee deportation."[6] Many viewed the controversial tactic as an illegal government-sponsored kidnapping, which would later haunt Wheeler's career.

Wheeler left the Rangers after he received a commission as a captain in the army and was being transported to France in April 1918 for assignment during the First World War when legal troubles arising from the Bisbee deportation called him back to Arizona. His lengthy absence from the army while preparing for trial as a defendant prompted the army to honorably discharge him in December. Wheeler and all others connected to the Bisbee incident were acquitted.

The next year Wheeler divorced his wife of twenty-one years and after only two months married an eighteen-year-old woman from Douglas, Arizona. He ran for sheriff of Cochise County in 1922 but was soundly defeated as many voters still questioned Wheeler's use of the overbearing tactics during the Copper Queen strike incident. On December 17, 1925, at the age of forty-nine, Harry Wheeler died of complications from pneumonia.[7]

Burt Alvord, the outlaw whose escapes from Ranger custody numbered one more than his arrests, hit a trail out of Arizona never to return following his third and final escape. He was supposedly sighted in far-off places such as Honduras, Venezuela, and Canada. Alvord died sometime in 1910, presumably in Honduras or possibly while living on a small island off the coast of Panama.[8]

Perhaps William Larkin "Billy" Stiles relied on his brief tenure in 1902 as an Arizona Ranger to seek employment in law enforcement, but Stiles found it prudent to leave Arizona and traveled to Nevada where he became a deputy sheriff. Deputy Stiles proved proficient at this rekindled trade. In 1908, Deputy Stiles was among a group of men who chased down and killed a Nevada cattle thief. The dead rustler's avenging brother caught Stiles in ambush and killed him in retaliation that same year.[9]

Gov. Nathan Oakes Murphy, the politically astute governor of the Arizona Territory who was responsible for the founding of the Arizona Rangers, served two terms as governor. He resigned in 1902 and spent much of his free time traveling throughout the United States and Europe. He especially enjoyed visiting California. On August 22, 1908, while visiting the Hotel Del Coronado, he died a sudden death. Initially buried in the Woodlawn Cemetery in San Diego, Murphy was reinterred at Rock Creek Cemetery in Washington, D.C., in December 1909. [10]

The last territorial governor who fought to keep the Rangers' force intact was Joseph Henry Kibbey. On February 15, 1909, after a lengthy and contentious battle with the territorial legislature, the Arizona Rangers were once and for all voted out of existence. Kibbey left office a few months after losing the battle to keep the Rangers. When he resigned on May 1, 1909, Pres. William Taft immediately nominated Richard Sloan. Kibbey lent his legal expertise to the Salt River Valley Water User's Association as its counsel for several years until he was again tapped by the Republican Party to reenter the political arena. In 1916, four years after statehood, he was nominated the party's candidate for U.S. Senate from Arizona but ran an unsuccessful campaign. Kibbey died in Phoenix on June 14, 1924, and is buried in Greenwood Memorial Park.[11]

Thomas H. Rynning was the second captain of the Arizona Rangers and then appointed prison superintendent at Yuma. He left that coveted position when the Democrats came to power in 1912 and began replacing Republican appointees. Rynning simply packed his bags and headed to San Diego, where he remained until the Arizona Republicans returned to power in 1921.[12] He regained his superintendent's post and resumed his duties at the new prison at Florence after Arizona gained statehood in 1912. When he retired he moved back to San Diego and received a commission as deputy U.S. marshal while also serving as under sheriff. The grizzled old lawman with three gunfights under his belt died of a heart attack at age seventy-five on June 18, 1941, while caring for his flowers.[13]

# Notes

**Introduction**

1. Breakenridge, 115.
2. Sheridan, *Arizona*, 26-27. In 1736, huge boulders of native silver weighing up to 2,500 pounds were found on a ranch owned by Bernardo de Urrea which was covered by oak trees and referred to as Arizona, roughly translated as "the good oak."
3. Trimble, *Arizona*, xiii.
4. Trimble, xx; Sheridan, 31.
5. Faulk, *Tombstone: Myth and Reality*, 6-7. Spanish missions remained in the area until 1846.
6. Trimble, xxi. Only Tucson escaped the depredations.
7. Sheridan, 126-27.
8. Sheridan, 129-30.
9. Sheridan, 137.
10. Pattie, 1.
11. Trimble, 83, 85.
12. Cooke, 197; Tyler, 282; Roberts, *The Mormon Battalion*, 53.
13. Roberts, 50.
14. Tyler, 204.
15. Cooke, 149, 151; Roberts, 50.
16. Cooke, 197; Tyler, 282; Roberts, 53.
17. Unfortunately, a map referenced in the treaty placed El Paso, Texas, north and east of its actual location. Although commissioners appointed by the two countries agreed on the necessary amendments, the American surveyor would not concur. The controversy was finally settled in the Gadsden Purchase of 1853.
18. Trimble, 89.
19. Ibid., 89-91
20. Ibid., 93-95.
21. Ibid.
22. Sides, 301-4, 379.
23. Ball, *U.S. Marshals*, 41-64.

24. Ball, 67-68.

25. Ernst, 90-91.

26. Ball, 74-76.

27. At least one writer has suggested that Curly Bill Brocius and C. Bill Graham were two different people. Marks, 103.

28. Marks, 126.

29. Ibid., citing Jacob R. Marcus, ed., "An Arizona Pioneer: Memoirs of Sam Aaron," *American Jewish Archives* 10, no. 1 (October 1958), 102.

30. Trimble, 101-3.

31. Faulk, 9.

32. Ibid., 11-12.

33. Yadon and Anderson, 53.

34. Trimble, 101-3.

35. Faulk, 13-14.

36. Trimble, 103.

37. Faulk, 18.

38. Ball, *U.S. Marshals,* 108-14.

39. The recollections of Ed Schieffelin have largely been extracted from Breakenridge, 138-51.

40. Camp Huachuca was established in 1877, became a fort, and eventually an important twentieth-century communications post.

41. Meaning unrefined ore.

42. The Homestead Act of 1862, providing 640 acres of public domain land in the desert in lieu of the standard 160 acres provided in more arable areas.

43. Richard Gird was destined to play a pivotal role in the development of Tombstone and Southern California.

44. A long abandoned mine and ghost town in west-central Arizona about forty miles east of Lake Havasu City.

45. Breakenridge, 146-54.

46. Sheridan, 152-53.

47. Marks, 414.


**Chapter 1**

1. Lubet, 4-5.

2. Boyer, ed., 238-42.

3. Marks, 116, citing Faulk, *Arizona: A Short History,* 94.

4. Breakenridge, 170.

5. Faulk, *Tombstone,* 115. Spicer defended Indian agent John Lee during his trial for the 1857 Mountain Meadows massacre of emigrants

from Arkansas and Missouri passing through Mormon country. Marks, 162. See Chapter 5 for more biographical information.

6. Parsons, *A Tenderfoot in Tombstone,* 151 n. 111, 155 n. 113.

7. Ibid., 66. The Parsons text actually confuses this place with the Occidental, which was on Allen.

8. Breakenridge, 171.

9. Earp, 178.

10. Breakenridge, 172. During the early Charleston years, Barton killed a customer named Jesus Gamboa, as well as his own business partner, a Mr. Merrill. After relocating to nearby Fairbank, Barton killed seventy-six-year-old E. J. Swift in 1887 and subsequently a Phoenix man but apparently was never convicted of those crimes. Martin, 63-66.

11. Adams, *More Burs,* 56.

12. Breakenridge, 8-30, 135.

13. Ibid., 37. Later, Geary used $13,200 in compensation from the federal government to build a hotel near Greeley.

14. Utley, 292-97.

15. Breakenridge, 94.

16. Ibid., 133-34; Ball, *Desert Lawmen,* 134.

17. Marks, 75-76.

18. Breakenridge, 137. According to his own account Wyatt Earp had arrived some twenty-six days earlier. Breakenridge related in his memoir that the first house in Tombstone was built in April 1879, about one mile from where the first miner's camp was established.

19. Marks, 25-29.

20. The time of Wyatt Earp's arrival is verified by William M. Breakenridge in *Helldorado,* 154. Earp apparently served as a Wichita policeman beginning April 21, 1875. Adams, *Burs,* 422.

21. Tefertiller, 4. However, his father and uncle were acquitted of the charge.

22. Boyer, ed., 38 n. 4.

23. Tefertiller, 5.

24. Marks, 79; Adams, *Burs,* 371. Bison hunting was one of the most lucrative short-term endeavors of the nineteenth century. Buffalo hides brought three dollars, and a skillful hunter could bring one down for the price of a twenty-five-cent cartridge. The most extensive (and profitable) season began in the fall of 1871 continued through to the next spring. Buffalo camps were virtual training grounds for the lawmen of that era due to the wide variety of weapons used and intensity of the hunting.

25. Adams, *Burs,* 246.

26. Marks, 82.

27. Newspaper accounts provide a chronological account of the Wyatt

Earp law-enforcement career before Tombstone: *Lamar (MO) Democrat,* September 6, 1957 Centennial Edition; *Wichita (KS) Daily Beacon,* May 24, 1876; *Dodge City (KS) Times,* October 14, 1876; and *Ford County (KS) Globe,* September 9, 1879.

28. Marks, 86; Adams, *Burs,* 19.

29. According to the *Prescott Weekly Miner,* Virgil Earp began a trip to Tombstone as early as November 14, so he may have arrived earlier. Readers should note that common law marriages, where allowed, are just as valid as those documented by licenses.

30. *San Francisco Examiner,* August 2, 1896.

31. Boyer, ed., 56 n. 5. One researcher relates that Virgil married again a Rosello Dragoo at Lamar, Missouri, in 1879.

32. Marks, 113, Adams, *Burs,* 329.

33. Dodge, 9.

34. Tefertiller, 4.

35. Sheridan, 118.

36. Boyer, ed., 7, 12-16.

37. Earp, 195-96. The emphasis is supplied.

38. Marks, 65; Adams, *Burs,* 547.

39. Ibid., 43.

40. Breakenridge, 205 n. 8.

41. Ibid., 170.

42. Marks, 92-93.

43. Ibid., 92.

44. Breakenridge, 166-67.

45. Ibid., 169-70.

46. Masterson, 40 n. 14.

47. Hurst was a lieutenant at the time of the incident. Marks, 90.

48. Breakenridge, 254. The date of the event was provided in Marks, 90.

49. Ball, *Desert Lawman,* 293.

50. Marks, 80.

51. Parsons, 111.

52. Breakenridge, 196-97. Breakenridge was incorrect in describing the death of Killeen as having occurred twenty days earlier, on June 2. George Perine testified he had been present during the killing, contrary to the testimony of Leslie and his amour. At least three different versions of this shooting have been recorded. Tefertiller, 47.

53. Parsons, 58.

54. Marks, 96-98.

55. Tefertiller, 47.

56. *San Francisco Examiner,* August 2, 1896.

57. Yadon and Anderson, 121.

58. Tefertiller, 49; Tanner, *Doc Holliday,* 144.

59. Parsons, 80.


**Chapter 2**

1. Earp, 65-70. Years later, William Breakenridge recorded the date of this incident as November 6 and stated that Virgil rather than Wyatt had put his arms around Curly Bill Brocius. Breakenridge, 157-58.

2. Earp, 333.

3. Marks, 106-7.

4. Marks, 119-20.

5. Accommodations were so limited in Tombstone that Sheriff Behan initially lived in the back of a tobacco shop. Ball, *Desert Lawmen,* 23.

6. Ball, *Desert Lawmen,* 23.

7. Breakenridge, 161 n. 7.

8. Marks, 115.

9. *San Francisco Examiner,* August 2, 1896.

10. Breakenridge, 161.

11. Marks, 119, 121.

12. Earp, 101-2.

13. Wyatt, 101-2.

14. Breakenridge, 192-94.

15. Parsons, 118.

16. Breakenridge, 201-2.

17. Breakenridge, 183; Young, 1.

18. Parsons, 119-20.

19. Parsons, 120-21.

20. Adams, *Burs,* 331, 552. Wyatt Earp has erroneously been placed at the scene through the years.

21. Parsons, 119.

22. One observer contends that Curly Bill and the cowboys were loosely allied with Clark and Gray. Sheridan, 154.

23. Marks, 117. Parsons, 107 n. 88; Adams, *Burs,* 330.

24. Marks, 118.

25. Earp, 21-22, 39.

26. Masterson, 55-56. Emphasis supplied.

27. Marks, 130.

28. Parsons, 129.

29. Another version of this robbery places one robber in the road to stop the stage. Marks, 134.

30. Breakenridge, 209. Breakenridge incorrectly described this as

the "Sandy Bob" stage robbery, which actually occurred the following September.

31. Marks, 136.

32. Emphasis supplied. One Len Redfield was reportedly lynched two years later in Florence after the fatal shooting of stagecoach guard Johnny Miller.

33. Breakenridge, 209-13.

34. Earp, 106.

35. Parsons, 136 n. 104.

36. Marks, 137.

37. Earp, 58.

38. Marks, 134.

39. Breakenridge, 211-12.

40. Marcus, ed., "An Arizona Pioneer," 103; Marks, 137.

41. Waters, 144.

42. Marks, 137-38, 142.

43. Gray, *When All Roads Led to Tombstone,* 54-55; Marks, 137.

44. Dodge, 246.

45. Waters, 134. Marks, 142.

46. Marks, 138.

47. Ibid., 141-42.

48. Ibid., 142.

49. *Tombstone Daily Nugget,* July 6. The affidavit was executed on July 5.

50. Marks, 162.

51. Breakenridge, 226-27.

52. Boyer, ed., 65-66.

53. Marks, 127-28.

54. This technique was known as the "road agent spin."

55. There is no known record of this.

56. Breakenridge, 230.

57. This is open to question, at least according to one biographer, who claimed that Ringo was rejected by his family on a trip to San Jose, California, in 1881 or 1882. Breakenridge, 232 n. 8.

58. Breakenridge, 232-33.

59. Ibid., 233-34.

60. Ibid., 240-41.


**Chapter 3**

1. Marks, 148.

2. Breakenridge, 278-81, 283-85, 297 n. 8.

3. Breakenridge, 281.

4. Adams, *More Burs,* 56; Tefertiller, 86.

5. Breakenridge, 211 n. 12. Other sources say their deaths occurred June 12 as Head and Leonard tried to ambush the Hasletts. Crane was killed during the Guadeloupe Canyon ambush of August 13, 1881. Earp, 45; Adams, *Burs,* 333.

6. Gray, *When All Roads Led to Tombstone,* 54-55; Marks, 164.

7. Breakenridge, 182.

8. Martin, 152.

9. Marks, 179. Deputy Stilwell operated livery stables in Bisbee and Charleston. His brother Simpson "Comanche Jack" Stillwell was a noted army scout. Neither was apparently related to Judge William H. Stillwell.

10. Dodge, 14.

11. *Tombstone Epitaph,* September 10, 1881.

12. Breakenridge, 237.

13. Marks, 180.

14. Breakenridge, 237-38. The Breakenridge manuscript references Pete Spence rather than Spencer.

15. Marks, 180.

16. Breakenridge, 238-39. Charles Ray, alias Pony Deal (Diehl) had been associated with the Jesse Evans gang in New Mexico about nine years before. Wallis, 128.

17. Earp, 80-85.

18. Ibid., 84.

19. Breakenridge, 268-69.

20. Ibid., 269.

21. Parsons, 179.

22. Breakenridge, 274-76. This apparently occurred between October 5 and October 12. Gen. George Crook obtained Geronimo's surrender later in Mexico. Parsons describes the rancher as Mr. Frinck and does not mention the rancher retrieving his own livestock. Parsons, 181.

23. Parsons, 178.

24. Earp, 60.

25. Breakenridge, 175-78.

26. Marks, 194.

27. Breakenridge, 242. Billy Clanton and Frank McLaury rode in from Charleston the next day and were in town by about one o'clock.

28. Dodge, 26. The spelling, punctuation, and grammar have been standardized.

29. Breakenridge, 242.

30. Marks, 200.

31. Earp, 88.

32. Marks, 200-1.
33. Ibid., 202.
34. Lubet, 48.
35. Ibid., 131-32.
36. Earp, 91-92.
37. Breakenridge, 244-46.
38. Ibid., xxii.
39. Ernst, 268-72.
40. Samuelson, 57-58.
41. Parsons,188.


**Chapter 4**
1. Marks, 235-36.
2. Bell, 78.
3. Lubet, 35. This chapter is largely based on *Murder in Tombstone: The Forgotten Trial of Wyatt Earp.*
4. *Tombstone Epitaph,* October 28, 1881. Spellings have been modernized.
5. Boyer, 97.
6. Lubet, 59.
7. Ibid., 60-61. Virgil Earp was actually chief of police at the time of the gunfight.
8. Ibid., 61.
9. Ibid., 66.
10. Lubet, 65.
11. *Tombstone Nugget,* October 30, 1881.
12. Parsons, 189.
13. Lubet, 60.
14. Ibid., 82-83.
15. Ibid., 80.
16. Breakenridge, 255 n. 7; Lubet, 75-79.
17. A second set of charges were filed at Contention by Ike Clanton on February 9, 1882. Probate Judge J.H. Lucas, who had testified as a witness at the first preliminary hearing, promptly granted habeas corpus to the Earps and Holliday because the charges had been found without merit the first day of December of the prior year. Ramon Adams and others have noted that Judge Spicer was friendly with the Earps and their associate John Clum. Adams, *Burs,* 372.
18. Lubet, 87-88.
19. Ibid., 106.
20. Ibid., 107.

21. Ibid., 110.

22. Breakenridge, 246-47.

23. Lubet, 117-28, 130.

24. Ibid., 132.

25. One researcher indicates the law allows a verbal statement but that Spicer expanded on the rule to permit Wyatt Earp the opportunity to submit a written statement without cross-examination. Alexander, *John H. Behan,* 146. Alexander also points out that none of Wyatt's statement was corroborated by anyone and Spicer might have been related to the Earps by marriage. Alexander, *John H. Behan,* 142 n. 6, 150-51.

26. Alexander, *John H. Behan,* 153. Behan also related that there were eight to ten shots fired before he saw weapons in the hands of Frank McLaury and Billy Clanton. Alexander, *John H. Behan,* 129.

27. Statement of Wyatt Earp as recorded in the *Tombstone Epitaph,* November 18, 1881.

28. Boyer, ed., 92, as cited in Alexander, *John H. Behan,* 154.

29. Alexander, *John H. Behan,* 154.

30. Lubet, 154-55.

31. Ibid., 162-63.

32. Ibid., 165.

33. Alexander, *John H. Behan,* 164-67.

34. The Lucas and Sills testimony is summarized in Breakenridge, 252-53.

35. Breakenridge, 255.

36. Lubet, 65.

37. Ibid., 256. Emphasis supplied.

38. Ibid., 260.

39. Thus eminent legal historian Steven Lubet described the results of this hearing, 223.


**Chapter 5**

1. Ball, *The United States Marshals,* 123; Alexander, 118.

2. Breakenridge, 197-98.

3. Another authority states the Bird Cage opened on December 23. Faulk, 116.

4. Breakenridge, 261-62. This event apparently occurred in December 1881 or the next month.

5. Ibid., 170-71, 286 n. 4.

6. Parsons, 198-99.

7. Ibid., 198 n. 129. Wyatt Earp requested authority to commission deputy U.S. marshals the day after Virgil was shot. Wyatt Earp claimed

in an 1896 *San Francisco Examiner* article that five double-barreled shotguns were used in the attempt. Others believed that the five shots came from three shotguns.

8. Earp, 59. Arrest warrants were later issued for Pony Deal, A. T. Tiebot, and Charlie Haws.

9. Ibid., 130. The date of the attempted resignations was February 1, 1882.

10. Breakenridge, 265 n. 265, citing Larry D. Ball, *The United States Marshals*, 123, 132. However, one source indicates that the Earp posse was deputized by U.S. Marshal Dake himself. Adams, *Burs*, 187.

11. Breakenridge, 215.

12. Ibid., 265-67.

13. Parsons, 212.

14. Earp, 120; Breakenridge, 285.

15. Earp, 124. The April 13, 1884, letter is in the possession of the Arizona Historical Society.

16. Marks, 346-47.

17. Adams, *Burs*, 373.

18. Breakenridge, 286-87.

19. The Breakenridge account implies that the Stilwell killing occurred on March 19. Modern authorities assume that the incident actually occurred on the evening of March 20. Ball, *The United States Marshals*, 124.

20. Earp was also apparently incorrect in stating to the *Denver Republican* that year that he stumbled into Clanton in the Tucson train yards. Adams, *Burs*, 373.

21. Ibid., *Burs*, 572-73.

22. Breakenridge, 287-88.

23. Marks, 350. This account is largely taken from *And Die in the West*.

24. *Tombstone Epitaph*, March 22, 1882.

25. Ibid.

26. This is the most commonly accepted date of the incident. Marks, 356. Since the exact location is unknown and most literature describes the place as Iron Springs, that designation is used here. Earp did not identify the specific place in his story, but at the time, the *Tombstone Epitaph* identified it as Burleigh Springs, which was about eight miles south of Tombstone. To make matters more confusing, Mescal Springs is several miles from Iron Springs. An investigation in 2008 revealed that the incident may have happened at Cottonwood Springs. Evans, "Gunfight in the Whetstone Mountains." Nobody really knows what happened to Curly Bill. One researcher reported that a Judge Hancock and several

newspapers verified that Curly Bill Brocius left Arizona Territory some six months before the Iron Springs gunfight supposedly occurred. Adams, *Burs,* 573. This of course would not eliminate the possibility that Curly Bill returned to Arizona in time to get himself killed.

27. Wyatt Earp interview with the *San Francisco Examiner,* August 2, 1896, as reported in Earp, 124-25.

28. *Denver Republican,* May 14, 1893, as related in Earp, 144-45.

29. The *Tombstone Epitaph* reported the incident March 25, 1882, on information received from the Earp posse. One can only say that no primary source documenting Curly Bill's presence in Arizona after 1882 has yet been discovered. That could mean he was killed as Wyatt Earp claimed but could also mean that he found anonymity elsewhere.

30. Breakenridge, 292-93; Breakenridge made little effort to disguise the partiality for Curly Bill, which is apparent throughout his memoir.

31. Dodge, 231-33.

32. Ball, *The United States Marshals,* 125; John Ringo was found dead on July 14, either murdered or a victim of suicide. Some attribute this death to Wyatt Earp and Doc Holliday.

33. *San Francisco Examiner,* August 2, 1896, as quoted in Earp, 123.

34. Breakenridge, 294.

35. Marks, 367.

36. Parsons, 213-15.

37. Breakenridge, 298-99.

38. Ibid., 301-12.

39. Ibid., 302.

40. Ibid.

41. Ibid., 304-5.

42. Ibid., 308.

43. Marks, 368.

44. Ibid., 374.

45. Ball, *The United States Marshals,* 126. See also Walker, "Retire Peaceably to Your Homes," 7.

46. Marks, 379-80. The destinations of McMasters, Johnson, and the rest of the party besides the Earps and Holliday has never been definitively established.

47. *Denver Tribune,* May 17, 1882, as quoted in Earp, 325-30.

48. Earp, 342-34.

49. Spellings modernized from "McLowry." The original punctuation has been retained.

50. This reference to "Billy the Kid" probably meant Billy Claiborne, but one wonders if Warren Earp or the reporter wanted to create a better

story by leaving the false impression that *the* Billy the Kid, known to most readers of the time, was involved. William H. Bonney (real name Henry McCarty) had been dead almost a year by the time of the interview.

51. Tefertiller, 323.

52. Boyer, 108.

53. Breakenridge, 320. Five years later, a fire destroyed a pump system that controlled the seepage in two of the major mines. When the mine owners could not agree on how to divide the cost of repairs, deep mining in Tombstone ended. A temporary mining resurgence which began in 1902 ended seven years later.

54. Alexander, *Dangerous Dan Tucker,* 128, 139; Metz, *Encyclopedia,* 114; O'Neal, *Encyclopedia,* 22; Breakenridge, 324-28. Former deputy sheriff Breakenridge noted in his memoir that he had seen five men hanged by vigilance committees but not a single legal execution. The Goldwater proprietors were the grandfather and great-uncle of United States senator Barry M. Goldwater.

55. Marks, 405-7.

56. Earp, 114.

57. Ibid., 116-18.

58. Ibid., 175. Wyatt gave a deposition in Los Angeles on behalf of Carlotta Cockburn in litigation over the estate of Lotta Crabtree, a famous and wealthy actress of the 1880s. Carlotta unsuccessfully attempted to break the terms of a four-million-dollar charitable trust, claiming to be a niece of Lotta Crabtree.

59. Earp, 175.

60. The term cowboy has been substituted for cow boys, as in many other places, for continuity.

61. Lubet, 219; Alexander, *John H. Behan,* 205, 210.

62. Yadon and Anderson, *200 Texas Outlaws and Lawmen,* 123.

63. Tefertiller, 268.

64. Marks, 410.

65. Breakenridge, 138; Tefertiller, 281.

66. Tefertiller, 281.

67. Marks, 421.

68. Ibid., 416; Adams, *More Burs,* 16.

69. Breakenridge, 185.

70. Ibid., 262 n. 3.

71. Marks, 413-14.

72. Barra, 340.

73. Marks, 422.

74. Breakenridge, 208 n. 8.

75. Parsons, xiii-xv.

76. Dodge, xiii.

77. Boyer, ed., 252. One researcher has noted that there are significant variations between this work and a manuscript Josephine Earp worked on with two of Wyatt Earp's relatives between 1936 and her death in 1944. Barra, 385.

78. Tanner, *Doc Holliday*, 223-24.

79. Breakenridge, 198 n. 3.

80. Marks, 402-3.

81. Ibid., 402-33; Breakenridge, 199 identifies the ranch hand as O'Neil.

82. Adams, *More Burs*, 21.

83. Breakenridge, 198-200; Sonnichsen, 43.

84. Adams, *Burs* 538; Adams, *More Burs*, 15, 22.

**Chapter 6**

1. Fish, Joseph. Papers. Folder 7, 688.

2. Ibid.

3. O'Neal, *Cattlemen vs Sheepherders*, 18.

4. The term "weapons of grass destruction" was coined by coauthor Laurence Yadon.

5. Monaghan, ed., 290.

6. O'Neal, *Cattlemen vs. Sheepherder*, 23.

7. *San Angelo (TX) Standard-Times*, February 3, 1889.

8. *The New Handbook of Texas Online*, "Sonora, Texas."

9. 18th Texas Legislature, *Title 99a. Wool-Growing Interest*, 42.

10. Ibid.

11. *San Angelo (TX) Standard-Times*, December 12, 1941.

12. Gammel, 567, 569.

13. Shirley, *Shotgun for Hire*, 56.

14. O'Neal, *Cattlemen vs. Sheepherder*, 2.

15. Ibid., 68.

16. *Biographical Directory of the United States Congress*, "Ross, Edmund Gibson, (1826-1907)."

17. O'Neal, *Cattlemen vs. Sheepherder*, 67-68.

18. Department of the Interior, Census Office, Tenth Census.

19. Edmund G. Ross Collection, 491.

20. Monaghan, ed., 290.

21. Edmund G. Ross Collection, 491.

**Chapter 7**

1. Barnes, "The Pleasant Valley War," 7.

2. Barnes, *Arizona Place Names*, 413.

3. O'Neal, *Cattlemen vs Sheepherders,* 46-47.
4. Ibid., 46.
5. Barnes, "The Pleasant Valley War of 1887: Part II," 36.
6. Fish, Joseph. Papers. Folder 7, 652-763.
7. O'Neal, *Cattlemen vs Sheepherders,* 47.
8. Fish, Joseph. Papers. Folder 7, 687.
9. *Cococino (AZ) Sun,* September 10, 1887, quoted Mrs. John Blevins (Eva) as saying that Andy "took the name of 'Cooper' when [he was] an outlaw in Texas."
10. McKinney, "Reminiscences" (April 1923), 37.
11. Ibid., 46.
12. Ibid.
13. Ibid., 48.
14. Ibid., 51.
15. Barnes, "The Pleasant Valley War of 1887: Part II," 24-25.
16. Barnes, "The Pleasant Valley War," 33.
17. Barnes, "The Pleasant Valley War of 1887: Part II," 36.
18. Ibid., 52.
19. O'Neal, *Cattlemen vs Sheepherders,* 51.
20. Fish, Joseph. Papers. Folder 7, 652-763.
21. Barnes, "The Pleasant Valley War of 1887: Part II," 38.
22. *Flagstaff (AZ) Champion,* September 10, 1887.
23. Ibid.
24. Barnes, "The Pleasant Valley War of 1887: Part II," 32.
25. *Prescott Journal-Miner,* September 9, 1887.
26. Joseph T. McKinney to Mrs. George F. Kitt, January 16, 1929, Tucson. "Joseph T. McKinney, 1858- [biofile]."
27. Drago, 122.
28. O'Neal, *Cattlemen vs Sheepherders,* 53.
29. Drago, 122.
30. *New York Times,* September 3, 1887; *Prescott Journal-Miner,* September 2, 1887.
31. O'Neal, *Cattlemen vs Sheepherders,* 51.
32. Drago, 122.
33. Barnes, "The Pleasant Valley War," 7.
34. McKinney, "Reminiscences" (April 1923), 50.
35. *Prescott Journal-Miner,* September 9, 1887.
36. *Arizona Silver Belt,* October 1, 1887.
37. Barnes, "The Pleasant Valley War of 1887: Part II," 33.
38. O'Neal, *Cattlemen vs Sheepherders,* 56.
39. Barnes, "The Pleasant Valley War," 7.
40. Dedera, 240-41.

## Chapter 8

1. Gravley, Ernestine, "Fifty Years Ago in Shawnee and Pottawatomie County," in *The Chronicles of Oklahoma* 31, no. 4, 381 ff.
2. Fortson, *Pott County*, 20.
3. Schooley, R.B., Indian-Pioneer Papers.
4. Cantelou, Jennie Watts.
5. Fortson, 20 ff.
6. Cantelou, Jennie Watts, Indian-Pioneer Papers, Letter from Santa Fe.
7. *Daily Oklahoman,* July 5, 1895.
8. *Edmond (OK) Sun-Democrat,* 1895.
9. Ibid.
10. *Daily Oklahoman,* July 1, 1895.
11. Burton, Jeff, *Black Jack Christian.*
12. Ibid.
13. Haley, 268.
14. Wilson, *An Unwritten History.*
15. Ibid., 53.
16. Haley, 270.
17. Ibid., 275-76
18. Burton, Jeff, *Black Jack Christian.*
19. Ibid.


## Chapter 9

1. Traywick, *Chronicles of Tombstone,* 154.
2. Cunningham, 299.
3. Erwin, *The Southwest of John H. Slaughter,* 199.
4. O'Neal, *Encyclopedia,* 287.
5. Cunningham, 299.
6. Burns, 1-200.
7. Ibid., 311.
8. Traywick, *Chronicles of Tombstone,* 141.
9. Erwin, 199.
10. Cunningham, 303.
11. Ibid., 304.
12. Traywick, *Chronicles of Tombstone,* 142; Burns, 313.
13. Erwin, 225.
14. Ibid., 199, quoting from the *Los Angeles Times,* September 1, 1940.
15. Burns, 328.
16. Traywick, *Chronicles of Tombstone,* 143; Burns, 321.
17. Cunningham, 309.

18. Traywick, *Chronicles of Tombstone,* 143.
19. Cunningham, 308.
20. Traywick, *Chronicles of Tombstone,* 145.
21. Erwin, 266-67, but acknowledging the other versions of the Kid's death.
22. O'Neal, 289.


## Chapter 10

1. Haley, 12.
2. Ibid., 30-31.
3. Ibid., 103.
4. Ibid., 97.
5. Ibid., 185.
6. Ibid., 77.
7. Ibid., 218.
8. Ibid., 220.
9. DeArment, *George Scarborough,* 278 n. 8.
10. Ibid., 104.
11. Haley, 245; DeArment, *George Scarborough,* 124.
12. Traywick, *Legendary Characters,* 118.
13. DeArment, *Deadly Dozen,* 72.
14. Wilson, *Encyclopedia,* 122ff.


## Chapter 11

1. Breakenridge, 115.
2. Ibid., 395-404.
3. Wilson, *Great Stagecoach Robberies,* 151, citing the *Arizona Star.*
4. Hart, "An Arizona Episode," 673-77.
5. Ibid., 675.
6. Cleere, 100.
7. Hart, "An Arizona Episode," 675.
8. Horan, *Desperate Women,* 294.
9. Hart, "An Arizona Episode," *Cosmopolitan,* 677.
10. Wilson, *Great Stagecoach Robberies,* 156.
11. Horan, 297.
12. Cleere, 103.
13. Horan, 304.
14. Ibid., 303.
15. McClintock, "Train Robbers."

16. Faulk, 159.
17. McClintock, "Train Robbers."
18. Rasch, Desperadoes, 77.
19. DeArment, *Deadly Dozen,* 117.
20. Rasch, *Desperadoes,* 77.
21. DeArment, *Deadly Dozen,* 138.
22. Ibid.
23. Ibid., 149.
24. Rasch, *Desperadoes,* 158.
25. Ibid., 161.
26. Cleere, 64ff.
27. Ibid., 66.
28. Ibid., 67-68.
29. Ibid., 71.

**Chapter 12**

1. Biographical Directory of the United States Congress, "Nathan Oakes Murphy, 1849-1908."
2. O'Neal, *The Arizona Rangers,* 6.
3. Ibid., 2.
4. Burton C. Mossman interview, *Arizona Daily Star,* January 9, 1947.
5. *Bisbee (AZ) Daily Review,* November 16, 1901.
6. Sharp, "The Maxwells of Arizona," 34-35, 46.
7. O'Neal, *The Arizona Rangers,* 14.
8. Hunt, 153.
9. O'Neal, *The Arizona Rangers,* 21, 190 n. 3; Barnes, "The Pleasant Valley War of 1887: Part II," 23.
10. *Tucson Citizen,* August 19 and 21, 1902.
11. "Thomas H. Rynning [biofile]."
12. O'Neal, *The Arizona Rangers,* 34.
13. Twenty-Second Legislative Assembly, 104-6.
14. O'Neal, *The Arizona Rangers,* 49.
15. Ibid., 51.
16. "Thomas H. Rynning [biofile]."
17. *Nogales (AZ) Border Vidette,* February 27, 1904.
18. Wagoner, 194-97.
19. *Bisbee (AZ) Daily Review,* June 2, 1906. The capitalization used in this message was common practice when sending a telegram.
20. Cananea Consolidated Copper Company records, ca. 1893-1930.
21. O'Neal, *The Arizona Rangers,* 116.

22. Wheeler, Harry, to Gov. Joseph H. Kibbey, August 7, 1908, Arizona Rangers Files.

23. O'Neal, *The Arizona Rangers,* 139.

24. Wheeler, Harry, to Gov. Joseph H. Kibbey, August 7, 1908, Arizona Rangers Files.

25. Ibid.; *Bisbee (AZ) Daily Review,* April 7, 1908.

26. O'Neal, *The Arizona Rangers,* 164-65.

27. *Journal of the Twenty-fifth Legislative Assembly, 1909,* 94-111; *Acts, Resolutions, and Memorials, Twenty-fifth Legislative Assembly, 1909,* Chapter 4:3.

**Afterword**

1. Slayton, "Ghosts Celebrating 100 Years near the "Red Light" District at Grill."

2. "Testimony taken in the cause of the killing of Houston Blevins, Mose Roberts, and Andy Cooper"; O'Neal, *Cattlemen vs Sheepherders,* 51-54; Ball, Desert Lawmen, 195-97.

3. Barnes, William Croft, 1858-1936. Papers, 1878-1945.

4. Hunt, 221-40.

5. O'Neal, Arizona Rangers, 173.

6. *Bisbee (AZ) Daily Review,* June 27, 1917; *Los Angeles Times,* July 13, 1917.

7. O'Neal, *Arizona Rangers,* 174.

8. Ibid., 175.

9. Ibid., 176.

10. Golf, 148.

11. Wagoner, *Arizona Territorial Officials,* Vol. 2, chapter 16.

12. O'Neal, *The Arizona Rangers,* 174.

13. *Phoenix Sun,* June 19, 1941.

# Bibliography

**Books**

Adams, Ramon F., *Burs Under the Saddle, a Second Look at Books and Histories of the West*. Norman: University of Oklahoma Press, 1964.
————. *More Burs Under the Saddle, Books and Histories of the West*. Norman: University of Oklahoma Press, 1979.
Alexander, Bob. *Desert Desperadoes: The Banditti of Southwestern New Mexico*. Silver City, NM: Gila Books, 2006.
————. *Dangerous Dan Tucker*. Silver City, NM: High-Lonesome Books, 2001.
————. *Fearless Dave Allison: Border Lawman*. Silver City, NM: High-Lonesome Books, 2003.
————. *John H. Behan: Sacrificed Sheriff*. Silver City, NM: High-Lonesome Books, 2002.
————. *Lawmen, Outlaws and SOBs*. Vol. 2. Silver City, NM: High-Lonesome Books, 2007.
Ball, Larry D. *The United States Marshals of New Mexico and Arizona Territories, 1846-1912*. Albuquerque: University of New Mexico Press, 1978.
————. *Desert Lawmen: The High Sheriffs of New Mexico and Arizona, 1846-1912*. Albuquerque: University of New Mexico Press, 1992.
Barnes, Will C., *Arizona Place Names*. Tucson: University of Arizona Press, 1988.
Barra, Allen. *Inventing Wyatt Earp: His Life and Many Legends*. New York: Carroll and Graff Publishers, Inc., 1999.
Bell, Bob Boze. *The Illustrated Life and Times of Wyatt Earp*. Phoenix: TriStar-Boze Publications, Inc., 1995.
Boggs, Johnny D. *Great Murder Trials of the Old West*. Plano: Republic of Texas Press, 2003.
Boyer, Glenn G., ed. *I Married Wyatt Earp: The Recollections of Josephine Sarah Marcus Earp*. Tucson: University of Arizona Press, 1976.
Breakenridge, William M. *Helldorado: Bringing the Law to the Mesquite*. Boston: Houghton Mifflin Company, 1928.

Breihan, Carl W. *Great Gunfighters of the West*. South Yarmouth, MA: Curley Publishing, Inc., 1978.

Burns, Walter Noble. *Tombstone*. New York: Grossett and Dunlap, n.d.

Burnham, Frederick Russell. *Scouting on Two Continents*. New York: Doubleday, Page & Company, 1926.

Burton, Jeff. *Black Jack Christian, Outlaw*. Santa Fe: Press of the Territorian, 1967.

Burton, Jeffrey. *The Deadliest Outlaws*. Portsmouth, England: Palamino, 2007.

Carlson, Chip. *Tom Horn: Blood on the Moon: Dark History of the Murderous Cattle Detective*. Glendo, WY: High Plains Press, 2001.

Chaput, Don. *The Odyssey of Burt Alvord*. Tucson: Westernlore Press, 2000.

Cleere, Jan. *Outlaw Tales of Arizona*. Guilford, CT: Two Dot Books, 2006.

Cooke, Phillip St. George. *The Conquest of New Mexico and California*. Albuquerque: Horn and Wallace, 1964.

Cunningham, Eugene. *Triggernometry*. Caldwell, ID: The Caxton Printers, 1989.

DeArment, Robert K. *Bat Masterson, the Man and the Legend*. Norman: University of Oklahoma Press, 1979.

———. *Deadly Dozen: Twelve Forgotten Gunfighters of the Old West*. Norman: University of Oklahoma Press, 2003.

———. *Deadly Dozen: Forgotten Gunfighters of the Old West*. Vol. 2. Norman: University of Oklahoma Press, 2007.

———. *George Scarborough: The Life and Death of a Lawman on the Closing Frontier*. Norman: University of Oklahoma Press, 1992.

———. *Knights of the Green Cloth: The Saga of the Frontier Gambler*. Norman: University of Oklahoma.

———. ed. *Outlaws and Lawmen of the Old West: The Best of Nola*. Cave Creek, AR: True West Publishing, 2001.

Dedera, Don. *A Little War of Our Own: The Pleasant Valley Feud Revisited*. Unknown Binding, 1988.

DeNevi, Donald P. *Western Train Robberies*. Millbrae, CA: Celestial Arts, 1976.

DeSoucy, M. David. *Arizona Rangers (Images of America)*. Charleston, SC: Arcadia Publishing, 2008.

Dodge, Fred. *Under Cover for Wells Fargo: The Unvarnished Recollections of Fred Dodge*. Ed. Carolyn Lake. New York: Ballantine, 1973; reprint, Norman: University of Oklahoma Press, 1998.

Drago, Harry Sinclair. *The Great Range Wars: Violence on the Grassland*. Lincoln: University of Nebraska Press, 1985.

Dunlop, Richard. *Doctors of the American Frontier*. Garden City, NY: Doubleday & Company, 1965.

Earp, Wyatt. *Wyatt Earp Speaks!* Cambria, CA: Fern Canyon Press, 1998.

Ernst, Robert. *Deadly Affrays: The Violent Deaths of the United States Marshals, 1789-2004.* Phoenix, AZ: Scarlet Mask Enterprises, 2005.

Erwin, Allen A. *The Southwest of John H. Slaughter.* Norman, OK: Arthur H. Clark Company, 1997.

Faulk, Odie B. *Arizona: A Short History.* Norman: University of Oklahoma Press, 1970.

———. *Tombstone: Myth and Reality.* New York: Oxford University Press, 1972.

Forest, Earle R. *Arizona's Dark and Bloody Ground.* Caldwell, ID: The Claxton's Printers, 1936.

Forston, John. *Pott Country and What Has Come of It: A History of Pottawatomie County.* Shawnee, OK: Pottawatomie Historical Society, 1936.

Gammel, H. P. N. *The Laws of Texas, 1822-1897.* Vol. 9. Austin: The Gammel Book Publishing Company, 1898.

Golf, John S. *Arizona Territorial Officials, Vol. 3: Delegates to Congress, 1863-1912.* Cave Creek, AZ: Black Mountain Press, 1985.

Haley, J. Evetts. *Jeff Milton: A Good Man with a Gun.* Norman: University of Oklahoma Press, 1948.

Harkey, Daniel R. "Dee". *Mean as Hell: The Life of a New Mexico Lawman.* Albuquerque: University of New Mexico Press, 1948.

Hatley, Allen G. *Murders and Myths: Crime and Violence in the Old West.* XLIBRES, 2008.

Hausladen, Gary J., ed. *Western Places, American Myths: How We Think About the West.* Reno: University of Nevada Press, 2003.

Horan, James David. *Desperate Women.* New York: Putnam, 1952.

Horn, Tom and Dean Krakel. *Life of Tom Horn: Government Scout and Interpreter.* Norman: University of Oklahoma Press, 1985.

Hunt, Frazier. *Cap Mossman: Last of the Great Cowmen.* New York: Hastings House, 1951.

Hunter, J. Marvin. *The Trail Drivers of Texas.* Austin: University of Texas, 1985.

Johnson, David D. *John Ringo.* Stillwater, OK: Barbed Wire Press, 1996.

Lubet, Steven. *Murder in Tombstone: The Forgotten Trial of Wyatt Earp.* New Haven: Yale University Press, 2004.

Marks, Paula Mitchell. *And Die in the West: The Story of the O.K. Corral Gunfight.* Norman: University of Oklahoma Press, 1996.

Martin, Douglas D. *Tombstone's Epitaph: The History of a Frontier Town as Chronicled in its Newspaper.* Norman: University of Oklahoma Press, 1958.

Masterson, W. B. "Bat." *Famous Gunfighters of the Western Frontier.* 75th Anniversary Edition. Annotated and Illustrated by Jack DeMattos. Monroe, WA: Weatherford Press, 1982.

McClintock, James Harvey. "Train Robbers" in *Arizona: The Youngest State*. Chicago: S.J. Clarke, 1913, available at http://files.usgwarchives. org/az/statewide/history/1916/arizonay/trainrobbers.txt.

Metz, Leon C. *Pat Garret: The Story of a Western Lawman*. Norman: University of Oklahoma Press, 1974.

———. *The Encyclopedia of Lawmen, Outlaws and Gunfighters*. New York: Checkmark Books, 2003.

———. *The Shooters: A Gallery of Notorious Gunmen from the American West*. New York: Berkley Books, 1996.

Monaghan, Jay, ed. *The Book of the American West*. New York: Simon and Schuster, 1963.

O'Neal, Bill. *An Encyclopedia of Western Gun-fighters*. Norman: University of Oklahoma Press, 1979.

———. *Cattlemen vs Sheepherder: Five Decades of Violence in the West*. Austin: Eakin Press, 1989.

———. *The Arizona Rangers*. Austin: Eakin Press, 1987.

Parsons, George Whitwell, and Lynn R. Bailey, ed. *A Tenderfoot in Tombstone: The Private Journal of George Whitwell Parsons: The Turbulent Years, 1880-82*. Tucson, AR: Westernlore Press, 1996.

Patterson, Richard M. *The Train Robbery Era: An Encyclopedic History*. Boulder, CO: Pruett Press, 1991.

———. *Historical Atlas of the Outlaw West*. Boulder, CO: Johnson Publishing Company, 1985.

Pattie, James O. *The Personal Narrative of James O. Pattie of Kentucky*. Cincinnati: E. H. Flint, 1933.

Rasch, Phillip J. *Desperadoes of Arizona Territory*. Laramie, WY: NOLA Press, 1999.

———. *The Hunting of Billy the Kid*. N.P.: Western Brand Books, Vol. XI, January 1969.

Roberts, Brigham Henry. *The Mormon Battalion: Its History and Achievements*. Salt Lake City, UT: The Deseret News, 1919.

Samuelson, Nancy B. *Shoot from the Lip*. Eastford, CT: Shooting Star Press, 1998.

Sheridan, Thomas E. *Arizona: A History*. Tucson: University of Arizona Press, 1995.

Shirley, Glenn, *Shotgun for Hire*. Norman: University of Oklahoma Press, 1970.

———. *West of Hell's Fringe*. Norman: University of Oklahoma Press, 1978.

Sides, Hampton. *Blood and Thunder: An Epic of the American West*. New York: Doubleday, 2006.

Sonnichsen, C. L. *Billy King's Tombstone: The Private Life of an Arizona Boomtown*. Tucson: University of Arizona Press, 1972.

Tanner, Karen Holliday. *Doc Holliday: A Family Portrait*. Norman: University of Oklahoma Press, 1998.

Tanner, Karen Holliday, and John D. Tanner. *Last of the Old-Time Outlaws*. Norman: University of Oklahoma Press, 2002.

Tefertiller, Casey. *Wyatt Earp: The Life Behind the Legend*. New York: John Wiley and Sons, 1997.

Theobald, John, and Lillian Theobald. *Wells Fargo in Arizona Territory*. Tempe: Arizona History Foundation, 1978.

Thrapp, Dan L. *Encyclopedia of Frontier Biography*. Spokane, WA: Arthur H. Clark Company, 1990.

Traywick, Ben T. *The Chronicles of Tombstone*. Tombstone: Red Marie's Bookstore, 1990.

———. *Legendary Characters of Southeast Arizona*. Tombstone: Red Marie's Bookstore, 1991

Trimble, Marshall. *Arizona: A Cavalcade of History*. Tucson, AR: Treasure Chest Publications, 1989.

———. *The Law of the Gun*. Phoenix: *Arizona Highways* Book Division, 1999.

Tyler, Daniel. *A Concise History of the Mormon Battalion in the Mexican War*. Chicago: Rio Grande Press, 1964.

Utley, Robert. *Frontiersmen in Blue*. New York: Macmillan Co., 1967.

Wagoner, Jay J. *Arizona Territory, 1863-1912: A Political History*. Vol. 1 and 2. Tucson: University of Arizona Press, 1970.

Walker, Dale L. *Rough Rider: Buckey O'Neill of Arizona*. Lincoln: University of Nebraska Press, Bison Books Ed., 1997.

Wallis, Michael. *Billy the Kid: The Endless Ride*. New York: W.W. Norton & Company, 2007.

Waters, Frank. *The Earp Brothers of Tombstone: The Story of Mrs. Virgil Earp*. Lincoln: University of Nebraska Press, 1976.

Weddle, Jerry. *Antrim Is My Stepfather's Name*. Phoenix: Arizona Historical Society, 1993.

Weir, William. *Written with Lead*. Lanham, MD: Cooper Square Press, 2006.

Wilson, Edward. *An Unwritten History: A Record from the Exciting Days of Early Arizona*. Sante Fe, NM: Stagecoach Press, 1966.

Wilson, R. Michael. *Encyclopedia of Stagecoach Robbery in Arizona*. Las Vegas: RaMa Press, 2003.

———, ed. *Wells Fargo & Company's Report of Losses from Stage Coach and Train Robbers, 1870-1884: 125th Anniversary Edition*. Las Vegas: RaMa Press, 2008.

———. *Great Train Robberies of the Old West*. Guilford, CT: Two Dot Books, 2007.

————. *Great Stagecoach Robberies of the Old West.* Guilford, CT: Two Dot Books, 2007.

Yadon, Laurence J., with Dan Anderson. *200 Texas Outlaws and Lawmen: 1835-1935.* Gretna, LA: Pelican Publishing Company, 2008.

Young, Roy B. *Johnny Behind the Deuce: Guilty Until Proven Innocent: The True Story of Mike O'Rourke.* Apache, OK: Young & Sons, 2007.


## Articles


Barnes, Will C. "The Pleasant Valley War: Its Genesis, History and Necrology." *Arizona Historical Review* 4, no. 3 (October 1931).

————. "The Pleasant Valley War of 1887: Part II." *Arizona Historical Review* 4, no. 4 (January 1932).

Benz, Donald. "Alias Black Jack Christian." *Old West* (Spring 1970).

Clark, Wayne. "Inventing History." *National Association for Outlaw and Lawman History, Inc., Quarterly* 31, no. 1 (January-March 2007).

DeArment, Robert. "Barney Riggs, Man of Violence." *Old West* (Fall 1983).

Diaz-Gonzalez, Darlinda. "Billy Claiborne: Arizona's Billy the Kid." *National Association for Outlaw and Lawman History, Inc., Quarterly* 29, no. 3 (July-September 2005).

Evans, Bill. "Gunfight in the Whetstone Mountains." *Wild West History Association Journal* 1, no. 6 (December 2008).

Franzi, Emil. "A Whirl with Pearl." Review of *I, Pearl Hart,* by Jane Candia Coleman. *Tucson Weekly,* August 13-19, 1998.

Garate, Donald. "Arizonac: A Twentieth-Century Myth." *Journal of Arizona History* 46, no. 2 (Summer 2005).

Haley, J. Evetts, "Jim East: Trail Hand and Cowboy." *Panhandle-Plains Review* 4 (1931).

Hart, Pearl. "An Arizona Episode." *Cosmopolitan* 27, no. 6 (October 1899).

Johnson, David. "The Fifth Ace: H.F. Sills and His Testimony." *National Association for Outlaw and Lawman History, Inc., Quarterly* 31, no. 2 (April-June 2007).

Marcus, Jacob R., ed."An Arizona Pioneer: Memoirs of Sam Aaron." *American Jewish Archives,* 10, no. 1 (October 1958).

McKinney, Joe T. "Reminiscences." *Arizona Historical Review* 5, no. 1 (April, July, October 1932).

Myers, Roger. "Between Wichita and Dodge: The Travels and Friends of Kate Elder." *National Association for Outlaw and Lawman History, Inc., Quarterly* 31, no. 2 (April-June 2007).

Potter, Pam. "Remembering the McLaurys." *National Association for Outlaw and Lawman History, Inc., Quarterly* 30, no. 4 (October-December 2006).

Sharp, Patricia Maxwell. "The Maxwells of Arizona: Trackers and Lawmen." *Frontier Times* (July 1972).

Slayton, Marie. "Ghosts Celebrating 100 Years Near the 'Red Light District' at the Grill." Days Past, *Prescott Daily Courier,* September 9, 2001.

Smith, Chuck. "One More for Morg." *National Association for Outlaw and Lawman History, Inc., Quarterly* 24, no. 4 (October-December 2005).

Smith, Robert Barr. "Jeff Milton." *Wild West Magazine* (July 1994).

———. "The West's Deadliest Dentist." *Wild West Magazine* (April 1994).

———. "Texas John's Odyssey." *Wild West Magazine* (December 1993).

———. "Born Bad: The Outlaw Christian Brothers." *Wild West Magazine* (December 2000).

Walker, Henry P. "Retire Peaceably to Your Homes: Arizona Faces Martial Law, 1882." *Journal of Arizona History* 10 (Spring 1969).

**Manuscript Collections**

"Alexander Oswald Brodie, 1849-1918 [biofile]." Biographical Files, Arizona Historical Society Library and Archives, Tucson.

Barnes, William Croft, 1858-1936. Papers, 1878-1945. MS 0017. Arizona Historical Society Library and Archives, Tucscon.

Cananea Consolidated Copper Company Records, ca. 1893-1930. MS 1311. Arizona State Archives, Phoenix.

Cantelou, Jennie Watts. Indian-Pioneer Papers. University of Oklahoma Western History Collection, Norman.

Edmund G. Ross Collection, 1856-1907. Kansas State Historical Society, Topeka.

Fish, Joseph. Papers, 1840-1926. MS 257. Arizona Historical Society, Library and Archives, Tucson.

Gray, John Pleasant. "When All Roads Led to Tombstone." Typescript, Arizona Historical Society Library and Archives, Tucson, n.d.

"Joseph T. McKinney, 1858- [biofile]." Biographical Files, Arizona Historical Society Library and Archives, Tucson.

Schooley, R.B. Indian-Pioneer Papers, Anadarko, Oklahoma, 22 March 1938. University of Oklahoma Western History Collection, Norman.

"Testimony taken in the cause of the killing of Houston Blevins, Mose Roberts, and Andy Cooper, within the Territory of Arizona in the County of Apache in the city of Holbrook, before Justice of the Peace B. G. Harvey on September, 4, 5, and 15, 1887." Arizona State Archives, Phoenix.

"Thomas H. Rynning [biofile]." Biographical Files, Arizona Historical Society Library and Archives, Tucson.
Wheeler, Harry, to Gov. Joseph H. Kibbey, August 7, 1908. Arizona Rangers Files, Box Two, Arizona State Archives, Phoenix.


Newspapers

*Arizona Daily Star* (Tucson, AZ)
*Arizona Silver Belt* (Globe, AZ)
*Arizona Weekly Star* (Tucson, AZ)
*Bisbee (AZ) Daily Review*
*Cococino (AZ) Sun*
*Daily Oklahoman* (Oklahoma City, OK)
*Dodge City (KS) Times*
*Edmond (OK) Sun Democrat*
*Flagstaff Champion*
*Ford County(KS) Globe*
*Gunnison (CO) Daily News-Democrat*
*Lamar (MO) Democrat*
*Los Angeles Times*
*National Police Gazette*
*New York Times*
*Nogales (AZ) Border Vidette*
*Phoenix Sun*
*Prescott Journal-Miner*
*Prescott Weekly Miner*
*San Francisco Examiner*
*Tombstone Daily Nugget*
*Tombstone Epitaph*
*Tucson Daily Citizen*
*Wichita (KS) Daily Beacon*


Other Sources

Department of the Interior. Census Office, Tenth Census, June 1, 1880, Table I b, page 4.
Eighteenth Texas Legislature, "Title 99a, Wool-Growing Interest," April 4, 1883.
Biographical Directory of the United States Congress, 1174-Present, available at http://bioguide.congress.gov/biosearch/biosearch.asp.
The Handbook of Texas Online, available at http://www.tshaonline.org/.
*Territory v. Ketchum,* 65 Pac. 169 (1901).
Twenty-Fifth Legislative Assembly (Arizona) 1909. "Acts, Resolutions, and Memorials," chapter 4:3.
Twenty-Fifth Legislative Assembly (Arizona) 1909. *Journal of the Twenty-Fifth Legislative Assembly, 1909,* 94-111
Twenty-Second Legislative Assembly (Arizona) 1903. "Acts, Resolutions, and Memorials," Act 64, sections 1-10.

# Index

354     ARIZONA GUNFIGHTERS

Brocius, Curly Bill, 64, 66, 68, 73, 77,
    79-80, 87, 90-92, 95-96, 98-100,
    105, 134, 139-42, 148-50, 152, 223,
    255, 278
Brodie, Alexander O., 305, 309, 313
Brooks, Johnny, 310, 312
Brown, John, 184-85
Burnett, James, 74
Burton, Jim, 54
Butler, Benjamin F., 149
Butte, Montana, 62

Campbell, John, 296-97, 309
Campbell, R. J., 109
Cantelou, Jennie, 208
Carr, W. H. "Bill", 210
Carver, Will, 272
Casey, Jim, 208
Casey, Vic, 208
Central City, Colorado, 55
Chacón, Augustine, 272, 280, 282-90,
    304
Chadborn, Buck, 278
Cheyenne, Wyoming, 169
Chisum, John, 226-28
Chivington, Colorado, 56
Christian, Bill "Black Jack", 205,
    207, 209-10, 212, 216, 218-19,
    221, 249-50, 272
Christian, Bob, 205, 209, 211-12,
    220
Christian, Old Man, 207
Ciprico, George M., 54
Claiborne, William Harrison "Billy
    the Kid", 111, 122-24, 131, 156,
    161
Clancie, Ike, 309
Clanton, William "Billy", 51, 68, 75,
    77, 96, 109-13, 115-18, 122-25,
    128-30, 151, 156
Clanton, Ike, 51, 57, 64, 75, 88, 95,
    102-3, 106-11, 113, 115, 117-20,
    122-26, 128, 134, 136, 142-43,
    151, 155-56, 158, 230, 255
Clanton, Newman H. "Old Man", 57,
    92, 100, 230, 269
Clanton, Phineas, 57, 143
Clark, Ben, 219
Clark, Ed, 53

Clark, James S., 81
Clark, Yavapai, 57, 187, 238
Clayton, New Mexico, 221
Clements, Mannen, 60, 65
Cleveland, Grover, 175, 294
Clifton, Arizona, 218, 249
Cloverdale, New Mexico, 86
Clum, John, 64, 81, 86, 104, 160
Clum, Mary, 69
Cody, William "Buffalo Bill", 55
Coffeyville, Kansas, 259
Colcord, William, 200
Coleman, R. F., 108, 117
Collins, J.B., 77
Colorado City, Texas, 243
Colton, California, 159
Cook, George, 302
Cooley, Scott, 65
Corbett, Jim, 160
Council Bluffs, Iowa, 61
Crane, James "Slim Jim", 64, 86,
    99-100, 103
Creaghe, St. George, 322
Crook, George, 53
Crosby, Lorenzo, 298
Crouch, Charles "Sandy Bob",
    101
Cruz, Florentino "Indian Charlie",
    138, 142
Cullen, Ed, 272
Cummings, George M., 161

Daggs, P. P., 181
Dake, Crawley P., 61, 134
Dallas, Texas, 71-72, 152, 154
Datile, New Mexico, 184
Davis, Jefferson, 190, 243, 284
Deal, Pony, 102-3, 150, 278-79
DeBrille Poston, Charles, 62
Delaney, William, 154
Delano, Kansas, 60
Deming, New Mexico, 97, 251, 254
Denison, Texas, 71
Denver, Colorado, 55, 149-50, 152
Dessart, John, 213
Diamond A Ranch, 217-18, 323
Dick, Lloyd, 77-78
Dodge, Fred, 62, 64, 102, 107, 116,
    142, 160, 276